Counseling Survivors
of Traumatic Events

Counseling Survivors of Traumatic Events

A Handbook for Pastors and Other Helping Professionals

Andrew J. Weaver
Laura T. Flannelly
John D. Preston

Abingdon Press
Nashville

COUNSELING SURVIVORS OF TRAUMATIC EVENTS
A HANDBOOK FOR PASTORS AND OTHER HELPING PROFESSIONALS

This book is printed on acid-free paper.

Library of Congress Cataloging-in-Publication Data

Weaver, Andrew J., 1942-
    Counseling survivors of traumatic events : a handbook for pastors and other helping professionals / Andrew J. Weaver, Laura T. Flannelly, John D. Preston.
    p. cm.
Includes bibliographical references.
    ISBN 0-687-05243-2 (pbk. : alk. paper)
    1. Post traumatic stress disorder—Patients—Pastoral counseling of. I. Flannelly, Laura T., 1962- II. Preston, John D., 1950- III. Title.

BV4461.W42 2003
253.5—dc21

2003010066

03 04 05 06 07 08 09 10 11 12—10 9 8 7 6 5 4 3 2 1

MANUFACTURED IN THE UNITED STATES OF AMERICA

To my brother in Christ, Richard L. Binggeli—AJW

To my husband, Kevin J. Flannelly—LTF

To the Reverend Mary Manna Maaga—JDP

Acknowledgments

We are grateful to the Reverend Carolyn L. Stapleton for her exceptional editing and research skills that added immeasurably to the quality and usefulness of the text. We are thankful to Dr. Sarah Fogg for her fine contribution to the book in her chapter on pregnancy loss. Thanks to Karen G. Costa and Michelle Housh for their help in preparing and editing the manuscript.

I called on your name, O LORD, from the depths of the pit; you heard my plea, "Do not close your ear to my cry for help, but give me relief!" You came near when I called on you; you said, "Do not fear!"

—Lamentations 3:55-57

Contents

Foreword

Counseling Survivors of Traumatic Events is a beckoning to help and be helped by those who have experienced something unforgettable. Being helped ourselves through our helping others is bearing witness to the wonder of the human spirit. This is the paradox of helping the traumatized.

I began my journey as a traumatologist out of frustration. I had witnessed considerable trauma as a U.S. Marine early in the Vietnam War. When I left the service, my intention was to focus on child psychology. I had loved working with children in Vietnam as a volunteer in the Vietnam-Marine Corps people-to-people program in DaNang. It was a wonderful opportunity to turn my attention away from destruction and killing to activities of love and nurturing. As an undergraduate at the University of Hawaii, my hatred of the war I fought in peaked when Martin Luther King, Jr., was killed in 1968. By the time I was in graduate school in 1970, I became politically active and began to organize fellow veterans who shared my rejection of the war. My first demonstration against the war was my last. That same day I became a trauma researcher.

I arrived in Washington, D.C. on a crisp and chilly March day in 1971 as a member of the Vietnam Veterans Against the War.[1] We were there to change the world, or at least to change U.S. policies and stop the war in Southeast Asia. I quickly became disenchanted with being a protester and turned my attention to the traumatic effects of war on the hundreds of young men around me. Like an investigative journalist, I began to circulate among my fellow vets and to use the research interviewing skills I had acquired in my graduate program at Pennsylvania State University. I quickly realized that my calling was as a chronicler of the costs of war being paid by those who fought in Vietnam. I decided to leave the demonstrating to those with a more political bent and the necessary personality and skills.

My first interview was with a combat veteran I'll call Mike. He was a young man who had, like me, lost friends in Vietnam and came home disillusioned. Unlike me, however, his life had gone from bad to worse. He had been married twice and was then divorced. He abused both drugs and alcohol. Until we spoke, he had never once talked about his time in Vietnam. In contrast, I had written about my experiences both during the war and afterwards. As I listened to Mike speak of his combat experiences and what followed, I realized how fortunate I was. He was clearly traumatized by what had happened and was unable to let go of the emotions stuck to his memories. Another thing I learned from Mike was that he was searching for answers to some fundamental questions, answers that, perhaps, would give him peace.

I went on to interview and survey thousands of survivors of trauma. Over the years, I have learned that the questions Mike was struggling to answer were not unlike those of others who have been traumatized. Everywhere I go, I am asked about the best way to counsel survivors of traumatic events. People want me to boil down all of the research, theory, and practical knowledge into a set of strategies that will work. The trick, of course, is finding the best method for a particular person at the right time under the right conditions. Yet even the ideal counseling approach that enjoys the best evidence of effectiveness cannot cure traumatic stress unless a survivor can find the answers he or she is seeking. Even though we have devised extraordinary drugs and techniques to manage the symptoms of traumatic stress, there is no genuine peace until a survivor is able to address with satisfaction at least three universal questions. These are:

- Why did this happen?
- Why did it happen to me (us)?
- How can I ever put my life back together again and feel okay after knowing what I know?

It is at this point that a person is face-to-face with a counselor, seeking the answers to these fundamental questions when science, technology, practice skills, and all of the other competencies of modern counseling are silent. The answers must come from the survivor's own spirituality and faith. There is no one better prepared to enable these persons to search and find the answers than the clergy who read this book.

It is likely that you, the reader, are a pastor. This volume is about helping those who have been touched by frightening or disturbing experiences. The authors wrote it especially for you because you are the most likely person to whom survivors of trauma will turn. Natural disasters, car crashes, suicide, torture, rape, combat, and other traumatic events challenge our faith or make it stronger (or both). This book provides an extraordinary amount of knowledge—not only about what survivors have endured, but also about what they need not just to endure, but to thrive by transforming their tragedies into triumphs.

This wise and varied team of practitioners represents numerous work contexts and approaches. They have designed a one-stop reference source for helping the traumatized. And there are lots of good examples—of both problems and solutions. Each chapter addressing the sixteen traumatic events includes information not only about psychological counseling, but also how a pastor (no matter the culture, nationality, language, or denomination) can utilize faith and the religious community to serve as a resource for healing and can facilitate answering those fundamental questions.

I know this volume will also help you assist those who serve in combat in the future and those they leave behind. Perhaps as a result, fewer lives in the times ahead will be broken or broken as long as they were in previous wars.

After thirty years of research on how people are affected by trauma—in both good and bad ways—and how they can be transformed, we know that faith and pastoral care matter. Religion and spirituality can provide the necessary stepping stones for the traumatized struggling to answer the haunting questions that, if left unaddressed, will be major stumbling blocks to peace of mind and experiencing God's presence.

God bless you in your important work. Please contact me or the Green Cross Foundation (www.GreenCross.org) if we can help you.

—Charles R. Figley, Ph.D.

---

1. One of the coordinators was John Kerry, who is currently a U.S. Senator from Massachusetts.

Charles R. Figley, Ph.D., is a professor in the School of Social Work at Florida State University. He is former editor of the *Journal of Traumatic Stress* and current editor of the international journal *Traumatology*. He is author of more than 150 scholarly works, including eighteen books, and the recipient of numerous awards from universities and learned societies throughout the world.

How to Use This Book

Counseling Survivors of Traumatic Events: A Handbook for Pastors and Other Helping Professionals is designed to be a text for those in training for pastoral ministry, as well as a practical resource for women and men already serving in ministry. The volume addresses the aftermath of a wide array of traumatic events (such as natural disasters, criminal violence, catastrophic accidents, life-threatening illnesses) and the mental health difficulties, especially post-traumatic stress disorder (PTSD), that may be experienced as a result. In the light of the threat of global terrorism, it is especially important that those in ministry understand how to help guide persons through very difficult places.

Part 1 offers information about the important role that clergy and the faith community serve in the mental health care of persons who have survived an intensely horrifying or deeply disturbing event. This section spells out the need for special expertise by pastors and other religious professionals as to how to recognize and address psychological trauma. The scientific evidence that nonpunitive, nurturing religious beliefs and practices serve a healing function for those traumatized is summarized.

The heart of the book is the case studies found in Part 2, which use real-life situations and highlight practical implications for pastors working with the traumatized. This format incorporates relevant research and identifies the needs of persons suffering from psychological trauma. The case studies are multidisciplinary in approach, integrating clinical knowledge in pastoral care, psychology, nursing, psychiatry, gerontology, sociology, medicine, social work, and marriage and family therapy, along with current scientific findings on the role of religion in mental and physical health care. The volume recognizes that the difficulties individuals face in the aftermath of horrific life events do not stand in isolation from one another, but are interrelated. For example, the chapter involving psychological trauma in police officers addresses PTSD, substance abuse, and depression.

The book is designed so that a reader can easily locate information on specific issues related to psychological trauma for which individuals and families seek help. It is a practical, easy-to-use guide on how to assess problems and respond to them. The table of contents provides the subject matter of sixteen traumatic events that often affect human beings.

Each case provides an example of a person who has survived a specific traumatic event and is in need of help. Included in each chapter is information about how a religious professional would assess the problem, what aspects of the situation are most important, how to identify the major issues, specific directions for what pastors and congregations can do, when to refer for professional assistance, and resources that can provide help. National organizations (often with toll-free numbers and Internet addresses) that supply information and support for individuals and families facing these issues are identified for each concern addressed. Cross-cultural aspects are discussed as well

Part 3 of the book has a section on responding to different types of crisis situations as well as guidelines on self-care for religious professionals working with traumatized persons. There is also a section on how and when to make a referral. Technical terms are defined in the glossary at the end of the book.

The text is written for people of all faiths, with an appreciation for the richness of the intergenerational and multicultural diversity found in religious communities. The authors are persons of faith with specialties in mental health.

Dr. Weaver is a clinical psychologist and ordained United Methodist minister who has served rural and urban parishes. He is the Director of Research at The HealthCare Chaplaincy in New York City. He has written over ninety scientific articles and book chapters and has coauthored eight books. Dr. Flannelly is a Roman Catholic laywoman and Associate Professor of Nursing at the University of Hawaii. She has worked extensively as a clinical nurse specialist and has written several articles on the role of spirituality in nursing. Dr. Preston is Associate Professor of Psychology at Alliant University in Sacramento, California, and an active layman in The United Methodist Church. He has written over thirty scientific articles and book chapters and has authored or coauthored fourteen books.

PART ONE

Introduction

Clergy, Faith, and Psychological Trauma

Clergy need the skills to recognize and assist those who come to them for counsel in the aftermath of psychological trauma. Many of these persons may be suffering what mental health professionals have identified as post-traumatic stress disorder, or PTSD. The word "trauma" is derived from the Greek word meaning "wound." Just as a physical trauma can cause suffering by wounding and disabling the body, a psychological trauma can cause suffering by overwhelming the thoughts and feelings.

Graphic accounts of the effects of extreme stress on human beings have been documented in literature since Homer's *Odyssey* and Samuel Pepys's diary of the disastrous London fire of 1666 (Daly, 1983). Freud recognized the effects of psychological trauma in childhood during the nineteenth century, but it has only been in the wake of the devastating wars of the twentieth century—particularly the return of Vietnam War veterans to the United States—that a concerted scientific effort has been marshaled to create an effective model to understand the symptoms that result from extreme stress (Van der Kolk, 1987). Most recent, the model for understanding psychological trauma, or PTSD, has been applied to understanding reactions to the criminal victimization that plagues our society, such as rape, robbery, assault, child abuse, elder abuse, and spouse battering (Herman, 1992).

Post-traumatic stress should usually be considered a normal reaction to an abnormally stressful situation (Lifton, 1988). PTSD is not a sign of being "emotionally weak" or "mentally ill." Virtually anyone exposed to the "shock effect" of extreme stress will find ordinary coping processes are overwhelmed. Post-traumatic stress disorder is diagnosed when a person responds with intense fear, helplessness, or horror to a traumatic experience that involves actual or threatened death, serious injury, or a threat to the physical well-being of self or others (APA, 2000). The traumatic event is reexperienced in specific ways, such as in recurrent and intrusive distressing recollections or dreams of the event. Additionally, the person often persistently avoids situations associated with the trauma and has emotional numbness in general. Often there is hypervigilance and irritability. Post-traumatic stress disorder becomes the diagnosis when these symptoms persist for more than one month.

Research has revealed that exposure to several categories of traumatic stressors can precipitate the symptoms of PTSD, including life-threatening illnesses, criminal victimization (rape, assault, robbery, spouse battering, child abuse, kidnapping, elder abuse), natural disasters (floods, wildfires, earthquakes, hurricanes, tornadoes), human-made disasters (war, death camps, torture, terrorism, gang violence), catastrophic accidents (automobile, airplane, industrial), and workplace exposure for rescue workers, firefighters, health care personnel, and police officers (APA, 2000). Clergy who are increasingly being exposed to dangerous situations will also be vulnerable to the effects of extreme stress (Weaver, 1992a). When these stressors involve a serious threat to one's life or physical integrity, one's children, spouse, close relatives, or friends; sudden destruction of one's home or community; or seeing another person who has been, or is being, seriously injured or killed as the result of an accident or physical violence, PTSD symptoms may result (APA, 2000).

Many People Suffer from Psychological Trauma

PTSD represents a significant public health concern and warrants the attention of clergy and the religious community. Research has discovered that about 60 percent of men and 50 percent of women have at least one traumatic experience in their lifetimes, while 10 percent of men and 6 percent of women have four or more traumatic experiences. About 8 percent of Americans have PTSD at some point in their lives, making it the fourth most common psychiatric disorder (Kessler et al., 1995). According to the National Center for PTSD, every year as many as 17 million people in North America survive or provide relief services for disasters such as earthquakes, floods, hurricanes, tornadoes, wildfires, chemical explosions, toxic spills, riots, mass killings, and terrorist acts. In addition, in any given year, one in one hundred Americans will be injured in a motor vehicle accident, and about 9 percent of them will develop PTSD (Blanchard and Hicking, 1997).

Churches, mosques, and synagogues have many veterans who are suffering from psychological trauma. Among Vietnam-era veterans, a study found that 15.2 percent of men and 8.5 percent of women suffer from PTSD fifteen or more years following their military service (Weiss et al., 1992). It is estimated that 830,000 Vietnam veterans (49 percent) "still experience clinically significant distress and disability from the symptoms of PTSD" (Weiss et al., 1992, p. 365).

It is also becoming clear that for some elderly veterans, the experience of combat has far-reaching effects on mental health. Almost 25 percent of American men aged sixty-five or older served in combat in the Second World War or Korea (Spiro, Schnurr, and Aldwin, 1993), and many of these men continue to suffer from the experience, especially those who were prisoners of war (Sutker and Allain, 1996).

In addition, high numbers of young Americans suffer from PTSD as a result of criminal violence. Exposure to violence among teens in the U.S. is at near epidemic levels. The rate of violent victimization for those aged twelve to nineteen is twice that of adults over the age of twenty-five (Bureau of Justice Statistics, 1993). Adolescent males from large urban areas are at the highest risk of victimization and of witnessing severe violence, such as stabbings and shootings. In a study of adolescents and young adults (aged fourteen to twenty-three) in Detroit, Michigan, 42 percent had seen someone shot or stabbed, and 22 percent had seen someone killed. Nine percent had seen more than one person killed (Shubiner, Scott, and Tzelepis, 1993). A national study of more than eleven thousand eighth and tenth graders found a high exposure to violence. A full one-third of the students had been threatened with bodily harm, while 15 percent had been robbed, and 16 percent had been assaulted in their neighborhoods. School offered little safety according to this study—34 percent of the students had been threatened, and 13 percent had been assaulted at school during the preceding year (American School Health Association, 1989). It is not surprising that in a random sample of adolescents, aged sixteen to nineteen, in Detroit, Michigan, it was discovered that 4 of 10 had been exposed to a traumatic event that qualifies as a PTSD stressor. The rate of PTSD in this group of urban young adults was almost 1 in 4 (Breslau, Davis, Andreski, and Peterson, 1991).

Between 1975 and 1987 alone, an estimated 700,000 refugees from Southeast Asia settled in the United States (Mollica, Wyshak, and Lavelle, 1987). Many refugees who immigrate to North America and Europe have suffered maltreatment and torture (Mollica, 2000). Researchers have documented that approximately one-half of the refugees coming to the United States from the war-torn areas of Central America, Central Europe, Africa, and Southeast Asia—groups with whom many religious communities have become actively involved—are suffering PTSD (Cervantes, de Synder, and Padella, 1989; Fox and Tang, 2000).

Children also suffer from psychological trauma and can have the full constellation of PTSD symptoms. Children and, as a result, their family members often experience psychological trauma from serious injury in a motor vehicle accident (Boyer et al., 2000). PTSD is also common among children who are abused or neglected (Duber and Motta, 1999) or who are put in grave danger (Garbarino, Kostelny, and Dubrow, 1991; La Greca et al., 1996). These children can have much the same set of PTSD features as adults, although expressed in somewhat different ways. One of the primary researchers in the area of childhood trauma, Dr. Lenore Terr, suggests that four characteristics are often seen in traumatized children: "Visualized or otherwise repeatedly perceived memories of the traumatic event, repetitive behaviors, trauma-specific fears, and changed attitudes about people, life, and the future" (1990, p. 10).

Who Is Most Vulnerable to PTSD?

The strongest single predictor of PTSD is the severity of the traumatic experience (Foy, 1992). Generally, the greater the exposure to the traumatic event or events, the greater the percentage of people with symptoms of PTSD (Shore, Tatum, and Vollmer, 1986). After a devastating disaster, 50 to 80 percent of those exposed can develop PTSD symptoms (Andreasen, 1985). Suffering from PTSD is more pronounced when the trauma is intentionally inflicted by another person, rather than when it is accidental (Peterson, Prout, and Schwarz, 1991). A completed rape, the perception of one's life being threatened during a crime, and physical injury during a crime all increase the likelihood of PTSD (Kilpatrick et al., 1989).

Though PTSD can appear at any age, it is most prevalent among young adults as a result of the higher incident rate of precipitating stressors. In general, children and older adults have more difficulty coping with traumatic stress than persons in midlife. Young children have not developed adequate coping skills, and older people may be physically frail and less able to maintain coping strategies. A lack of adequate social support and additional stress will make a person more vulnerable to PTSD (Brewin, Andrews, and Valentine, 2000). It is more prevalent in persons who are single, divorced, widowed, economically disadvantaged, or socially isolated. It appears that previous child physical or sexual abuse or severe marital or family dysfunction may increase the risk of PTSD (Foy, 1992). Certain psychiatric disorders, including major depression and anxiety disorders in the family of origin, may predispose persons to PTSD (Breslau, Davis, Andreski, and Peterson, 1991).

People with Psychological Trauma Seek Clergy Counsel

It is important that clergy be skilled in recognizing PTSD symptoms, given that research over several decades has demonstrated that millions of Americans call upon clergy for help in times of crisis (Weaver, 1995). A University of Michigan research group published results of a survey using a representative sample of 2,267 Americans. The study revealed that about 4 of 10 Americans reported that they sought counsel from a member of the clergy when they had a personal problem. Among people who stated they attended religious services once a week, the number rose to 53 percent. Even among people who said they never attended religious services, 16 percent reported that they sought guidance from clergy for assistance with personal problems. Particularly relevant to the subject of PTSD is the finding that persons in "crisis" involving the "death of someone close" reported almost five times more likelihood of seeking the aid of a clergyperson than of all other mental health professionals (psychiatrists, psychologists, social workers, and marriage and family therapists) combined (Veroff, Kulka, and Douvan, 1981).

Researchers at Yale University surveyed 214 Catholic, Protestant, and Jewish clergy in New Haven, Connecticut. Eighty-five percent of the clergy surveyed reported they had counseled dangerous or suicidal persons, and most clergy stated they did some crisis intervention counseling in the course of their pastoral work. These authors summarized their study with this comment: "Parish-based clergy, especially the black clergy, function as a major mental health resource to communities with limited access to professional mental health services" (Mollica et al., 1986, p. 323).

In 1988, the psychiatrist David Larson and colleagues published research findings from a national survey of 18,495 adults. The study revealed that a person was as likely to seek out a clergyperson as a mental health professional for counsel when suffering a wide range of serious psychiatric disorders, including major depression, which is strongly associated with PTSD. The article concluded that "the clergy are coping, with or without the assistance of mental health professionals, with parishioners who have a broad spectrum of psychiatric disorders" (p. 1068).

One study examined the role of clergy as counselors, in which the majority of the persons seeking assistance were Mexican Americans. Among the 534 persons in this study who sought help or who were likely to seek help, clergy were the primary resource. In fact, the study found that the degree of identification with Mexican ethnicity was strongly related to seeking pastoral help. The study states, "For El Paso, Texas, residents the clergy are by far the most popular source of help for a personal problem. In decreasing order of popularity (after clergy at 41 percent) are doctors (29 percent), psychiatrists and psychologists (21 percent), and social service agencies (including social workers at 18 percent)" (Chalfant et al., 1990, p. 308).

In 1999, researchers studied African American pastors in ninety-nine churches in urban areas of Connecticut (Williams et al., 1999). Ninety-four of the congregations offered community outreach programs for those in need. Most of the programs offered services to persons who suffer from conditions that place them at risk for PTSD, including homelessness and hunger, child abuse, domestic violence, substance abuse, AIDS, and imprisonment.

Pastoral care and mental health publications have documented that clergy are responding with pastoral counseling to persons exposed to a wide range of extreme stressors that can precipitate PTSD. These publications document clergy's responses to natural disasters such as floods (Smith et al., 2000) and tornadoes (Chinnici, 1985); catastrophic accidents such as large fires (Lindy, Grace, and Green, 1981) and plane crashes (Black, 1987); criminal assault including rape (Golding, Siegel, Sorenson, Burham, and Stein, 1989), spouse battering (Bowker, 1988; Cwik, 1997), child abuse (Weaver, 1992b), and elder abuse (Weaver and

Koenig, 1997); and human-created disasters including death camps (Cohen, 1989), war (Zimmerman and Weber, 2000), and torture (Lernoux, 1980; Daries, 1990).

People Use Faith to Cope with PTSD

With psychological trauma, an individual's sense of order and continuity of life is shattered. Questions of meaning and purpose arise as a person experiences a loss of control over his or her destiny. Religious faith is a primary coping strategy for many people suffering from psychological trauma, with one-half to three-quarters of PTSD sufferers indicating that their faith helps them cope (Weaver, Koenig, and Ochberg, 1996). Scientists have found that surveyed combat veterans (Green, Lindy, and Grace, 1988), natural disaster survivors (Weinrich, Hardin, and Johnson, 1990), adult survivors of severe child abuse (Lawson et al., 1998), and young people in a war zone (Zeidner, 1993) frequently use their faith as a positive coping strategy. Fathers of children being treated for cancer in a hematology hospital clinic were asked about various methods of coping. Among twenty-nine separate coping strategies used, prayer was both the most common and the most helpful for the fathers (Cayse, 1994).

In addition to offering the social support of community, nurturing religion provides a healing means of addressing a traumatic experience. Faith can facilitate faster and more effective emotional recovery (Pargament, 1997). In a rigorously designed long-term study of 124 parents who lost a child to sudden infant death syndrome, McIntosh, Silver, and Wortman (1993) found that greater religious participation was related to increased emotional support by others and increased meaning found in the loss of the child. This is no small finding given the high level of trauma that follows the sudden death of an infant. Religion appears to provide for these trauma-stricken parents a clinically effective means to make sense of the loss and enhances well-being, lowers distress, and may facilitate faster and more effective cognitive restructuring when integrating severe loss and emotional trauma. In another well-designed study of persons grieving the death of a family member or very close friend, it was discovered that there is a strong link between the ability to make sense of the loss through religious practices and positive psychological adjustment (Davis, Nolen-Hocksema, and Larson, 1998). Researchers in Great Britain found that people with strong religious beliefs coped better with the loss of a loved one or close friend over a fourteen-month period than did those without faith (Walsh et al., 1999).

Unique Role of Clergy

With adequate training, clergy are in an ideal position to recognize and assist those suffering from psychological trauma. Pastors are often in long-term relationships with individuals and their families, giving them ongoing contacts by which they can observe changes in behavior that can assist in the assessment and treatment of PTSD. Clergy are most often called upon in crisis situations associated with grief, depression, or trauma reactions such as personal illness or injury, death of spouse, death of a close family member, divorce or marital separation, change in health of a family member, or death of a close friend (Fairchild, 1980). Highlighting the prominent role that clergy have in community mental health, the U.S. Surgeon General's 2000 *Report on Mental Health* found that each year, 1 of 6 adults obtains mental health services either from a health care provider, the clergy, or a social service agency (Satcher, 2000).

Researchers have discovered that 1 of 5 persons (700,000 survivors) who are victimized in a violent crime (for example, rape, attempted rape, robbery, aggravated assault, or simple assault) seeks the counsel of a clergy-person (Norris, Kaniasty, and Scheer, 1990). This is the same number seeking help from all other mental health professionals or medical doctors combined (Norris, Kaniasty, and Scheer, 1990). Undoubtedly persons in distress go to clergy in such large numbers because accompanying the stressful state for many individuals are questions of meaning and purpose uniquely addressed by communities of faith. It is estimated that 1.8 million women are abused each year by husbands or intimate partners (Branner et al., 1999). A national survey of one thousand battered wives found that 1 of 3 received help from clergy, and 1 of 10 abusive husbands was counseled by clergy (Bowker, 1988).

Clergy and other religious professionals need to know how best to help people who have been affected by traumatic events. Pastors are accessible helpers within communities that offer a sense of continuity with centuries of human history and an experience of being a part of something greater than oneself. Clergy are visible and available leaders who communicate with a language of faith and hope in communities. Rabbis, priests, imams, and ministers are also in a unique position of trust in which they can assist persons by referring them to support systems available through their faith communities and beyond (Weaver, Revilla, and Koenig, 2001).

Summary

Accounts of the effects of traumatic stress have been documented over the history of humankind. Post-traumatic stress is a normal reaction to an abnormally stressful situation and represents a significant public health concern that warrants the attention of the religious community. Churches, synagogues, and mosques have many persons who are suffering from psychological trauma and need help. Religious faith is a primary way people cope with its negative effects. Faith communities can offer both the social support and a healing means of addressing a traumatic experience.

To become more effective helpers, clergy need skills to recognize and assist those who seek them for counsel in the aftermath of psychological trauma.

References

American Psychiatric Association (2000). *Diagnostic and Statistical Manual of Mental Disorders* (Fourth Edition, Text Revised). Washington, DC: American Psychiatric Association.

American School Health Association (1989). *The National Adolescent Student Health Survey: A Report on the Health of America's Youth*. Oakland, CA: Third Party Publishing Company.

Andreasen, N. C. (1985). Post-traumatic stress disorder. In H. I. Kaplan and B. J. Sadock (Eds.), *The Comprehensive Textbook of Psychiatry* (4th ed.) (pp. 918-924). Baltimore: Williams and Wilkins.

Black, J. W. (1987). The libidinal cacoon: A nurturing retreat for the families of plane crash victims. *Hospital and Community Psychiatry, 38(12)*, 1322-1326.

Blanchard, E. B., and Hicking, E. J. (1997). *After the Crash*. Washington, DC: American Psychological Association.

Bowker, L. H. (1988). Religious victims and their religious leaders: Services delivered to one thousand battered women by the clergy. In A. L. Horton and J. A. Williamson (Eds.), *Abuse and Religion: When Prayer Isn't Enough* (pp. 229-234). Lexington, MA: D.C. Heath.

Boyer, B. A., Knolls, M. L., Kafkalas, C. M., Tollen, L. G., and Swartz, M. (2000). Prevalence and relationship of posttraumatic stress in families experiencing pediatric spinal cord injury. *Rehabilitation Psychology, 45(4)*, 339-355.

Branner, S. J., Bradshaw, R. D., Hamlin, E. R., Fogarty, J. P., and Colligan, T. W. (1999). Spouse abuse: Physician guidelines to identification, diagnosis, and management in the uniformed services. *Military Medicine, 164(1)*, 30-36.

Breslau, N., Davis, G. C., Andreski, P., and Peterson, E. (1991). Traumatic events and posttraumatic stress disorder in an urban population of young adults. *Archives of General Psychiatry, 48*, 216-222.

Brewin, C. R., Andrews, B., and Valentine, J. D. (2000). Meta-analysis of risk factors for posttraumatic stress disorder in exposed adults. *Journal of Consulting and Clinical Psychology, 68(5)*, 748-766.

Bureau of Justice Statistics (1993). *Criminal Victimization in the United States, 1992*. Washington, DC: U.S. Department of Justice. Publication NCJ-144776.

Cayse, L. N. (1994). Fathers of children with cancer: A descriptive study of the stressors and coping strategies. *Journal of Pediatric Oncology Nursing, 11(3)*, 102-108.

Cervantes, R. C., de Synder, U. N. S., and Padella, A. M. (1989). Post-traumatic stress in immigrants from Central America and Mexico. *Hospital and Community Psychiatry, 40*, 615-619.

Chalfant, H. P., Heller, P. L., Roberts, A., Briones, D., Aguirre-Hochbaum, S., and Farr, W. (1990). The clergy as a resource for those encountering psychological distress. *Review of Religious Research, 31(3),* 305-313.

Chinnici, R. (1985). Pastoral care following a natural disaster. *Pastoral Psychology, 33(4),* 245-254.

Cohen, M. S. (1989). The rabbi and the holocaust survivor. In P. Marcus and A. Rosenberg (Eds.), *Healing Their Wounds: Psychotherapy with Holocaust Survivors and Their Families* (pp. 167-176). New York: Praeger.

Cwik, M. S. (1997). Peace at home? *Journal of Psychology and Judaism, 21(1),* 7-67.

Daly, R. J. (1983). Samuel Pepys and post-traumatic stress disorder. *British Journal of Psychiatry, 143,* 64-68.

Daries, J. M. (1990). Baptists and human liberation: South Africa. *American Baptist Quarterly, 9(4),* 307-309.

Davis, C. G., Nolen-Hocksema, S., and Larson, J. (1998). Making sense of loss and benefiting from the experience two construals of meaning. *Journal of Personality and Social Psychology, 75(2),* 561-574.

Duber, A. E., and Motta, R. W. (1999). Sexually and physically abused foster children and post-traumatic stress disorder. *Journal of Consulting and Clinical Psychology, 67(3),* 367-373.

Fairchild, R. W. (1980). *Finding Hope Again: A Pastor's Guide to Counseling Depressed Persons.* New York: Harper and Row.

Fox, S. H., and Tang, S. S. (2000). The Sierra Leonean refugee experience: Traumatic events and psychiatric sequelae. *Journal of Nervous and Mental Disease, 188(8),* 490-495.

Foy, D. W. (Ed.) (1992). *Treating Post-Traumatic Stress Disorder: Cognitive-behavioral Strategies.* New York: Guilford Press.

Garbarino, J., Kostelny, K., and Dubrow, N. (1991). What children can tell us about living in danger. *American Psychologist, 46(4),* 376-383.

Golding, J. M., Siegel, J. M., Sorenson, S. B., Burham, M. A., and Stein, J. A. (1989). Social support services following sexual assault. *Journal of Community Psychology, 17,* 92-107.

Green, B. L., Lindy, J. D., and Grace, M. C. (1988). Long-term coping with combat stress. *Journal of Traumatic Stress, 1(4),* 399-412.

Herman, J. L. (1992). *Trauma and Recovery.* New York: Basic Books.

Kessler, R. C., Sonnega, A., Bromet, E., Hughes, M., and Nelson, C. B. (1995). Post-traumatic stress disorder in the National Comorbidity Survey. *Archives of General Psychiatry, 52,* 1048-1060.

Kilpatrick, D. G., Saunders, B. E., Amick-McMullan, A., Best, C. L., Veronen, L. J., and Resnick, H. S. (1989). Victim and crime factors associated with the development of crime-related post-traumatic stress disorder. *Behavior Therapy, 20,* 199-214.

La Greca, A. M., Silverman, W. K., Vernberg, E. M., and Prinstein, M. J. (1996). Symptoms of post-traumatic stress in children after Hurricane Andrew: A prospective study. *Journal of Consulting and Clinical Psychology, 64(4)*, 712-723.

Larson, D. B., Hohmann, A. A., Kessler, L. G., Meador, K. G., Boyd, J. H., and McSherry, E. (1988). The couch and the cloth: The need for linkage. *Hospital and Community Psychiatry, 39(10)*, 1064-1069.

Lawson, R., Drebing, C., Berg, G., Vincellette, A., and Penk, W. (1998). The long-term impact of child abuse on religious behavior and spirituality in men. *Child Abuse and Neglect, 22(1)*, 369-379.

Lernoux, P. (1980). *Cry of the People.* Garden City, NJ: Doubleday.

Lifton, R. J. (1988). Understanding the traumatized self: Imagery, symbolization, and transformation. In J. P. Wilson, Z. Harel, and B. Kahana (Eds.), *Human Adaptation to Extreme Stress: From the Holocaust to Vietnam* (pp. 7-31). New York: Plenum.

Lindy, J. D., Grace, M. C., and Green, B. L. (1981). Survivors: Outreach to a reluctant population. *American Journal of Orthopsychiatry, 51(3)*, 468-478.

McIntosh, D. N., Silver, R. C., and Wortman, C. B. (1993). Religious role in adjustment to a negative life event: Coping with the loss of a child. *Journal of Personality and Social Psychology, 65(4)*, 812-821.

Mollica, R. F. (2000). Waging a new kind of war: Invisible wounds. *Scientific American, 282(60)*, 54-57.

Mollica, R. F., Streets, F. J., Boscarino, J., and Redlich, F. C. (1986). A community study of formal pastoral counseling activities of the clergy. *American Journal of Psychiatry, 143(3)*, 323-328.

Mollica, R. F., Wyshak, G., and Lavelle, J. (1987). The psychosocial impact of war trauma and torture on Southeast Asian refugees. *American Journal of Psychiatry, 144*, 1567-1572.

Norris, F. H., Kaniasty, K. Z., and Scheer, D. A. (1990). Use of mental health services among victims of crime: Frequency, correlates, and subsequent recovery. *Journal of Consulting and Clinical Psychology, 58(5)*, 538-547.

Pargament, K. I. (1997). *The Psychology of Religion and Coping: Theory, Research, Practice.* New York: Guilford Press.

Peterson, K. C., Prout, M. F., and Schwarz, R. A. (1991). *Post-Traumatic Stress Disorder: A Clinician's Guide.* New York: Plenum Press.

Satcher, D. (2000). Mental health: A report of the Surgeon General-executive summary. *Professional Psychology: Research and Practice, 31(1)*, 5-13.

Shore, J. H., Tatum, E. L., and Vollmer, W. M. (1986). Psychiatric reaction to disaster: The Mount St. Helens experience. *American Journal of Psychiatry, 143*, 590-596.

Shubiner, H., Scott, R., and Tzelepis, A. (1993). Exposure to violence among inner-city youth. *Journal of Adolescent Health, 14(3)*, 214-219.

Smith, B. W., Pargament, K. I., Brant, C., and Oliver, J. M. (2000). Noah revisited: Religious coping by church members and the impact of the 1993 Midwest flood. *Journal of Community Psychology, 28(2)*, 169-186.

Spiro, A., Schnurr, P. P., and Aldwin, C. M. (1993). Combat-related posttraumatic stress disorder symptoms in older men. *Psychology and Aging, 9(1)*, 17-26.

Sutker, P. B., and Allain, A. N. (1996). Assessment of PTSD and other mental disorders in World War II and Korean Conflict POW survivors and combat veterans. *Psychological Assessment, 8(1)*, 18-25.

Terr, L. (1990). *Too Scared to Cry.* New York: Basic Books.

Van der Kolk, B. A. (1987). *Psychological Trauma.* Washington, DC: American Psychiatric Press.

Veroff, J., Kulka, R. A., and Douvan, E. (1981). *Mental Health in America: Patterns of Help-Seeking from 1957 to 1976.* New York: Basic Books.

Walsh, K., King, M., Jones, L., Tookman, A., and Blizard, R. (2002). Spiritual beliefs may affect outcome of bereavement: Prospective study. *British Medical Journal, 324*, 1551-1554.

Weaver, A. J. (1992a). Working with potentially dangerous persons: What clergy need to know. *Pastoral Psychology, 40(5)*, 313-323.

Weaver, A. J. (1992b). The distressed family and wounded children. *Journal of Religion and Health, 31*, 207-220.

Weaver, A. J. (1995). Has there been a failure to prepare and support parish-based clergy in their role as front-line community mental health workers? A review. *Journal of Pastoral Care, 49*, 129-149.

Weaver, A. J., and Koenig, H. G. (1997). Uncovering elder abuse: How to stop the hidden violence. *Christian Ministry, 28(4)*, 18-19.

Weaver, A. J., Koenig, H. G., and Ochberg, F. M. (1996). Post-traumatic stress, mental health professionals, and the clergy: A need for collaboration, training and research. *Journal of Traumatic Stress, 9(4)*, 861-870.

Weaver, A. J., Revilla, L. A., and Koenig, H. G. (2002). *Counseling Families Across the Stages of Life: A Handbook for Pastors and Other Helping Professionals.* Nashville: Abingdon Press.

Weinrich, S., Hardin, S. B., and Johnson, M. (1990). Nurses' response to hurricane Hugo: Victims' disaster stress. *Archives of Psychiatric Nursing, 4(3)*, 195-205.

Weiss, D. S., Marmar, C. R., Schlenger, W. E., Fairbank, J. A., Jordan, B. K., Hough, R. L., and Kulka, R. A. (1992). The prevalence of lifetime and partial posttraumatic stress disorder in the Vietnam theater veterans. *Journal of Traumatic Stress, 5(3)*, 365-376.

Williams, D. R., Griffins, E. H., Young, J. L., Collins, C., and Dobson, J. (1999). Structure and provision of services in black churches in New Haven, Connecticut. *Cultural Diversity and Ethnic Minority Psychology, 5(2)*, 118-133.

Zeidner, M. (1993). Coping with disaster. *Journal of Youth and Adolescence, 22*, 89-108.

Zimmerman, G., and Weber, W. (2000). Care for the caregivers: A program for Canadian military chaplains after serving NATO and the United Nations peacekeeping missions in the 1990s. *Military Medicine, 165(9)*, 687-690.

Defining Terms

Difficult life experiences, those ranging from the mild frustrations of daily life to intensely painful events, have been referred to by mental health specialists as stressors. Life is full of low-level stressors, encountered every day, and unfortunately punctuated at times by more serious ones. However, exposure to stressors does not necessarily cause problems. A key element in triggering stress is an individual's assessment of his or her ability to cope (for example, "Do I have what it takes to handle this? Do I feel competent and in control?"). When people feel confident and have a sense of mastery, stressors can be annoying, but they usually do not cause significant difficulties. However, the perception of a relative inability to cope leads to distress.

stressors + lack of confidence in one's ability to cope = distress

For an experience to be considered truly *traumatic*, two elements are generally necessary. The first is exposure to an intensely scary, horrifying, deeply disturbing, or awful event. The second is an individual's perception of a profound sense of powerlessness or helplessness (a complete inability to escape from a terrible situation or to cope with it).

overwhelming stressors + perception of extreme powerlessness = trauma

The intensity of reaction is always influenced by a person's unique level of emotional sensitivity.

Emotional Vulnerability

People are not created equal in terms of their psychological vulnerability. Several factors ultimately have great bearing on how persons perceive and react to very stressful life events.

Inborn emotional sensitivity. Numerous studies have clearly demonstrated that some individuals are born with nervous systems that are wired for exquisite sensitivity. Generally these infants (about 10 percent of all babies born) have no signs of brain damage or abnormal neurobiology.

They are just sensitive—somewhat like those who are born with fair skin that is especially susceptible to sunburn. From the start, these youngsters have a rough time: They are easily upset, they may cling to their parents, and they shy away from novel or unfamiliar situations. Excellent parenting can provide much needed comfort and soothing, but most of these children will continue to be psychologically sensitive for the rest of their lives.

Biological predisposition for psychiatric disorders. There is increasing evidence that some forms of mental illness are linked to abnormalities in brain chemistry and can be due in part to genetic factors. Such disorders include: schizophrenia, panic disorder, depression, obsessive-compulsive disorder, autism, bipolar (manic-depressive) disorder, and attention deficit hyperactivity disorder (ADHD). Each of these illnesses results in a variety of specific symptoms, and it is important to note that people with these disorders are generally more vulnerable to the effects of major stressors.

The role of early adverse life events. Child abuse or neglect can have a lifetime effect. Aside from the emotional scars, two additional effects are important to consider.

During the past ten years, research has revealed that *severe neglect*, especially during the first year of life, can result in persistent abnormal brain functioning. Current theories strongly support the idea that sufficient amounts of touching, holding, and rocking of young children (as well as all infant mammals) are essential stimuli necessary for normal brain development, a considerable amount of which continues well after birth. Without this, abnormal nerve cell development can leave a brain in a more or less permanent state of hypersensitivity, which results in persistent, excessive emotional vulnerability. Although loving, nurturing experiences later in childhood can help a child to some extent, such positive experiences do not appear able completely to undo the damage. The frequent result is lifelong psychological sensitivity and increased risk for anxiety and depression.

Severe child abuse (neglect, physical abuse, marked emotional maltreatment, and especially sexual molestation) can result in a large number of psychological problems, many of which will be addressed in later chapters. Clearly, most persons who experienced early child abuse, especially if it was ongoing, have persistent emotional sensitivity. But this is just the tip of the iceberg.

When abuse has been severe and prolonged, especially if at the hands of a parent, such experiences can damage the inner desire to attach to others, which is one of the most fundamental of human needs. When the desire for attachment is extinguished by brutal abuse early in life, the results are devastating. Such persons enter childhood, adolescence, and adulthood with deep-seated fears of closeness and intimacy, a sense of ever-present danger, and often profound mistrust (which is not surprising, given their first and earliest experiences with others). Most of these terribly wounded people never develop meaningful human relationships. Social interactions are usually superficial at best, which often leaves them with a lonely and barren existence. For persons who are traumatized later in life, the best hope for emotional healing and recovery is in the context of loving support from friends, family, clergy, and counselors. However, those with attachment problems usually do not seek out support from others because of their fears and mistrust, and they often have the most chronic and devastating outcomes following traumatic life events.

Sensitization from prior traumas. A final issue that can contribute to emotional vulnerability is exposure to repeated traumatic experiences.

Traumatic Events

How devastating a particular experience is must be understood from a person's own perspective. For a number of years, only life-threatening events were considered to be traumatic by psychological literature. However, recent studies have made it clear that a wide array of experiences can be traumatic, depending on the individual. Some events are so intensely frightening, horrible, or disturbing that anyone would feel overwhelmed—rape, assault, kidnapping, or witnessing the murder of a family member, to mention a few. Beyond this are a number of life experiences that do not make newspaper headlines but are traumatic and not infrequent, such as being told that one's child has a terminal illness, being the victim of a terrible accident, or experiencing the death of a close family member or friend (studies show that up to 14 percent of persons develop severe post-traumatic symptoms following the loss of a loved one).

The magnitude of traumatic events cannot be determined as one might rate the intensity of a hurricane or earthquake. The effect of an experience *always* depends on its personal meaning to individuals and their preexisting level of emotional sensitivity.

Other factors to consider. In general, the following factors must also be evaluated in understanding psychological trauma:

- *Is it an ongoing trauma versus a single event* (e.g., ongoing child abuse versus surviving a house fire)?
- *Is the trauma caused by humans versus an unavoidable, natural event* (e.g., rape or attempted murder versus tornado or flood)?
- *If the trauma occurs at the hand of another person, is that person a stranger or someone on whom one depends* (e.g., injury by a drunk driver versus domestic violence or child abuse by a parent)?
- *Was the event anticipated?* Even deaths following prolonged illnesses can be traumatic. However, the more unexpected an experience,

generally the less prepared a person is, and that can contribute to a greater sense of vulnerability or powerlessness.

Post-Traumatic Stress: How Common Is It?

All people react to traumatic life events, however the responses vary considerably. The more severe forms of reaction are called *post-traumatic stress disorder* (PTSD) and *acute stress disorder* (ASD), which has the same symptoms as PTSD but lasts for only a brief period (a few days to a month). The manifestations of these conditions will be discussed below, but first the frequency of these disorders will be examined.

It is estimated that 90 percent of people will have at least one experience that is overwhelmingly frightening or disturbing, yet not everyone will develop PTSD. In the United States, the lifetime prevalence rate for PTSD is at least 8 percent (Kessler et al., 1995); however, many experts believe that this figure underestimates its frequency. It is more likely to be 15 percent (Zisook, 1999).

One factor that influences the prevalence of these disorders is whether people are exposed to specific traumatic experiences and, if so, for how long. Fortunately, only a tiny percentage of persons in the U.S. are kidnapped or tortured; however, among those who are, 54 percent develop PTSD. The rate of chronic PTSD among holocaust survivors is extraordinarily high. Thirty-six percent of family members of suicide victims experience PTSD (Zisook, 1999). In communities struck by natural disasters, typically 30 percent of people develop PTSD.

The single most common traumatic event is the death of a loved one. Ten to fourteen percent of persons who face this experience develop PTSD or ASD (Zisook, 1999).

Rates of PTSD following a natural disaster vary considerably. One of the most studied disasters was the Buffalo Creek dam break and subsequent flood in West Virginia. Following that event, 59 percent of those affected exhibited symptoms of PTSD, and 25 percent continued to have symptoms when followed up fourteen years later (Green et al., 1992). Studies of refugees show PTSD rates that exceed 50 percent (McFarlane and De Girolamo, 1996, p. 143). Forty-eight percent of female rape victims experience PTSD (Kessler et al., 1995), while there is a 16 percent lifetime prevalence rate of PTSD among firefighters (McFarlane, 1998). There is variation among Vietnam War veterans; however, the best studies indicate that 15 percent of those who saw combat suffered PTSD (Kulka et al., 1990).

Every rabbi, priest, imam, or pastor will encounter in their congregations those who suffer from PTSD or ASD. Knowing how to recognize the disorders and responding appropriately is crucial.

Signs and Symptoms of PTSD

Almost all of those who develop PTSD initially react with extremely intense emotions, usually fear and denial manifest in disbelief ("It can't be true!"). This state of shock and of feeling overwhelmed may last from minutes to hours to a few days. It is then followed by one of two predominant reactions: *intrusion* or *numbing*.

Intrusion is a state characterized by emotions, thoughts, and vivid memories that enter a person's mind repeatedly throughout the day. They are termed intrusive because these experiences are clearly unwelcome—they force their way into awareness and are not under the individual's control. Intrusions are so awful and intense that most people with PTSD will do anything to avoid them, but they are usually unable completely to suppress the experiences. These survivors not only were powerless during a psychological trauma, but also afterward became powerless over their inner thoughts, feelings, and memories that erupt without warning. This contributes to an ongoing sense of helplessness. Individuals with phobias (for example, a fear of flying) often deal with them by avoidance (they simply do not fly), but persons cannot escape from their own minds.

Intrusive experiences can also include repetitive nightmares and "flashbacks," which are intensely vivid and highly emotion-laden memories. They often seem so real that persons experiencing flashbacks actually believe they are back in the psychological trauma for a moment or two.

The frequent, if not almost constant, state of being emotionally overwhelmed is aptly described as a "living hell" by many with PTSD. To make matters worse, often the nightmares are so disturbing that survivors become afraid to sleep. Ultimately, sleep deprivation further contributes to an escalating loss of emotional control. Attempted escape through alcohol abuse is an understandable and not uncommon response. Suicides also occur because the times of intrusion and of feeling overwhelmed can last for weeks or months and may seem never ending.

As will be discussed in the next chapter, low-level stressful experiences are ultimately worked through as people confront and acknowledge psychologically painful realities. Facing difficult truths is central to emotional healing. However, it must be emphasized that in PTSD, the feelings and memories that sweep over survivors are often too intense to be processed. Rather than being beneficial, these tidal waves of emotional pain overwhelm; each new explosion of suffering actually retraumatizes a person. For this reason, true PTSD rarely resolves on its own and often becomes increasingly severe. The adage that "time heals all wounds" simply does not apply to this condition.

Living with horrible intrusions for months takes a devastating toll on people and may eventually lead to a major depression. Then a person has PTSD *and* depression, which increases the risk of substance abuse and suicide.

The second most common psychological state is *numbing*. It manifests in a number of ways, including: profound emotional deadness or emptiness, marked withdrawal from social interactions, and avoidance of situations that may be reminders of the traumatic event (for example, if the trauma was a terrible automobile accident, some with PTSD may be afraid to ride in a car; if the trauma occurred at night, survivors may intensely fear leaving their homes after dark).

Another common symptom is *dissociation*. This is a strange state of detachment, in which people report feeling groggy, "fuzzy-headed," "spaced out," mildly confused, or disoriented. Often survivors say that it "feels like I'm on drugs" even though they are not. Some also suffer from a related symptom: *derealization*—another peculiar experience in which a person feels as if the world is odd, distorted, or in other ways unfamiliar and unreal. Strong evidence suggests that dissociation and derealization are due to bio-chemical changes in the brain. Finally, alcohol and other substances are frequently abused, which contributes to this state of numbness.

Often persons experiencing dissociation or emotional numbing are perplexed. They know that something bad has happened to them, but there is a conspicuous lack of emotion. It seems odd, and some individuals begin to feel guilty ("I should be feeling more. What's wrong with me?").

In the weeks or months following traumatic events, those with PTSD often vacillate between these two markedly different states of mind. The oscillation between intrusion and numbness strikes not only the sufferer, but also friends and family, as inexplicable. For example, a rape victim may have been in a constant state of numbness for six months. By outward appearances she looks shut down and detached but not upset. Then, suddenly nightmares and intrusive experiences reemerge for no apparent reason. It is not surprising that many of these survivors and their loved ones begin to question their sanity.

Additional problems. The following are additional common symptoms seen in PTSD: feeling constantly tense and on edge; a tendency to startle easily; irritability; depression and substance abuse; occasionally self-mutilation (for example, intentionally burning or cutting oneself) or psychotic symptoms (such as hallucinations); and physical problems, such as insomnia, weight loss, and headaches.

Close relationships are almost always adversely affected by PTSD. Problems with intimacy and sexuality are especially common. A large number of persons experience significant difficulties at work or school, often due to difficulty with concentration and memory that is quite common in PTSD.

Existential and spiritual crises. In almost all PTSD cases, two fundamental existential beliefs are challenged, if not shattered: "The world is fair" and "The world is safe."

On a cognitive level, most intelligent adults are quick to acknowledge the inaccuracy of these assumptions. Yet the truth is that on a deep inner level, most people believe (or at least hope) that "bad things happen, but they won't happen to me or to my family if I lead a good life and believe in God." When trauma strikes, these beliefs crumble and one's worldview is radically shaken. And this often greatly contributes to a profound increase in one's sense of powerlessness and vulnerability.

Although many turn to God for support during difficult times, the relentless nature of PTSD symptoms wears survivors down and often leads to a spiritual crisis. "How can God let these bad things happen to people who love God?"

Bottom Lines

PTSD and its less chronic cousin, ASD, unfortunately are common. Although individuals often have incredible strength and resilience in overcoming difficult life experiences, those with PTSD are a different story. Without professional treatment, PTSD rarely disappears on its own and often becomes more severe over time. Yet good treatment is available if the disorder is recognized and appropriate referrals are made.

Clergypersons are in a position to become aware of PTSD when it occurs in the lives of congregants and to understand its tenacious, chronic course. Many in congregations are likely to show great and genuine concern when tragedy strikes a member. Yet most laypeople have a "you'll get over it—time heals all wounds" view, which is sincere, but naive.

Those suffering from PTSD often feel profoundly misunderstood and alone as they battle terrible emotional pain. Unfortunately, most of these survivors sooner or later hear others encouraging them to "put it behind you—get on with your life." Clergy's role in educating a congregation regarding psychological trauma and being available to counsel those suffering with PTSD or ASD can mean a lot to these emotionally wounded people.

The next chapter will examine key ingredients in recovery from psychological trauma. It will shed light on those experiences that facilitate healing and recovery. Then in subsequent chapters, there will be a closer examination of specific traumatic situations, with a focus on how clergy can intervene.

References

Green, B. L., Lindy, J. D., Grace, M. C., and Leonard, A. C. (1992). Chronic post-traumatic stress disorder and diagnostic co-morbidity in a disaster sample. *Journal of Nervous and Mental Disease, 180,* 700-766.

Kessler, R. C., Sonnega, A., Bromet, E., Hughes, M., and Nelson, S. B. (1995). Post-traumatic stress disorder in the National Co-Morbidity Survey. *Archives of General Psychiatry, 52(12),* 1048-1060.

Kulka, R. A., Fairbank, J. A., Jordan, K. B., Weiss, D., and Cranston, A. (1990). *Trauma and the Vietnam War Generations: Report of the Findings from the National Vietnam Veterans Readjustment Study*. New York: Brunner/Mazel.

McFarlane, A. C. (1988). The phenomenology of post-traumatic stress disorder following a natural disaster. *Journal of Nervous and Mental Disease, 176, 22-26*.

McFarlane, A. C., and DeGirolamo, G. (1996). The nature of traumatic stressors and the epidemiology of post-traumatic reations. In B. A. van der Kolk, A. C. McFarlane, and L. Weisaeth (Eds.), *Traumatic Stress: The Effects of Overwhelming Experience on Mind, Body, and Society* (pp. 129-154). New York: Guilford Press.

Zisook, S., Chentsova-Dutton, Y., and Shuchter, S. R. (1999). PTSD following bereavement. *Annals of Clinical Psychiatry, 10(4), 157-163*.

Treatment for Post-Traumatic Stress Disorder

Chapters that follow will address specific traumatic situations and explore particular treatment and referral options. This chapter will focus on general treatment approaches.

Realistic Support

Most people who encounter a traumatic life event have never experienced anything as intense, and the responses described in the previous chapter are frequently perplexing and frightening. Often when persons are engulfed by intrusive symptoms, they believe they are going crazy. Uncontrolled displays of emotion evoke feelings of shame and vulnerability for many who suffer from PTSD. Profound numbing can cause survivors to feel guilty that they are not experiencing what they consider to be appropriate emotions.

The first order of business must be to address these worries by helping a person (and the family) understand something about the nature of PTSD, to "normalize" it by teaching survivors that their symptoms are not unusual following severe trauma. It is also important to explain that many individuals do not quickly recover and that professional counseling is often helpful and necessary.

Create Safety and Reduce Demands

For many with PTSD, the world is now experienced as highly unpredictable and unsafe. Those things once counted upon for reassurance and protection seem no longer reliable. Existential anchors (such as beliefs that the world is fair) are shaken.

How can safety be created? One of the important first steps involves validation. If persons experience understanding and acknowledgment of their responses, they may begin to feel less alone and to develop a sense of connection. This in itself can reduce fear. However, it is crucial to listen carefully to come to an accurate understanding of a person's unique perceptions and feelings. Superficial comments, such as "I understand what you are going through," typically provide little real comfort. Conversely, such statements often leave a survivor feeling more estranged and isolated. Although one may gradually sense what a traumatic event was like for a given person, it is difficult completely to understand complex and highly individual experiences and emotions. Survivors do not need clichés or platitudes; they need someone who cares and is trying to understand.

Another way to help create safety is to explore with persons whether they are *currently* exposed to experiences that foster ongoing fear or stress. A survivor can be asked, "Is there anything going on *now* that is creating further stress in your life or requiring more of you than you can give?" For example, soldiers with PTSD are taken from the battlefront and removed from the sights and sounds of war to prevent retraumatization.

Consider two situations. Robert was a night clerk at a convenience store that was robbed, and his life was threatened. He continued to feel overwhelmed three days later but was told by his employer that he must return to work, even though he was afraid to do so. Since the robbery took place at night, a reasonable accommodation would be for Robert to be reassigned to the day shift. Such a solution may reduce some of the fear and vulnerability associated with working after dark. In a state of traumatization, many survivors may not even consider requesting such an adjustment, so to recommend this to them can be very helpful.

Ruth identified the seriously mutilated body of her mother who was killed in an especially terrible automobile crash. For the past month, Ruth has been haunted by intrusive memories and terrible nightmares. She is overwhelmed, and her daily life is further strained by her commitment to a number of volunteer activities (such as helping at a soup kitchen and teaching a Sunday school class). Since her sense of obligation is strong, she may not consider taking a breather from her normal responsibilities without encouragement. A reasonable strategy for her might be to remove some of the pressures until she is better able to cope.

In these examples, clergy can assist by helping survivors give themselves permission to make requests (such as Robert's change of shift) or restructure their lives, at least for a while. Persons often resist because they feel obligated or believe that it is inappropriate. Clergy can support survivors in constructing lives that reduce overload or that create a greater sense of safety.

Facing Painful Realities: Bit by Bit

Those who successfully recover from PTSD have invariably had to come to terms with the reality of traumatic events. This almost never occurs quickly, and it requires facing a truth that is always accompanied by tremendous suffering. But for this process to be effective, two basic elements are required: *reexposure without retraumatization* and *repetition*.

Some *reexposure without retraumatization* occurs naturally in the form of recurrent intrusive thoughts, memories, and dreams. It is as if the mind has its own self-healing mechanism. Although such experiences are unpleasant, they may be at the heart of emotional recovery. Each intrusive memory is like receiving a dose of reality.

Intrusions are automatic and involuntary. Beyond that, many survivors also feel the urge to think and talk about the trauma. This is an important element of emotional healing that must be understood. For some, the impulse to go over events again and again may seem morbid; for others, the need to talk about them repeatedly seems like "beating a dead horse." But there is a healthy motive behind these urges. When people have been traumatized, the terrifying images and memories *must* be confronted repeatedly. If done appropriately, the memories will gradually lose their power to overwhelm. After successful psychotherapy, those who had suffered from PTSD will still have occasional thoughts about their trauma. However, those memories will no longer dominate one's life; they become less frequent and the emotions become less intense.

If reexperiencing is to lead to healing, it must be done in a way that does not retraumatize, which is difficult to achieve without psychotherapy. Those trained to treat PTSD proceed cautiously as they encourage clients to discuss events surrounding their trauma. Typically a number of anxiety reduction techniques are taught to survivors to help them manage intense feelings. When learned, these skills provide some measure of control over otherwise overwhelming emotions. A regained sense of control is likely to be part of the recovery process in itself, since mastery is the best antidote to powerlessness.

A bit-by-bit revisitation of traumatic events helps survivors gradually process their experiences, place things in perspective, and, most important, face painful realities without being completely overwhelmed. A counselor who is caring and empathetic, yet not overwhelmed by the intense emotions, can serve as an anchor. This sturdy presence helps a traumatized person feel safe while navigating through turbulent memories and emotions.

It is important to emphasize that a common error in counseling those with PTSD is too aggressively encouraging the open expression of emotions or discussion of the traumatic event. Often, to do so will open up people too much. That experience, in and of itself, can be overwhelming, and a common consequence is that survivors then avoid future counseling. A therapist might say something like this:

> It is often necessary for people to be able to talk openly about terrible experiences. I am happy to listen now and at any time in the future, but please go at your own pace. And if it ever feels like it is becoming too intense, please tell me.

Repetition is also necessary. This must be conveyed to a traumatized person along with a counselor's patience and willingness to discuss experiences repeatedly. Often survivors believe that they are burdening others if they talk about events over and over again. It is likewise all too common for listeners to communicate in subtle (or not so subtle) ways that it is not okay to go on and on about a traumatic experience. This is the underlying message of such comments as, "You shouldn't dwell so much on the past— you need to put it behind you and get on with your life." Such remarks generally come from friends and family members who have good intentions, but do not understand the nature of PTSD and the need to process a devastating experience again and again.

Furthermore, it is simply difficult for most people to listen to another talk about what are often frightening or disturbing events. Even among well-trained psychotherapists, sometimes hearing gruesome details of a traumatic experience or witnessing extremely intense emotions can cause a sort of PTSD in the therapist (this has been called "secondary PTSD" and has many familiar symptoms, such as nightmares). Many good-hearted and competent clergy and counselors may not be able to listen to horrific stories without experiencing their own sense of being overwhelmed. When this is the case, a referral to a psychotherapist specifically trained to treat PTSD is in order.

The clergyperson or therapist who takes on the responsibility of counseling a traumatized person should explain that it is common for those with PTSD to need to go over events repeatedly. It is crucial for emotional healing, and survivors should not feel inhibited about needing to return to such discussions a number of times.

Dealing with Overwhelming Intrusive Symptoms

Frequently, traumatized persons will feel the urge to talk about intensely distressing events only to have that result in feeling completely overwhelmed. Two approaches have been shown to be helpful for these individuals.

The first is a technique first developed in the early 1990s known as Eye Movement Desensitization and Reprocessing (EMDR). This procedure, used by therapists who have taken specialized training, involves the use of eye movements with other sensory and motor techniques rapidly to de-escalate intense feelings (Foa, Keane, and Friedman, 2000). EMDR is done in the context of otherwise traditional approaches to psychotherapy.

A second technique that is often helpful in reducing intrusive symptoms and feelings of being overwhelmed is medication. Occasionally tranquilizers and/or antipsychotic drugs may be used. However, the class of medications considered most effective in treating PTSD is the selective-serotonin antidepressants (such as Prozac, Paxil, Celexa, Zoloft, Serzone). These drugs often reduce nightmares, anxiety, and intrusive symptoms, as well as depression. In general, they enhance overall emotional control. Antidepressant medications are not habit-forming and are safe and often effective for treating certain symptoms of PTSD. Once antidepressants are prescribed, it generally takes two to four weeks before the first signs of improvement are noticed. After the drugs begin to take effect, typically they will be used for a period of at least one year.

A clear advantage of these medications is that antidepressants generally do not cause the sedation or psychological numbing that can occur with tranquilizers. Antidepressant drugs improve emotional control so that people are better able to face painful realities and talk about them with less likelihood of it leading to feeling overwhelmed (Preston, O'Neal, and Talaga, 2001). Medication is used not to pacify or dull the person, but to enhance the chances that psychotherapy will work.

Numbing and Denial

Some numbing and denial can be understood as adaptive and a welcomed respite from being psychologically overwhelmed. However, if extreme or prolonged, this state can result in emotional paralysis, withdrawal from life, and occupational dysfunction. Among the most devastating results of chronic numbing are loneliness and withdrawal from connection or intimacy with others.

When this psychological state is pronounced or prolonged, antidepressants and psychotherapy have been found to be helpful. Many experts believe that numbing is a defense against feeling overwhelmed. Thus, when medications begin to shore up inner emotional controls, it then becomes safe enough to lift the defenses and survivors begin to come back to life.

Additional Goals for Psychotherapy

In addition to the core emotions of fear, sadness, and loss, other feelings can interfere with post-traumatic healing and contribute significantly to increased suffering. Leading the list of offenders are guilt, shame, anger, and existential anxiety.

Guilt can be traced to a person's belief that he or she should have done more to avoid or prevent the traumatic event. Reassurances such as "It wasn't your fault" or "There was nothing you could have done" rarely assuage guilt. In therapy, what typically helps is the counselor encouraging a survivor to talk very specifically about details leading up to the trauma. Often, only by rehashing an experience can a person with PTSD come to a clear understanding of what realistically could and could not have been done to prevent the tragedy. Guilt almost always carries an underlying theme of "badness" of the self. Often what gradually becomes clear is that a survivor had no ability to foresee events, few realistic options, and almost no bad intentions. Transforming guilt into regret is healing, as is the dawning awareness of human limitations in preventing many forms of trauma. It is important to note that highly resistant and unrealistic guilt often accompanies major depression, a condition that must be treated.

Shame often accompanies the loss of emotional control that is experienced frequently with PTSD. Over a period of time, a counselor's non-judgmental stance may be the single most helpful element in reducing feelings of shame. Although the words may not be spoken directly, a compassionate attitude without judgment can convey that "these terrible events would shake anyone to the core—your intense emotions may be unfamiliar and profoundly upsetting, but they are understandable and honest reactions."

Anger can be triggered by numerous sources: the drunk driver, the incompetent doctor, an impersonal health care system, the family member who committed suicide, oneself for perceived emotional weakness, God for having created a world that can be dangerous or unfair. It is important for survivors to find a voice for their rage. If not expressed, honored, and understood, anger can poison; it can result in bitterness, erupt into violence or chronic irritability, and cause serious health problems (most notably, high blood pressure).

One common pathway for the resolution of anger is through forgiveness. But as noted psychiatrist M. Scott Peck explains, many persons engage in "cheap forgiveness," which is shallow and does little actually to extinguish root feelings (Peck, 1992). According to Dr. Peck, individuals must first find someone guilty before they can be pardoned. The road to meaningful forgiveness often requires an open acknowledgment of one's deep anger—facing it, getting clear about the sources, and sharing it with a counselor. The heart of forgiveness may be the letting go of rage in such a way that it does not continue to dominate and contaminate one's inner emotional life.

Existential anxieties are almost never alleviated by platitudes (such as life will go on, time heals all wounds, just trust in God and you'll be okay). In the wake of traumatic events, survivors do not need advice, but they do benefit from experiencing genuine support and a human connection. Clichés and "good advice" often leave a traumatized person feeling cold and isolated, realizing that a concerned friend or family member just does not understand. Patience, care, love, and continued availability are the responses that afford the greatest chance of reducing the suffering of survivors facing existential crises.

You Can Help

Most persons who experience traumatic stress receive no professional treatment and little real help from friends and family. They are cast adrift in emotional turmoil that often feels unending. Those with PTSD suffer terribly, relationships are often ruined, and many are confronted by a crisis of faith. Clergy can do much to educate a congregation about emotional trauma, provide counseling, and make appropriate referrals for treatment. The more a person understands about the many aspects of traumatic stress, the better he or she is able to recognize it and to respond appropriately.

The remaining chapters will explore in detail a number of traumatic experiences, how they are manifest, how they are treated, and suggested responses on the part of religious leaders.

References

Foa, E. B., Keane, T. M., and Friedman, M. J. (2000). *Effective Treatments for PTSD*. New York: Guilford Press.

Peck, M. S. (1992) *Further Along the Road Less Traveled: Blame and Forgiveness*. New York: Simon and Schuster.

Preston, J. D., O'Neal, J. H., and Talaga, M. (2001). *Handbook of Clinical Psychopharmacology for Therapists*. Oakland, CA: New Harbinger.

PART TWO

Case Studies

Motor Vehicle Accident

"It was a miracle she survived the crash"

Grace, a twenty-six-year-old single woman, was driving to a church fellowship meeting on a Saturday evening. In order to get there, she entered the freeway planning to travel three exits. As she left the on-ramp, her car was struck at high speed in the rear by a large recreational vehicle. The driver was an eighteen-year-old with little driving experience. It was later discovered that he was drinking alcohol and attempting to adjust his CD player at the time of the accident.

Grace's car was totally demolished, but she survived because she was wearing her seat belt and the vehicle had air bags. However, she was trapped for several hours before she could be extricated. Her injuries were extensive, and it took four months of rehabilitation and convalescence before she could return to her job. Unfortunately, she continued to suffer from chronic back pain and had problems focusing at work. Before the accident she had been open, adventurous, and gregarious. Afterward, she had little interest in participating in the social, athletic, and church activities she formerly enjoyed. Her pastor, the Rev. Susan Osborn, observed that Grace had become detached and withdrawn from others, especially her family and close friends. She refused to drive and was nervous, on edge, and easily upset as a passenger, particularly if a large vehicle came near. In addition, she had intense nightmares about the accident.

Rev. Osborn consulted with Rabbi Zahara Springer, the chaplain who had ministered to Grace in her convalescence at the medical center. The rabbi had extensive training in clinical pastoral education and was able to help Rev. Osborn recognize the signs of post-traumatic stress disorder (PTSD). The chaplain knew that PTSD sometimes develops following a traumatic event and can be a debilitating condition.

Pastoral Care Assessment

Grace continued to reexperience the terrifying event in recurrent and intrusive nightmares. She avoided situations associated with the accident and experienced a general emotional numbness. Grace was also hypervigilant and uncharacteristically irritable. Post-traumatic stress disorder is diagnosed when these symptoms persist for more than one month and create significant impairment in a person's ability to live normally (APA, 2000).

Relevant History

According to a recent study by the University of North Carolina Highway Safety Research Center, an estimated 284,000 distracted drivers are involved in serious crashes each year (Stutts, Reinfurt, Staplin, and Rodgman, 2001). Researchers found that drivers were most often distracted by something outside their vehicles (29.4 percent), followed by adjusting a radio or CD player (11.4 percent). Drivers under the age of twenty were especially likely to be distracted by tuning a radio or changing CDs.

Diagnostic Criteria

Motor vehicle accidents (MVAs) are probably the single most common form of trauma that causes PTSD (Norris, 1992). A survey of four cities in the U.S. and Canada found that almost 1 in 4 individuals had experienced an MVA at some time during his or her life. Although the majority of persons who survive a serious MVA do not develop mental health difficulties, many do. In studies of the general population, approximately 1 in 11 MVA survivors develops PTSD (Norris, 1992), with higher rates among those seeking psychological treatment. A study of almost one thousand patients treated shortly after an MVA at an emergency clinic in England found that PTSD was present in 23 percent after three months and almost 17 percent after one year. In the study, chronic PTSD was correlated to trauma severity, perceived threat, dissociation during the accident, female gender, and previous emotional problems (Ehlers, Mayou, and Bryant, 1998).

Of those who have PTSD, symptoms usually begin within three months of an accident, and the course of the illness varies. Some recover within six months, although others have symptoms that last much longer. Occasionally, the illness does not show up until years after the traumatic event. Things that remind survivors of the crash can be very distressing, which may cause them to avoid places or situations that bring back those memories. Ordinary events can serve as reminders of the trauma and can trigger flashbacks or intrusive images. A person having a flashback (which can come in the form of images, sounds, smells, or feelings) may lose touch with reality and believe that the accident is happening again. Anniversaries of the traumatic event are often very difficult (APA, 2000).

Major depression and anxiety disorders are also common among MVA survivors (Blanchard and Hickling, 1997). Almost 7 percent of men and 16 percent of women have had an anxiety disorder in the form of a specific phobia at some point in their lives (Kessler et al., 1994). A specific phobia, such as an accident phobia in reaction to an MVA, is an intense fear of something that poses little or no actual danger. If an individual comes in contact with the feared object or situation, he or she may experience panic symptoms (such as increased heart rate, sweating, nausea, shortness of breath, faintness, negative thoughts). Such phobias are not extreme fear; rather they are an irrational fear of a particular thing (APA, 2000). Although adults with accident phobias may realize that these fears are irrational, they often find that facing, or even thinking about facing, the feared situation (for example, driving a car) brings on a panic attack or severe anxiety. Grace also has the symptoms of a person with accident phobia in addition to PTSD.

Response to Vignette

One aspect of MVA-related PTSD that is different from many other traumas is the increased likelihood of being injured or of developing chronic pain following the event. As the degree of physical injury and fear of dying because of the MVA increase, the greater the likelihood of developing PTSD. Research shows that persons with poor coping skills, mental health problems (such as depression, anxiety disorders), and poor social support before the traumatic event have sometimes been linked to the development of PTSD following severe MVAs (Blanchard and Hickling, 1997). However, Grace did not have a history of mental health problems, possessed good coping skills, and had a good social support network at her job and in her church. When a trauma is very severe, almost anyone can develop PTSD.

PTSD is common among persons who require rehabilitation after a trauma. Unfortunately it is often overlooked or attributed to other sources, such as pain or physical injury (Asmundson, Norton, and Norton, 1999). Persons in rehabilitation with chronic pain resulting from an MVA are three times more likely to have PTSD and accident phobia than those not involved in an MVA (Kuch, Evans, Watson, Bubela, and Cox, 1991). Those with accident phobias after an MVA often have anxiety and avoidance along with extreme fear of new events resembling the accident.

It is important to identify PTSD and accident phobias quickly and to encourage persons to seek appropriate treatment. If left untreated, these conditions can become chronic. Taylor and Koch (1995) found that anxiety symptoms in combination with medical conditions increased the number of days persons spent in bed with a disability by nearly fourfold (18.0 versus 4.8 average days).

Social support from friends and family and the active reengagement of the survivor in work and other activities are very important to those suffering from psychological trauma. To the extent that limitations will allow, Grace should be encouraged to maintain as much of her pre-accident lifestyle as she is able. Rev. Osborn understood the positive role that she and members of the church could have in encouraging Grace in her efforts to reengage in church activities. Support from her family and friends in the church is vital, and it has been associated with positive mental health outcomes (Koenig, McCulloch, and Larson, 2001).

The substantial number of preventable MVAs in the United States and other industrialized countries is a serious social issue that deserves the attention of the religious community. According to the National Highway Traffic Safety Association (NHTSA, 1999), each year, motor vehicle accidents claim nearly forty-two thousand lives and are responsible for more than three million personal injuries. These crashes cost over $150 billion in property loss, medical bills, and productivity loss (NHTSA, 1999).

Alcohol use is the leading cause of motor vehicle deaths. Only 7 percent of all accidents involve alcohol, but nearly 4 in 10 fatal crashes result from it (NHTSA, 1999). Despite the more than 2,300 anti-drunk-driving laws that have been passed since 1980, traffic crashes are the greatest single cause of death of those aged six through thirty-three. In addition, it is estimated that 2.6 million drunk driving accidents each year victimize four million innocent people who either are injured or have their vehicles damaged.

Fatigue is the second priority issue for highway safety advocates because sleep deprivation is common among drivers of large trucks. In 1995, the National Transportation Safety Board reported that fatigue may be a factor in 30 to 40 percent of all truck accidents, making it the primary cause of heavy truck crashes. In a 1992 survey, almost 1 in 5 truck drivers said they had fallen asleep at the wheel in the previous month (Elisa et al., 1992).

In 1999, according to the federal government (NHTSA, 2000), 5,362 people died in 451,000 accidents involving large trucks. An estimated 136,000 more individuals were injured, and a third of those suffered severe brain damage or the loss of a limb. More than one million people were affected by these crashes. The National Traffic Safety Board has recommended a change in regulations so that truck drivers are able to get the sleep they need (NTSB, 1995). These safety concerns must be brought to the attention of the religious community for its advocacy in order to improve the safety of our highways and to prevent unnecessary injuries and fatalities.

Effective treatments for phobias and other anxiety disorders are available, and research is yielding new, improved therapies that can help most people with anxiety disorders lead productive, fulfilling lives (DeRubeis and Christoph, 1998). If a pastor thinks someone in his or her congregation has symptoms of persistent anxiety, advising a visit to the family physician is usually the best place for the parishioner to start. A physician can help determine whether the symptoms are due to an anxiety disorder, some other medical condition, or both. The next step in getting treatment for an anxiety disorder is referral to a mental health professional.

There are a number of different approaches that have proved effective for MVA-related PTSD. Treatments include behavior therapy, cognitive therapy, and medications (Blanchard and Hickling, 1997). Some psychologists and psychiatrists specialize in treating PTSD. It may also be important to work with a chronic pain specialist to help manage the pain caused by the injury. Often the treatments are provided in conjunction with one another.

Specific phobias, such as accident phobias, are generally highly treatable with carefully targeted psychotherapy. Treatment is typically sought when the fear interferes with one's functioning. The most successful is called exposure-based therapy (McMullin, 2000), which works by gradually bringing an individual into contact with the feared situation, until he or she can face the threat with little or no fear. Medication can be useful in controlling phobia symptoms, but it is most effective in combination with exposure therapy.

A number of medications that were originally used to treat depression have been found to be effective for anxiety disorders. Some of the newest antidepressants, called selective serotonin reuptake inhibitors (SSRIs), act in the brain on a chemical messenger called serotonin. SSRIs tend to have fewer side effects than older antidepressants (Preston and Johnson, 1997). Another group of antianxiety medications, benzodiazepines, relieve symptoms quickly and have few side effects, although drowsiness may be a problem. Benzodiazepines are generally prescribed only for short periods of time because people can develop a tolerance for them that can lead to addiction (Preston and Johnson, 1997).

Many persons with phobias or other anxiety disorders benefit from joining a self-help group and sharing their problems and successes with others. Talking with trusted friends or clergy can also be very helpful, although it is not a substitute for mental health care.

Family members are of great importance in the recovery of an individual with a phobia. Ideally, loved ones will be supportive without helping perpetuate the person's symptoms. If a family tends to trivialize the disorder or demand improvement without treatment, that will exacerbate the problem. Stress management techniques may help a person be calmer and increase the benefits of therapy. Some people find group therapy to be another helpful form of treatment.

Drunk driving is a problem found in all ethnic groups, but there are differences among them. For example, MVAs are higher among Hispanics than among European and African Americans. MVAs are the leading cause of death for Hispanics up to the age of twenty-four, and the second leading cause of death for those aged twenty-five through forty-four. The third leading cause of death for Hispanics of all ages is MVAs, surpassed only by heart disease and cancer (CDC, 1997). Asian/Pacific Islanders have the lowest rate of drinking and driving problems and the lowest rates of traffic injuries and fatalities among all ethnic groups. Chinese have the least rate of alcohol-related traffic fatalities among the Asian/Pacific Islander groups.

Resources

—AAA Foundation for Traffic Safety Administrative Office; 1440 New York Avenue, NW, Suite 201, Washington, DC 20005; (800) 305-SAFE; www.aaafoundation.org; is an independent, publicly funded, charitable research and educational organization founded by the American Automobile Association in 1947. Its mission is to prevent traffic deaths and injuries by conducting research into their causes and by educating the public about strategies to prevent crashes.

—Advocates for Highway and Auto Safety; 8730 George Avenue, Suite 600, Silver Spring, MD 20901; (240) 485-1001; www.saferoads.org; is an alliance of consumer, health, and safety groups and insurance companies working to create safer roads. The organization encourages the adoption of federal and state laws and programs that save lives and reduce injuries. It seeks to build coalitions of a wide array of groups to increase the participation in public policy initiatives that advance highway and auto safety.

—Anxiety Disorders Association of America; 8730 Georgia Avenue, Suite 60, Silver Spring, MD 20901; (240) 485-1001; www.adaa.org; promotes the prevention and cure of anxiety disorders and works to improve the lives of all who suffer from them. It is made up of professionals who conduct research and treat anxiety disorders and individuals who have an interest in learning more about such disorders.

—Association for Advancement of Behavior Therapy; 305 Seventh Avenue, 16th Floor, New York, NY 10001-6008; (212) 647-1890; www.aabt.org; is a professional, interdisciplinary organization concerned with the application of the behavioral and cognitive sciences to understanding human behavior, developing interventions to enhance the human condition, and promoting the appropriate use of these interventions.

—CRASH Foundation (Citizens for Reliable and Safe Highways); P.O. Box 14380, Washington, DC 20044-4380; www.truck-safety.org; (888) 353-4572; is a nationwide grassroots nonprofit organization committed to improving overall truck safety in the U.S. and eliminating the unnecessary deaths and injuries caused by trucks. It is dedicated to providing immediate compassionate support to truck crash survivors and the families of victims. It provides referrals to grief counseling, medical services, and truck crash experts; phone support; conferences; advocacy; First Response Program; and Survivors Network.

—Freedom from Fear; 308 Seaview Avenue, Staten Island, NY 10305; (718) 351-1717; www.freedomfromfear.com; is a national not-for-profit mental health advocacy association founded in 1984. Its mission is to aid and counsel individuals who suffer from anxiety and depressive illnesses and their families.

—Mothers Against Drunk Driving (MADD); 511 East John Carpenter Freeway, Suite 700, Irving, TX 75062; (800) GET-MADD; www.madd.org; is an educational and advocacy organization with over six hundred chapters devoted to heightening awareness of the dangers of impaired driving. It has a newsletter, chapter development guidelines, and programs designed to support victims of drunk driving.

—National Highway Traffic Safety Administration; 400 Seventh Street, SW, Washington, DC 20590; (888) 327-4236; www.nhtsa.dot.gov; under the authority of the U.S. Department of Transportation, is responsible for reducing deaths, injuries, and economic losses resulting from motor vehicle crashes. It establishes and enforces safety performance standards for motor vehicles and, through grants to states, conducts local highway safety programs. It investigates safety defects in motor vehicles; helps states and local communities reduce the threat of drunk drivers; promotes the use of safety belts, child safety seats, and air bags; and provides consumer information on motor vehicle safety topics.

—Remove Intoxicated Drivers (RID); P.O. Box 520, Schenectady, NY 12301; (518) 372-0034; www.rid-usa.org; is a national organization with 152 chapters in forty-one states and was founded in 1978. It advocates against drunk driving, educates the public, seeks reforming legislation, and aids victims of drunk driving.

Helpful Books

After the Crash: Assessment and Treatment of Motor Vehicle Accident Survivors (Edward B. Blanchard and Edward J. Hickling, Washington, DC: American Psychological Association, 1997).

Crash Course: A Self-Healing Guide to Auto Accident Trauma and Recovery (Diane Poole Heller and Laurence Heller, Berkeley, CA: North Atlantic Books, 2001).

Surviving an Auto Accident: A Guide to Your Physical, Emotional, and Economic Recovery (Robert Saperstein and Dana Saperstein, Ventura: Pathfinder Publishing of California, 1994).

References

American Psychiatric Association (2000). *Diagnostic and Statistical Manual of Mental Disorders* (Fourth Edition, Text Revised). Washington, DC: American Psychiatric Association.

Asmundson, G. J. G., Norton, P. J., and Norton, G. R. (1999). Beyond pain: The role of fear and avoidance in chronicity. *Clinical Psychology Review, 19,* 79-97.

Blanchard, E. B., and Hickling, E. J. (1997). *After the Crash.* Washington, DC: American Psychological Association.

Centers for Disease Control and Prevention (1997). *Monthly Vital Statistics Report for 1995*. Atlanta: CDC.

DeRubeis, R. J., and Christoph, P. C. (1998). Empirically supported individual and group psychological treatments for adult mental disorders. *Journal of Consulting and Clinical Psychology, 66(1)*, 37-52.

Ehlers, A., Mayou, R. A., and Bryant, B. (1998). Psychological predictors of chronic posttraumatic stress disorder after motor vehicle accidents. *Journal of Abnormal Psychology, 107*, 508-519.

Elisa, R., Braver, E. R., Preusser, C. W., Preusser, D. F., Baum, H. M., Beilock, R., and Ulmer, R. (1992). Long hours and fatigue: A survey of tractor-trailer drivers. *Journal of Public Health Policy, 13(3)*, 341-366.

Kessler, R. C., McGonagle, K. A., Zhao, S., Nelson, C. B., Hughes, M., Eshleman, S., Wittchen, H. U., and Kendler, K. S. (1994). Lifetime and 12-month prevalence of DSM-III-R psychiatric disorders in the United States: Results from the National Co-morbidity Survey. *Archives of General Psychiatry, 51(1)*, 8-19.

Koenig, H. G., McCulloch, M., and Larson, D. B. (2001). *Handbook on Religion and Health*. Oxford: Oxford University Press.

Kuch, K., Evans, R. J., Watson, P. C., Bubela, C., and Cox, B. J. (1991). Road vehicle accidents and phobias in 60 patients with fibromyalgia. *Journal of Anxiety Disorders, 5*, 273-280.

Marcus, S. C., Olfson, M., Pincus, H. A., Shear, M. K., and Zarin, D. A. (1997). Self-reported anxiety, general medical conditions, and disability bed days. *American Journal of Psychiatry, 154(12)*, 1766-1768.

McMullin, R. E. (2000). *The New Handbook of Cognitive Therapy Techniques*. New York: W. W. Norton and Company.

National Highway Traffic Safety Administration (1999). *National Center for Statistics, Analysis, Research & Development*. Washington, DC: NHTSA.

National Highway Traffic Safety Administration (2000). *Fatal Accident Reporting System*. Washington, DC: NHTSA.

National Transportation Safety Board. (1995). *Safety Study: Factors That Affect Fatigue in Heavy Truck Accidents*. Washington, DC: NTSB.

Norris, F. H. (1992). Epidemiology of trauma: Frequency and impact of different potentially traumatic events on different demographic groups. *Journal of Consulting and Clinical Psychology, 60*, 409-418.

Preston, J., and Johnson, J. (1997). *Clinical Psychopharmacology Made Ridiculously Simple*. Miami: MedMaster.

Stutts, J. C., Reinfurt, D. C., Staplin, L., and Rodgman, E. A. (2001). *The Role of Driver Distraction in Traffic Crashes*. Washington, DC: American Automobile Association Foundation for Traffic Safety.

Taylor, S., and Koch, W. J. (1995). Anxiety disorders due to motor vehicle accidents: Nature and treatment. *Clinical Psychology Review, 15*, 721-738.

Natural Disaster (Hurricane)

"Debris became flying missiles"

Hurricane Lucy, with sustained winds of over 140 miles per hour, slammed into the coastal community in the middle of a late–summer night at high tide. Hurricane-force winds destroyed buildings and mobile homes. Some structures along the beaches withstood the fierce gusts until their foundations were weakened by erosion and they, too, collapsed. Signs and roofing material became flying missiles. Extensive damage to trees, towers, water and underground utility lines (from uprooted trees), and fallen poles caused considerable disruption. Lucy produced a huge storm surge that, along with the rainfall, brought extensive inland flooding in communities hundreds of miles from the coast. In addition, the hurricane spawned several tornadoes that added to the storm's destructiveness.

In the weeks following the hurricane, some Sunday school teachers reported to Pastor Martinez that many of the students were having problems not seen before. Some of the parents noticed that their children were clingy, wet their beds, and had changes in their appetites. Other youngsters were constipated, complained of headaches, had sleep disturbances, and were irritable. Some became scared of outsiders, apathetic, and withdrawn. Undue hostility toward others and pessimism about the future showed up in some children's play fantasy life. Pastor Martinez knew some additional expertise was needed so he consulted with a pediatrician, Dr. Roche, who was a member of the church. He agreed to help assess the children's needs.

A disaster, such as a hurricane, can have grave consequences that produce considerable damage and distress affecting a large population. There is often injury and loss of life. Hurricanes are traumatic enough to

Pastoral Care Assessment

induce stress in anyone, especially children. The emotional effect of a disaster can persist well after the physical consequences. Dr. Roche explained to Pastor Martinez and the Sunday school teachers that children often show symptoms related to a disaster at home, church, or school. These are normal reactions to an abnormal situation; therefore, it is important for those working with children to know how to recognize the emotional consequences in order to help children and their families. Parents and teachers should be assured that these changes are normal reactions to a psychological trauma and that punishment and shame are not appropriate.

A basic method for assessing the extent to which children have been affected by a hurricane is to ask them, their Sunday school teachers, and parents about such things as: changes in sleep patterns, lack of motivation, regressive behavior (bed-wetting, biting, thumb-sucking, fear of darkness), changes in relationships with family members or peers (clingy and dependent or withdrawn and isolated), hostile behavior, changes in grades at school, along with fears and worries.

It is also important to gauge the level of healthiness in a family to understand the adaptation of a child. Parental adjustment to a disaster is an important factor in the child's response (Miller, 1999). If there are serious preexisting family conflicts, such as domestic violence or addiction, these can slow down adaptation to circumstances brought on by a disaster.

Relevant History

The word "hurricane" comes from the Caribbean *Hurican*, meaning "God of Evil." It is a fitting name, given the high seas, devastating winds, torrential rains, and unpredictable course of these storms. If the right conditions persist long enough, a tropical storm will become a hurricane when the weather system reaches sustained winds of 74 mph or higher. Hurricanes are categorized according to the strength of their winds—a Category 1 hurricane has the lowest velocity, while a Category 5 hurricane has winds at greater than 155 mph. According to the Federal Emergency Management Agency, hurricanes are the primary reason that 90 percent of all federally declared disasters are weather-related, leading to nearly $14 billion in damage annually (FEMA, 2001).

Each year, an average of ten tropical storms develops over the Atlantic Ocean and Gulf of Mexico. Many remain over the ocean, but approximately six of these storms become hurricanes each year. In an average three-year period, roughly five hurricanes strike the United States coastline, killing approximately fifty to one hundred people from Texas to Maine. Of these storms, two are typically "major" or "intense" hurricanes, with winds greater than 110 mph.

The greatest loss of life during a hurricane is often from the storm surge—the massive amount of water that is pushed toward the shore by the force of the winds swirling around the storm. The advancing surge combines with the tides to create a hurricane storm tide, which can increase the mean water level fifteen feet or more. This rise in water level can cause severe flooding in coastal areas, particularly if the storm surge coincides with high tide. Since water weighs approximately 1,700 pounds per cubic yard, extended pounding by waves can demolish any structure not specifically designed to withstand such force.

Diagnostic Criteria

There are some differences in appropriate responses to PTSD in children as compared to adults. The primary effect of a disaster on youngsters is the loss of routine in their daily lives. It is important for parents and teachers quickly to establish and maintain a schedule that is as predictable as possible for children. Youngsters are resilient, but they need order, especially when their routines have been disrupted by a calamity. It is helpful if parents can spend extra time with their children in positive activities after such a disruption.

Very young children usually respond to emotional distress with increased dependency. They may also experience magical thinking, which results in them feeling that they are responsible for the disaster because of something "bad" they did. School-age children may show signs of psychological trauma in their talk and play about the disaster, hostility to peers and family members, and avoidance of previously enjoyed activities. Youngsters often express fear and helplessness through disorganized and agitated behavior. In young children, repetitive play reenacting themes or aspects of the disaster may occur. Children may suffer from separation anxiety, school phobias, fear of strangers, and recurrent nightmares. Sleep disturbances such as insomnia, resistance to bedtime, refusal to sleep alone, early rising, or excessive sleep are very common. Youngsters may also experience headaches, stomachaches, and other physical symptoms. Some children protect themselves against feelings of passivity and helplessness by aggression, while others transform their anger into self-hatred or depression.

The more that children are exposed to the effects of a disaster, the greater their likelihood of having symptoms of psychological trauma (Anthony, Lonigan, and Hecht, 1999). Therefore, after a major disaster many youngsters will show signs of posttraumatic stress; however, few will go on to develop the full-blown psychiatric disorder. A diagnosis of PTSD is made when a child has symptoms in three categories persisting for more than one month (APA, 2000):

- Intrusive, repeated reexperiencing of an event through play, in trauma-specific nightmares or in flashbacks, or distress with events that resemble or symbolize the trauma.
- Routine avoidance of reminders of an event or a general lack of responsiveness, such as diminished interests or sense of a foreshortened future.
- Increased general arousal, such as sleep disturbances, irritability, poor concentration, increased startle reaction, and regression.

Response to Vignette

After a disaster, many children must cope with loss. Destruction or damage to a home, house of worship, school, or possessions, as well as the death or injury of a loved one or even a pet, can cause grief. Sorrow, trying to make sense of what happened, and anger are normal reactions to loss and can be different for each youngster. School-age children and adolescents are able to talk about sadness and should be strongly encouraged to do so. The intensity of their grief will usually be at its peak shortly after the disaster and decrease during the next few weeks. However, the anniversary of the event may trigger bereavement and recurrent symptoms.

The provision of emotional support by family and the community for children's grief reactions is important (Miller, 1999). Unfortunately, a family's response may not always be helpful. Parents are also exposed to trauma in disasters, and they may experience denial, depression, and substance abuse. Grief reactions can last for several months. The primary goals are to keep the family together, to provide support, and to encourage family communication.

For children experiencing symptoms of PTSD, it is important to listen and to emphasize their strengths and abilities to cope with difficulties as demonstrated in the past. It is also helpful to reinforce a child's courage during the disaster. The goal is to decrease stress for a child and facilitate working through loss by listening and empathizing with the youngster and family. Sometimes encouraging children to make drawings helps them express their fears. Observing them at play can help adults sort out children's emotional states.

Treatment Within the Faith Community

The aftermath of a large-scale disaster places strains on the entire fabric of a community and its residents. The pastor and parsonage family may be both sources of assistance and survivors. Since faith is a source of comfort and renewal to many in the face of loss, it is important that churches, synagogues, and mosques become active in the recovery of their community during and after a natural disaster. Mutual referral between clergy, physicians, and mental health specialists should be established to aid families in coping.

Feelings of intense guilt are common after a natural disaster. Children and teenagers may experience guilt for surviving or for their families and homes remaining intact. They may also feel guilt about being unable to help or may blame parents or authority figures for being unprepared. Pastors can help alleviate such feelings by reassuring youngsters that the disaster was not their fault and that everything possible is being done to return life to normal. A pastoral word can remind parents and children that assigning blame is not helpful and that rebuilding lives, families, and communities is what is most constructive.

Religious leaders need to be informed about denominational disaster relief resources, as well as be active in their local communities. One important task for religious leaders is to help the community implement a disaster preparedness program prior to a hurricane. Such programs are critical in areas that are susceptible to these storms, such as Hawaii, the coasts of the Gulf of Mexico, and southeastern coasts of the U.S. According to a recent survey sponsored by the American Red Cross, nearly 6 in 10 residents living in coastal areas of the southern U.S. are concerned that they are in danger from hurricanes, but only half of them are prepared for a disaster. Almost half of the forty-eight million residents living along the U.S. coast from Maine to Texas do not have an evacuation plan or disaster supplies kit, and 30 percent have not made living arrangements in case of forced evacuations.

Hurricanes will continue to occur. A lack of education and planning increase the likelihood of major hurricane disasters. By knowing one's vulnerability and what actions to take, a family can reduce the effects of a hurricane. Assisting a community in preparing for disasters may include providing guidance to Sunday school teachers and presentations to parents in the congregation. Preparatory information would include: identifying shelters, reviewing first-aid tips, and discussing symptoms that may occur in children after a disaster.

Indications for Referral

Any of the symptoms seen in the Sunday school children in Pastor Martinez's church, such as wetting the bed, changes in appetite, headaches, sleep disturbances, irritability, fear of outsiders, and withdrawal, are within normal expectations—provided they last only a few weeks. Youngsters will need a referral to a mental health professional if significant problems persist beyond that time. Sometimes it is easier for parents to seek treatment for their children than to get treatment for themselves. These parents may take a distressed youngster to a physician or mental health specialist when they are the ones who need the care most.

Severe grief may last for many months. If symptoms persist beyond three to four, or if they are excessive with an inability to return to predisaster functioning, referral to a mental health professional is needed.

Treatment by Mental Health Specialist

It is important for emotional recovery that youngsters and their families be helped to work together as they deal with the aftermath of a disaster. When symptoms are prolonged, then individual, group, and/or family therapy is recommended for parents and children to help them recognize and understand one another's feelings. Other therapeutic approaches include play therapy, education, and anxiety management skills, such as breathing training and relaxation techniques (Pfefferbaum, 1997). The basic goal of the therapy is to decrease disruptions in a youngster's normal development. Parents and other family members must be involved, and early intervention is important.

A sense of sadness is common after a disaster. However, if a child or teenager has persistent symptoms of depression (such as sad mood, agitation, lack of pleasure, significant change in sleep or eating patterns), a mental health intervention is warranted. If there is preexisting depression or other mental health problems in a child or family, the disaster may exacerbate it and strongly hinder adequate recovery. Some young people may have suicidal thoughts or gestures, especially if a close relative has died. If a teenager expresses helplessness, hopelessness, suicidal thoughts, isolation, or other depressive symptoms, an evaluation by a mental health specialist is required.

Cross-Cultural Issues

A study conducted in Florida after a Category 4 hurricane (Andrew) compared predisaster and postdisaster symptoms of psychological trauma in fourth-, fifth-, and sixth-grade students. Youngsters with indications of anxiety before the hurricane were at greater risk of lasting psychological trauma symptoms, and African American children were at greater risk than non-African Americans (Le Greca, Silverman, and Wasserstein, 1998).

Resources

—American Academy of Child and Adolescent Psychiatry; 3615 Wisconsin Avenue, NW, Washington, DC 20016; (202) 966-7300; www.aacap.org; publishes a pamphlet series on child and adolescent mental health issues.

—American Academy of Pediatrics; 141 Northwest Point Boulevard, Elk Grove Village, IL 60000; (847) 434-4000; www.aap.org.

—American Association for Marriage and Family Therapy; 112 South Alfred Street, Alexandria, VA 22314; (703) 838-9808; www.aamft.org; offers continuing education programs for those who work with families.

—American Association of Pastoral Counselors; 9504A Lee Highway, Fairfax, VA 22031; (703) 385-6967; www.aapc.org; provides information on qualified pastoral counselors and church-related counseling centers.

—American Red Cross; National Headquarters, 431 Eighteenth Street, NW, Washington, DC 20006; (202) 303-4498; www.redcross.org; is not a government agency, although its authority to provide disaster relief was given by Congress in 1905. Currently operating on a budget of $2.7 billion, the Red Cross responds to more than sixty-seven thousand disasters, including house or apartment fires (the majority of disaster responses), hurricanes, floods, earthquakes, tornadoes, hazardous materials spills, transportation accidents, explosions, and other natural and human-caused disasters.

—Federal Emergency Management Agency (FEMA); 500 C Street, SW, Washington, DC 20472; (202) 566-1600; www.fema.gov; is an independent agency of the federal government founded in 1979. Its mission is to reduce loss of life and property from hazards of all types through a comprehensive emergency management program of preparedness and recovery assistance. Online visitors can create custom hazard maps by entering a zip code and selecting from a variety of hazard types to help determine disaster risks in any community. There is a section on FEMA's website devoted to children: www.fema.gov/kids.

—National Hurricane Center; Tropical Prediction Center; 11691 SW Seventeenth Street, Miami, FL 33165-2149; (305) 229-4470; www.nhc.noaa.gov; is a federal agency that works to save lives and mitigate property loss by issuing watches, warnings, forecasts, and analyses of hazardous tropical weather. The National Weather Service has designed an educational program to help communities with the communication and safety skills necessary to save lives and property.

Helpful Books

Hurricane Survival Guide: How to Prepare Your Family and Home for the Next Hurricane (Fort Lauderdale Sun Staff, Fort Lauderdale, FL: NTC Publishing Group, 1993).

Hurricane Survival Made Easy: A Guide for Hurricane Preparedness (Morris I. Taite and Joe Masia, Miami, FL: Wisdom Market Press, 1993).

Hurricanes: How to Prepare and Recover (Max Roberts, Miami, FL: Universal Press Syndicate Company, 1993).

References

American Psychiatric Association (2000). *Diagnostic and Statistical Manual of Mental Disorders* (Fourth Edition, Text Revised). Washington, DC: American Psychiatric Association.

Anthony, J. L., Lonigan, C. J., and Hecht, S. A. (1999). Dimensionality of post-traumatic stress disorder symptoms in children exposed to disaster: Results from confirmatory factor analysis. *Journal of Abnormal Psychology, 108(2)*, 326-336.

FEMA (2001). Federal Emergency Management Agency. *FEMA History*, www.fema.gov.

Le Greca, A. M., Silverman, W. K., and Wasserstein, S. B. (1998). Children's predisaster functioning as a predictor of posttraumatic stress following Hurricane Andrew. *Journal of Consulting and Clinical Psychology, 66(6)*, 883-892.

Miller, L. (1999). Treating posttraumatic stress disorder in children and families: Basic principles and clinical application. *American Journal of Family Therapy, 27*, 21-34.

Pfefferbaum, B. (1997). Posttraumatic stress disorder in children: A review of the past ten years. *Journal of the American Academy of Child and Adolescent Psychiatry, 36(11)*, 1503-1511.

Terrorism

"The second plane plowed into the towers"

On September 11, 2001, the Wilsons were having breakfast on the thirty-fourth floor in their New York City hotel room when the first plane hit the World Trade Center. The fiery blast from the impact was close enough that they felt the heat from the explosion. The Wilsons were vacationing from Ohio, celebrating their tenth wedding anniversary. They began to shoot the burning skyscraper with their video camera. Through the camera's lens, they saw people jumping from the building—a man and woman holding hands as they fell to the ground. While making the video, the second plane plowed into the towers. That was when they realized this was no accident.

Upon returning home a few days later, Mrs. Wilson experienced severe levels of fear and anxiety related to the terrorist acts. She had a difficult time focusing on her work, problems sleeping, and bouts of crying. She felt an intense sense of dread, apprehension, and vulnerability. Mrs. Wilson had recurrent thoughts and nightmares of the people she saw jumping from the buildings and began to suffer gastrointestinal distress. She found herself watching the television news about the terrorist attacks several hours a day. When their pastor, the Rev. Joan Grant, made a pastoral visit to Mrs. Wilson's home and saw the severity of her distress, she immediately referred Mrs. Wilson to her family physician, who in turn referred her to a psychologist who specialized in the treatment of anxiety disorders.

Some experts believe that millions across the U.S. were psychologically affected by the events of September 11, 2001 (Schuster et al., 2001). Based on research findings after the 1995 bombing of the Murrah Federal Building in Oklahoma City, it is estimated that approximately 35 percent of those who were directly exposed to the terrorist attacks will develop

Pastoral Care Assessment

post-traumatic stress disorder (PTSD) (North et al., 1999). In addition, many persons with prior exposure to psychological trauma may reexperience PTSD symptoms triggered by the horrific events and their distressing effects (Brewin, Andrews, and Valentine, 2000).

Before the September 11 attacks, studies of the prevalence of PTSD in the United States found that 5 to 6 percent of men and 10 to 14 percent of women have experienced PTSD at some point in their lives, making it the fourth most common psychiatric disorder (Kessler et al., 1995). Those most at risk for developing PTSD are people with direct, personal involvement in a traumatic event. This high-risk group includes not only individuals exposed to life-threatening danger themselves, but also those like the Wilsons who watched the situation unfold from a nearby vantage point. PTSD typically manifests itself in flashbacks or nightmares that replay a traumatic experience, an avoidance of reminders of the ordeal, or a hyper alert state (APA, 2000).

Studies show that rates of PTSD are greater following events caused by deliberate violence rather than after natural disasters. If an airplane had accidentally flown off course in a heavy fog in New York and taken down one of the towers, it would have been traumatic—but much less so than knowing that some persons wanted to kill everybody in those buildings.

Relevant History

Mrs. Wilson was physically and psychologically abused as a child by an alcoholic father, and she has a history of anxiety attacks. Individuals with previously diagnosed panic or anxiety disorders are more likely than others to suffer frequent and magnified symptoms after a catastrophic event such as a terrorist attack. More than twice as many women as men experience PTSD following exposure to trauma (Brewin, Andrews, and Valentine, 2000). It is unclear why women are more vulnerable to traumatic events than men. Possible reasons may involve genetics, hormonal influences, and socialization (Saxe and Wolfe, 1999).

Diagnostic Criteria

PTSD is an anxiety disorder triggered by memories of a traumatic experience, and symptoms typically appear within three months (APA, 2000). However, they may not emerge until years afterward. Symptoms can include: flashbacks and distressing dreams associated with the event; efforts to avoid thoughts, emotions, and activities associated with the trauma; feelings of detachment or estrangement from others; the inability to feel affectionate; hopelessness about the future; trouble sleeping; anger; difficulty concentrating; an exaggerated startle response; and bodily reactions to situations that are reminders of the traumatic event (APA, 2000). Physical responses can include an increase in blood pressure, rapid heart rate, muscle tension, shortness of breath, nausea, and diarrhea.

The severity and duration of a psychological trauma appear to be factors in triggering the disorder. Issues that can increase the likelihood of developing PTSD include: having a poor social support system, additional life stress, a history of depression or other emotional disorder, previous physical or sexual abuse, family history of anxiety, and alcohol or substance abuse (Brewin, Andrews, and Valentine, 2000; Widom, 1999).

Terrorism threatens a society by instilling anxiety and feelings of helplessness. It seeks to hold communities hostage by fear of harm. The violent actions are unprovoked and intentional, and they often target the defenseless. Trying to cope with irrational violence is beyond normal comprehension and can set off a series of psychological responses culminating in feelings of fear, vulnerability, and grief. Experiencing or learning about a traumatic event challenges a person's sense of safety, leading to feelings of powerlessness.

Response to Vignette

Another common response in those witnessing tragedies such as recent terrorist attacks will be anger. For some, rage and a desire for revenge may seem justified. For others, such emotions will be experienced as distressing (for example, "I shouldn't feel this way; I'm a Christian"). It is important to know that a common human reaction to feelings of fear and powerlessness is anger. Identifying those underlying emotions and acknowledging the legitimacy of the feelings (rather than condemning them) may actually help reduce anger or its manifestations (such as scapegoating, prejudice, hostility). No matter what the emotional response, the process of recovery requires acknowledgment of changes that have occurred as the result of a horrific event.

Recovery from acute stress requires confronting human vulnerability in a way that fosters the development of resilience. However, the body's physical responses in the aftermath of a catastrophic experience may leave one feeling scared, which interferes with a sense of safety. Living in constant fear can overwhelm a person's ability to cope and lead to the avoidance of thoughts and emotions associated with the trauma. If individuals have disturbing feelings for more than one week, if they are severe, or if survivors believe they are having trouble getting their lives under control, they should see a mental health professional.

A final element affecting recovery is the effect of repeated exposure to traumatic images (for example, frequently watching video clips on television). Viewing media pictures of carnage, devastation, and destruction intensify the shock and keep persons confused and isolated (Schuster et al., 2001). One might imagine that vulnerable or previously traumatized people simply would not watch upsetting images. In some instances this may be the case. However, more often than not, the need to know and the impulse to be watchful and vigilant can motivate those with PTSD to stay glued to television. Repeated exposure to traumatic scenes and violence has been found to increase the likelihood of overestimating the risk of victimization (Gerbner et al., 1994).

A nationally representative sample of U.S. adults was interviewed three to five days after September 11, 2001, about their reactions to the terrorist attacks (Schuster et al., 2001). Respondents throughout the country reported stress symptoms in themselves and their children. Nine of ten said that they had used their religion to some degree to cope with the situation.

As witnesses to horrors like those of September 11, most congregants' emotional distress will be evident. Additionally, some members are likely to be affected especially hard (such as those with preexisting vulnerabilities). Besides heightened levels of suffering, some will either believe that their reactions are signs of pending emotional collapse or feel shame ("Why am I reacting so intensely?"). Pastors can, in the context of sermons and on an individual basis, validate the fact that there will be strong responses. Acknowledging that some people will be affected in intense ways, especially those exposed to prior traumas or losses, can help normalize reactions to strong emotions and reduce shame and guilt.

Supportive networks, such as faith communities, are crucial resources for survivors of psychological trauma. They help people in the ongoing recovery process, both by the sharing of resources and practical assistance and through the emotional support they provide to deal with the disaster and its aftermath. Faith can help give interpretative meaning to life events that are harsh and unfair. Those with PTSD who believe that they are cared for by others and that help is available if needed fare better psychologically than do those who feel they are unloved and alone.

An important component of helping survivors is providing education about emotional trauma, which will help normalize reactions, improve coping, enhance self-care, foster recognition of significant problems, and increase knowledge of and access to services. Persons with PTSD and their families can be reassured about common responses to traumatic experiences and advised about positive and negative forms of coping. Pastors can help survivors understand that their symptoms represent psychological and physical reactions to overwhelming stress rather than character flaws or signs of weakness. Clergy and others can provide a nonjudgmental ear and emphasize that traumatized persons are not alone (Norris and Kaniasty, 1996). Clergy can also help people struggle through inevitable faith issues and questions. Although no one wishes for these moments, they can serve to deepen people's faith and commitment.

When evaluating for PTSD and referring a survivor to a mental health specialist, a pastor must keep in mind that depression, alcohol or other substance abuse, and other anxiety disorders (such as phobias) frequently occur concurrently with PTSD (Kessler et al., 1995). The likelihood of treatment success is increased when other such conditions are appropriately diagnosed and treated as well.

PTSD can be extremely debilitating. Fortunately, research has led to the development of treatments (Foa, Keane, and Friedman, 2000), usually involving a combination of medication and behavior therapy designed to help persons gain control of their anxiety. The objective is to reduce emotional distress and disturbances to sleep and daily living, helping persons better cope with the event that triggered the distress. Experts suggest that trying to return to some semblance of ordinary life is crucial.

Research has shown the benefits of cognitive-behavioral therapeutic approaches, group therapy, and stress management training (Foa, Keane, and Friedman, 2000). Studies have also found that several types of medication, particularly the selective serotonin reuptake inhibitors and other antidepressants, can help relieve the symptoms of PTSD (Preston, O'Neal, and Talaga, 2001).

Some trauma survivors benefit from ongoing psychotherapy. Likely candidates for long-term therapy would include those with a history of previous traumatization (for example, those who experienced childhood abuse) or who have preexisting mental health problems.

Treatment by Mental Health Specialist

To assess their exposure to the traumatic events and their psychological condition, a random sample of 1008 adults living in lower Manhattan was contacted five to eight weeks after the September 11, 2001, terrorist attacks. Twenty percent of those living near the site of the World Trade Center had PTSD. Hispanic ethnicity was associated with both PTSD and depression (Galea et al., 2002). Research with veterans of the Vietnam War found that Hispanics, especially Puerto Ricans, may have a higher prevalence rate of PTSD than persons of other racial or ethnic backgrounds (Ortega and Rosenheck, 2000).

Cross-Cultural Issues

—American Association of Pastoral Counselors; 9504A Lee Highway, Fairfax, VA 22031; (703) 385-6967; www.aapc.org; provides information on qualified pastoral counselors and church-related counseling centers.

—American Counseling Association; 5999 Stevenson Avenue, Alexandria, VA 22304; (800) 347-6647; www.counseling.org.

—American Psychiatric Association; 1000 Wilson Boulevard, Arlington, VA 22209; (703) 907-7300; www.psych.org.

—American Psychological Association; 750 First Street, NE, Washington, DC 20002-4242; (800) 374-2721; (202) 336-5510; www.apa.org; provides online services for professionals and the general public.

—Anxiety Disorders Association of America; 8730 Georgia Avenue, Suite 600, Silver Spring, MD 20910; (240) 485-1001; www.adaa.org.

—Gift from Within; 16 Cobb Hill Road, Camden, ME 04843; (207) 236-2818; www.giftfromwithin.org; is a nonprofit organization dedicated

Resources

to helping those who suffer from PTSD. It maintains a roster of trauma survivors who participate in a national network for peer support.

—International Society for Traumatic Stress Studies; 60 Revere Drive, Suite 500, Northbrook, IL 60062; (847) 480-9028; www.istss.org.

—National Center for Post-Traumatic Stress Disorder; VA Medical Center, 215 North Main Street, White River Junction, VT 05009; (802) 296-5132; www.ncptsd.org.

—Posttraumatic Stress Disorder Alliance, (877) 507-PTSD, www.ptsdalliance.org, is a multidisciplinary group that provides educational resources to health care professionals and those diagnosed with PTSD.

—Sidran Traumatic Stress Foundation; 200 East Joppa Road, Suite 207, Towson, MD 21286; (410) 825-8888; www.sidran.org; focuses on education, advocacy, and research related to the early recognition and treatment of traumatic stress disorders.

Helpful Books

Assessing and Treating Victims of Violence (John Briere, ed., San Francisco: Jossey-Bass, 1994).

Coping with Trauma: A Guide to Self-Understanding (Jon Allen, Washington, DC: American Psychiatric Press, 1995).

Helping Traumatized Families (Charles R. Figley, San Francisco: Jossey-Bass, 1989).

Post Traumatic Stress Disorder: The Latest Assessment and Treatment Strategies (M. J. Friedman, Kansas City, MO: Compact Clinicians, 2000).

Post-Traumatic Stress Disorder: A Clinician's Guide (K. C. Peterson, M. F. Prout, and R. A. Schwarz, New York: Plenum Press, 1991).

Post-traumatic Therapy and the Victims of Violence (Frank Ochberg, ed., New York: Brunner/Mazel, 1988).

The PTSD Workbook: Simple, Effective Techniques for Overcoming Traumatic Stress Symptoms (Mary Beth Williams and Soili Poijula, Oakland, CA: New Harbinger, 2002).

Trauma and Recovery: The Aftermath of Violence from Domestic Abuse to Political Terror (Judith L. Herman, New York: Basic Books, 1997).

References

American Psychiatric Association (2000). *Diagnostic and Statistical Manual of Mental Disorders* (Fourth Edition, Text Revised). Washington, DC: American Psychiatric Association.

Brewin, C. R., Andrews, B., and Valentine, J. D. (2000). Meta-analysis of risk factors for posttraumatic stress disorder in exposed adults. *Journal of Consulting and Clinical Psychology, 68*(5), 748-766.

Foa, E. B., Keane, T. M., and Friedman, M. J. (2000). *Effective Treatments for PTSD.* New York: Guilford Press.

Galea, S., Ahern, J., Resnick, H., Kilpatrick, D., Bucuvalas, M., Gold, J., and Vlahov, D. (2002). Psychological sequelae of the September 11 terrorist attacks in New York City. *New England Journal of Medicine, 346(13)*, 982-987.

Gerbner, G., Gross, L., Morgan, M., and Signorielli, N. (1994). Growing up with television: The cultivation perspective. In J. Bryant and D. Zillman (Eds.), *Media Effects: Advances in Theory and Research* (pp. 17-42). Hillsdale, NJ: Lawrence Erlbaum Associates.

Kessler, R. C., Sonnega, A., Bromet, E., Hughes, M., and Nelson, C. B. (1995). Post-traumatic stress disorder in the National Co-morbidity Survey. *Archives of General Psychiatry, 52*, 1048-1060.

Norris, F. H., and Kaniasty, K. Z. (1996). Received and perceived social support in times of distress: A test of the social support deterioration deference model. *Journal of Personality and Social Psychology, 71(3)*, 498-511.

North, C. S., Nixon, S. J., Shariat, S., Mallonee, S., McMillen, J. C., Spitznagel, E. L., and Smith, E. M. (1999). Psychiatric disorders among survivors of the Oklahoma City bombing. *Journal of the American Medical Association, 282(8)*, 755-762.

Ortega, A. N., and Rosenheck, R. (2000). Posttraumatic stress disorder among Hispanic Vietnam veterans. *American Journal of Psychiatry, 157(4)*, 615-619.

Preston, J. D., O'Neal, J. H., and Talaga, M. (2001). *Handbook of Clinical Psychopharmacology for Therapists*. Oakland, CA: New Harbinger.

Saxe, G., and Wolfe, J. (1999). Gender and posttraumatic stress disorder. In P. A. Saigh, and D. Bremner (Eds.), *Posttraumatic Stress Disorder: A Comprehensive Text* (pp. 160-179). Needham Heights, MA: Allyn and Bacon.

Schuster, M. A., Stein, B. D., Jaycox, L. H., Collins, R. L., Marshall, G. N., Elliott, M. N., Zhou, A. J., Kanouse, D. E., Morrison, J. L., and Berry, S. H. (2001). A national survey of stress reactions after the September 11, 2001, terrorist attacks. *New England Journal of Medicine, 345(20)*, 1507-1512.

Widom, C. S. (1999). Posttraumatic stress disorder in abused and neglected children grown up. *American Journal of Psychiatry, 156(8)*, 1223-1229.

School Violence

"Another girl threatened her with a box cutter"

Mr. and Mrs. Harris went to the Rev. Donna Lindsey's office to talk to her about their fifteen-year-old granddaughter who lives with them and attends high school. Erica is a sophomore with a 3.5 grade point average. She is a popular student, vice president of the honor society, and an active member of her church youth group. Her mother was killed by her father when she was six years old, and Erica's father is now in prison. She was repeatedly exposed to domestic violence as a young child.

Erica recently experienced a frightening episode when she was leaving school. Another girl kicked her and threatened her with a box cutter because she did not like the way Erica looked at her. She escaped without serious physical injury, but Erica was very upset and fearful afterwards. She has nightmares and trouble falling and staying asleep. She has recurrent stomachaches and difficulty concentrating on her studies.

Rev. Lindsey has been close to the Harris family since moving to the church ten years ago. She has had clinical pastoral education training and experience working with survivors of criminal victimization. The pastor was able to explain to Mr. and Mrs. Harris that when a severe psychological trauma occurs, such as a life-threatening assault, it is not unusual for a survivor to feel shaken, unsafe, and insecure for some time. Sleep disturbances, eating difficulties, feelings of irritability, anger, sadness, or guilt are very common, particularly if a person has experienced prior trauma. Emotional injury is essentially a normal response to an extreme event. It involves the creation of emotional memories, which arise through a long-lasting effect on structures within the brain. The more severe the exposure to a traumatic event, the higher the risk for emotional harm.

Pastoral Care Assessment

After meeting with the family and listening to Erica's story, Rev. Lindsey thought of the other people she had heard recite that same litany. She began seriously to suspect that Erica might be suffering from PTSD. Symptoms of the disorder include intrusive recollections of the event, flashbacks, nightmares, and efforts to avoid activities associated with the trauma. Knowing that severe stress causes physiological changes in the adrenal system, which often trigger heart palpitations, a sense of impending doom, and being overly sensitive to threat-related situations, Rev. Lindsey suggested to Erica's grandparents that they consult their doctor. The pastor stressed the gravity of this diagnosis and that a specialist should evaluate Erica before they could be sure she was suffering from PTSD.

When a person's basic sense of safety is altered, she may have trouble concentrating and falling or staying asleep. Erica may feel detached and numb, and her ability to trust others may be compromised. These responses may range from mild to intense. Severe symptoms may indicate that an individual is experiencing PTSD or depression. It has been demonstrated that the effect of a traumatic event is likely to be greatest on persons who previously have been victims of child abuse or other forms of violence (such as domestic abuse) or those who lack family support (Brewin, Andrews, and Valentine, 2000).

Relevant History

Although Erica does not have a history of alcohol or drug use, many teens who experience a psychological trauma self-medicate with such substances. Using a large national sample of adolescents, researchers found that those who had been physically or sexually assaulted, had witnessed violence, or had family members with alcohol or drug abuse problems had an increased risk for substance abuse (Kilpatrick et al., 2000). PTSD increases the risk of marijuana and hard drug abuse, with European Americans at the greatest risk of addiction.

Diagnostic Criteria

School violence includes a variety of acts, from verbal abuse of a peer or teacher to theft and physical assaults to shooting firearms at groups of persons. It is hostile behavior that results in physical or psychological pain, injury, or death. Violence in schools is significantly related to violence in U.S. society in general. Events of recent years, such as the catastrophic shootings at Columbine High School in Colorado, have focused national attention upon the issue.

A survey in 1999 reported that 1 in 4 students and 1 in 6 teachers had been the victim of a violent act that occurred in or around school, and elementary school students are just as likely as those in secondary schools to be victims (Metropolitan Life, 1999). Another study found that 10 percent of all public schools reported at least one incident of serious violence (including murder, rape, suicide, or physical attack with a weapon) to law enforcement officials in the 1996–97 school year (Heaviside et al.,

1998), for a total of almost sixteen thousand crimes per school day (Goldstein and Conoley, 1997).

In a recent federal government report, 9 percent of high school students indicated that they had carried a weapon on school property in the past month, while 7 percent of students were threatened or injured with a weapon at school in the past year (Snyder and Sickmund, 1999). Four percent of high school students stated that they had felt too unsafe to go to school at some point in the past thirty days (Snyder and Sickmund, 1999). Twenty percent of parents worry a great deal about their children's safety at school and en route. Those concerns are felt by parents living in both urban and rural areas in all parts of the nation (National Crime Prevention Council, 1999). Forty percent of students indicated that the behavior of other students in their school definitely or somewhat interfered with their performance (Horatio Alger Association, 1999). Peer group pressure is cited by half of seventh through twelve graders as a major factor contributing to school violence—drugs or alcohol are credited by 39 percent, lack of parental supervision is blamed by 36 percent, and lack of family involvement by 25 percent (Metropolitan Life, 1999).

Response to Vignette

Erica will likely need time to talk about the internal rage and shame that may not have been expressed at the time of trauma. It will be vital for Erica to receive plenty of nonjudgmental listening from her pastor, friends, and family. She may also need a chance to articulate the confusion, anger, and sadness that are often hidden inside, so that she can begin to dispel the overwhelming anxiety and helplessness associated with her attack. She will need strategies and skills to deal with her emotional turmoil and reassurance that she will be safe and taken care of. Erica will need care and stability in her interactions with others as she relearns that the world is safe and finds that shattered trust can be regained. It is important to reassure her that the assault was not her fault and that everything will be done to ensure that the student assailant will not be a threat to her in the future.

Feeling angry and wanting to strike back are normal reactions for many people. Finding appropriate ways to express feelings (such as talking to friends, family, and adults who are trusted) or working out frustration and anger with physical exercise can be helpful. Limiting activities that can increase restlessness and adding activities that help a person feel relaxed, such as recreation and listening to music, can reduce the stress. Strong emotions are normal responses to trauma, and dealing with them requires good judgment, self-control, and positive support from others.

Treatment Within the Faith Community

Unfortunately, Erica's experience is not unusual in the United States. Youth violence in the community and school and its negative effect is far too common. Researchers conducted a national telephone survey of adolescents aged ten through sixteen and found that 1 in 3 had been the victim of an assault at least once in his or her life (Boney-McCoy and Finkelhor, 1995). Nearly 20 percent of teenage males reported being victims of aggravated assault, and 13 percent of males said they had suffered violent assault to the genitals (such as being kicked during a fight). Adolescents who reported being victimized indicated significantly more psychological distress than nonvictimized teens, including increased PTSD symptoms, more sadness, and increased difficulties in school (for example, experiencing trouble with a teacher). Extrapolating from their findings in this random national sample, the researchers estimated that over 6.1 million adolescents aged ten though sixteen have suffered some form of assault, placing them at risk for psychological distress and school difficulties.

Faith communities can be helpful in preventing youth violence in schools, neighborhoods, and homes. The most effective programs involve long-term interventions providing a range of family services. They encompass the collaborative efforts of religious groups, social service and public health organizations, the business community, schools, and law enforcement agencies. For example, church programs in parenting and family relationships, particularly those focusing on nonviolent living skills and recovery from substance abuse, can protect youth from learning to use violence. Programs in conflict resolution and anger management that are designed for adolescents are effective at breaking the cycle of violence in the community (Cotten et al., 1994).

Congregational after-school programs can keep youth constructively engaged when their families are unavailable by providing them with attention from caring adults and good role models. They keep teens away from negative influences in the world and on television. Such programs can also offer educational enrichment and assistance with schoolwork and help participants develop positive religious values.

Helping young people find employment is an important way for religious communities to reduce property crime and to help build adolescents' self-esteem and sense of responsibility. Having a job also helps teens understand how important staying in school is to their future career plans.

Churches. mosques, and synagogues can assist with community efforts against gang involvement (which exist in all fifty states). Effective anti-gang programs include crisis intervention teams made up of the police, probation officers, and community leaders; intensive community, family, and youth education programs; alternative youth activities; and a long-term commitment.

Indications for Referral

Erica should be evaluated for PTSD by a school psychologist or other knowledgeable mental health specialist, given her early childhood exposure to violence from domestic abuse. It is important to understand that any adolescent or adult who is exposed to this level of stress is at risk for additional problems for which they need to be assessed, including depression, anxiety, alcoholism, and drug abuse.

The best clinical treatment for PTSD involves an integration of cognitive, behavioral, psychodynamic, and psychopharmacological interventions (Foa, Keane, and Friedman, 2000). Psychodynamic approaches, or "talk therapy," make up the majority of treatment currently offered to persons suffering from PTSD. This intervention emphasizes "working through" the emotions associated with a traumatic event and its relationship to current symptoms and experiences. Behavioral approaches typically attempt to desensitize the individual to situations that activate traumatic memories and affects. Cognitive treatments usually focus on working with cognitive distortions or "shattered" life assumptions, such as the loss of a sense of self-invulnerability, feeling that life is meaningless, and traumatic disturbances in one's worldview (McMullin, 2000). Psychopharmacology is primarily used as an adjunct aimed at reducing overwhelming intrusive and hyperarousal symptoms and at helping an individual function in daily life and to make better use of dynamic and cognitive-behavioral treatments. Medication may also be effective in treating related conditions, such as depression and anxiety (Preston, O'Neal, and Talaga, 2001).

Family therapy is often very important in working with traumatized youth, since family dynamics can facilitate or impede coping and the psychological development of teens. The onset of PTSD during adolescence can have serious negative implications for the acquisition of life skills necessary for independence in adulthood. This is a critical issue to be addressed in individual and family therapy.

Group therapy may also be helpful for youth who survive criminal victimization. If led by appropriately trained and experienced professionals, groups can help persons realize that other individuals in the same circumstances often have similar reactions and emotions.

Researchers at Arizona State University examined the prevalence of peer victimization in a sample of African American, Hispanic, and non-Hispanic European American urban elementary school-aged students (Hanish and Guerra, 2000). A study of almost two thousand children (40 percent African American, 42 percent Hispanic, 18 percent European American) attending public elementary schools located in the Midwest found that the risk for being victimized by peers varied by ethnicity and by school population. Hispanic youngsters had lower victimization scores than did either African American or European American children. These findings, however, were dependent on the type of school. Attending ethnically integrated schools was associated with a significantly higher risk of victimization for European American children and a slightly lower risk of victimization for African American youngsters and did not affect the risk of victimization for Hispanic children. In addition, African American youngsters were less likely than Hispanic and European American children to be repeatedly victimized by peers over time.

Treatment by Mental Health Specialist

Cross-Cultural Issues

Resources

—American Academy of Child and Adolescent Psychiatry; 3615 Wisconsin Avenue, NW, Washington, DC 20016; (202) 966-7300; www.aacap.org.

—American Psychological Association; 750 First Street, NE, Washington, DC 20002-4242; (800) 374-2721; (202) 336-5510; www.apa.org; provides online services for professionals and the general public.

—Center for Mental Health in the Schools; Department of Psychology, P.O. Box 951563, Los Angeles, CA 90095; (310) 825-3634; smph.psych.ucla.edu.

—Center for Mental Health Services; Knowledge Exchange Network (KEN), 5600 Fishers Lane, Room 17-99, Rockville, MD 20857; provides information about mental health through a toll-free telephone number: (800) 789-2647. Staff are skilled at listening and responding to questions from the public and professionals, quickly directing callers to federal, state, and local organizations dedicated to treating and preventing mental illness. KEN also has information on federal grants, conferences, and other events.

—Center for the Prevention of School Violence; 1803 Mail Service Center, Raleigh, NC 27699; (800) 299-6054; www.ncsu.edu/cpsv; was established in 1993 as a public agency focusing on ensuring that schools are safe. The Center acts as a resource for information, program assistance, and research about school violence prevention.

—International Association of Chiefs of Police: Guide for Preventing and Responding to School Violence; 515 North Washington Street, Alexandria, VA 22314; (800) THE-IACP; www.theiacp.org/pubinfo/pubs/pslc/svindex.htm; provides recommendations for preventing and responding to school violence.

—Keep Schools Safe, www.keepschoolssafe.org, was developed by the National Association of Attorneys General and the National School Boards Association to address the escalating problem of youth violence. It is dedicated to promoting a mutual response to violence and to working together to find solutions to these problems.

—National Alliance for Safe Schools; Ice Mountain, Slanesville, WV 25444-0290; (888) 510-6500; www.safeschools.org; is a nonprofit corporation that provides technical assistance, training, and research to school districts interested in reducing school-based crime and violence.

—National Association of School Psychologists; 4340 East West Highway, Suite 402, Bethesda, MD 20814; www.nasponline.org; (301) 657-0270.

—National Crime Prevention Council; 1000 Connecticut Avenue, NW, 13th Floor, Washington, DC 20036; (202) 466-6272; www.ncpc.org; is a nonprofit educational organization that aims to reduce violence by and against young people and to change community conditions that cause crime.

—National Organization for Victim Assistance; 1730 Park Road, NW, Washington, DC 20010; (800) TRY-NOVA; www.try-nova.org; is a nonprofit organization of victim and witness assistance programs and practitioners, criminal justice agencies and professionals, mental health professionals, researchers, former victims and survivors, and others committed to the recognition and implementation of victim rights and services.

—National Youth Violence Prevention Resource Center; (866) 723-3968; www.safeyouth.org.

Helpful Books

The Conflict Resolution Handbook: A Guide to Building Quality Programs in Schools (Donna K. Crawford and Richard J. Bodine, New York: Jossey-Bass, 1997).

Counseling Troubled Teens and Their Families: A Handbook for Pastors and Youth Workers (Andrew Weaver, John Preston, and Leigh Jerome, Nashville: Abingdon Press, 1999).

Ready-to-Use Social Skills Lessons and Activities for Grades 7-12 (Ruth Weltmann Begun, ed., Paramus, NJ: The Center for Applied Research in Education, 1997).

Ready-to-Use Violence Prevention Skills Lessons and Activities for Elementary Students (Ruth Weltmann Begun and Frank J. Huml, eds., Paramus, NJ: The Center for Applied Research in Education, 1999).

Reducing School Violence Through Conflict Resolution (David W. Johnson and Roger T. Johnson, Alexandria, VA: Association for Supervision and Curriculum Development, 1995).

Talk It Out: Conflict Resolution in the Elementary Classroom (Barbara Porro and Peaco Todd, Alexandria, VA: Association for Supervision and Curriculum Development, 1996).

Violence in American Schools: A New Perspective (Delbert S. Elliott, Beatrix A. Hamburg, and Kirk R. Williams, eds., Cambridge: Cambridge University Press, 1998).

Youth Violence: Current Research and Recent Practice Innovations (Matthew O. Howard and Jeffrey M. Jenson, eds., Washington, DC: National Association of Social Workers Press, 1999).

References

Boney-McCoy, S., and Finkelhor, D. (1995). Psychosocial sequelae of violent victimization in a national youth sample. *Journal of Consulting and Clinical Psychology, 63,* 726-736.

Brewin, C. R., Andrews, B., and Valentine, J. D. (2000). Meta-analysis of risk factors for posttraumatic stress disorder in trauma-exposed adults. *Journal of Consulting and Clinical Psychology, 68(5),* 748-766.

Cotten, N. U., Resnick, J., Brown, D. C., Martin, S. L., McCarraher, D. R., and Woods, J. (1994). Aggression and fighting behavior among

African American adolescents: Individual and family factors. *American Journal of Public Health, 84(4)*, 618-622.

Foa, E. B., Keane, T. M., and Friedman, M. J. (2000). *Effective Treatments for PTSD*. New York: Guilford Press.

Goldstein, A. P., and Conoley, J. C. (1997). *School Violence Intervention*. New York: Guilford Publications.

Hanish, L. D., and Guerra, N. G. (2000). The roles of ethnicity and school context in predicting children's victimization by peers. *American Journal of Community Psychology, 28(2)*, 201-223.

Heaviside, S., Rowand, C., Williams, C., and Farris, E. (1998). *Violence and Discipline Problems in U.S. Public Schools: 1996–1997*. U.S. Department of Education, National Center for Educational Statistics, NCES 98-030. Washington, DC: U.S. Government Printing Office.

Horatio Alger Association (1999). State of Our Nation's Youth. Alexandria, VA: The Horatio Alger Association.

Kilpatrick, D. G., Acierno, R., Saunders, B., Resnick, H. S., Best, C. L., and Schnurr, P. P. (2000). Risk factors for adolescent substance abuse and dependence: Data from a national sample. *Journal of Consulting and Clinical Psychology, 68(1)*, 19-30.

McMullin, R. E. (2000). *The New Handbook of Cognitive Therapy Techniques*. New York: W. W. Norton and Co.

Metropolitan Life (1999). *The Metropolitan Life Survey of the American Teacher: Violence in the American Public School—Five Years Later*. New York: The Metropolitan Life Insurance Company.

National Crime Prevention Coalition of America (1999). *Are We Safe? The 1999 National Crime Prevention Survey*. Washington, DC: National Crime Prevention Council, www.ncpc.org.

Preston, J. D., O'Neal, J. H., and Talaga, M. (2001). *Handbook of Clinical Psychopharmacology for Therapists*. Oakland, CA: New Harbinger.

Snyder, H. N., and Sickmund, M. (1999). *Juvenile Offenders and Victims: 1999 National Report*, NCJ 178257. Washington, DC: U.S. Department of Justice, Office of Justice Programs, Office of Juvenile Justice and Delinquency Prevention.

The Suicide of a Child

"They were walking around in a fog of disbelief"

It was after one in the morning when Jacob Adams, aged sixteen, took a loaded pistol and the keys to his father's car. Jacob had been distraught about not making the high school football team and about his girlfriend breaking up with him. He had become irritable and withdrawn in recent months, and his grades had begun to suffer. He drove around for several hours, drinking beer and calling friends on his cell phone, before he went to the high school parking lot. Jacob pointed the gun at his head and pulled the trigger.

Janet and Kevin Adams were in shock and disbelief over the sudden and traumatic death of their only child. It was incomprehensible and horrifying; they felt like they were walking around half awake in a fog. They were unable to read, watch television, or talk for more than a few minutes before the recollection of his death would impinge upon their thoughts.

For weeks, they found themselves looking in Jacob's bedroom in the morning, expecting that he had come back during the night. When school let out for the day, Janet found herself watching for him to come down the street along with the other teenagers. The parents felt as though they were just going through the motions of their daily lives and none of it made much sense. After the funeral, they told Rev. Choy that they felt as if they were having a bad dream and that if they woke up from it, they would find that nothing had really happened.

Rev. Choy had twenty-five years of experience as a pastor. He knew that some events in life can be devastating and that the suicide of a family member is such an occurrence. The bereavement process following the unexpected and violent loss of a loved one can take years (Lehman et al., 1989). Sudden death is especially difficult for those who are left behind

Pastoral Care Assessment

because there is no time to prepare for it. In the past, parents had described the death of a child to the pastor as "overwhelming suffering," "intensely painful," and "creating lasting changes" in their families.

Although each person's experience of grief is unique, there are common emotions among survivors of suicide. The most immediate response is shock, numbness, and a sense of disbelief. Many people experience dramatic swings from one emotional state to another. Feelings may include depression, anger at the deceased for dying, guilt about what might have been done to prevent the death, irritability, anxiety, and extreme sadness. In their intense grief and shock, some survivors say they are afraid that they may go insane. Others become suicidal as a result of their deep depression. Survivors may also experience physical symptoms, such as pain, gastrointestinal upset, lack of energy, sleeplessness, and appetite disturbances.

Relevant History

The main reason that young people kill themselves is that they are suffering from a major depression—one of the most pervasive emotional problems of adolescents. Experts estimate that about 1 in 20 teens has significant depressive symptoms (Reynolds, 1995), which are underreported, undertreated, and dangerous (about 15 percent of young people with an untreated major depression commit suicide). Two-thirds of adolescents who take their lives use firearms. The presence of guns in a home, even when stored and locked, increases the risk of suicide by teens (Brent et al., 1991). Substance abuse is also a significant factor in one-third to one-half of youth who take their lives (Burstein et al., 1993).

Suicide is an act born of mental illness or despair. Individuals who take their lives are primarily trying to get rid of overwhelming emotional pain. At the time of the suicide, they have no hope that the hurt will ever disappear. The desire to eliminate their pain is greater than the will to live.

A major depression can constrict awareness of the feelings of others to the degree that one becomes focused only on one's own intense inner pain. Those who take their lives very often do not realize how much their death will hurt others.

Diagnostic Criteria

Suicide is the second leading cause of death among those under the age of twenty-one, and 73 percent of the self-inflicted deaths of those aged fifteen through twenty-four are by European American males. For fifteen- to nineteen-year-olds, the suicide rate in 1950 was only 2.7 per 100,000. By 1990, a mere two generations later, the rate had grown to 11.1—an increase of over 400 percent (National Center for Health Statistics, 1993). More teenagers and young adults take their lives than die of cancer, heart disease, AIDS, birth defects, stroke, pneumonia, and chronic lung disease combined (NSSP, 2001). For each completed adolescent suicide, there are fifty to one hundred attempts (Reynolds, 1995).

There are approximately thirty thousand suicides recorded each year in the United States. Assuming that there are an average of four survivors in each immediate family, then 120,000 new survivors are created annually—1.2 million each decade. If extended family members and close friends directly affected by the death are counted, the number of survivors is in the tens of millions. Every faith community contains someone who has been affected in a personal way by suicide (NSSP, 2001).

Parents, especially mothers, who lose a child to suicide are at risk of developing post-traumatic stress disorder (PTSD), further complicating the grieving process. In a study of 171 mothers and 90 fathers who lost a child in a violent death, four months after the event, 40 percent of the mothers and 14 percent of the fathers reported experiencing the full spectrum of PTSD symptoms. Intrusive thoughts, nightmares, reminders of how the child died, and distress at holidays and other family events were the most reported symptoms by parents. Two years after the deaths, 71 percent of the mothers and 32 percent of the fathers in the group that did not receive treatment still reported experiencing symptoms. Twenty-one percent of the mothers and 14 percent of the fathers continued to have the full criteria for PTSD two years after the deaths (Murphy et al., 1999).

Response to Vignette

The suicide of a young person presents unique circumstances that intensify and prolong a parent's mourning. Denial, feelings of shock, guilt, anger and depression are part of any grief reaction, but the self-inflicted death of a child greatly intensifies them. A son's or daughter's suicide raises painful questions, doubts, and fears. The knowledge that one's parenting was not enough to save one's child and the fear that others will judge one to have been an unfit parent can raise intense feelings of failure.

Suicide is different from other deaths in several ways. Surviving parents experience feelings of rejection and abandonment, which separate them from others who mourn the death of a loved one. It is common in the grief process for survivors to search for the reason the suicide occurred. Survivors attempt to piece together various reasons that a person chose to end her or his life. Before they can begin to accept the loss, survivors must deal with the reasons for it—and with the gradual recognition that they may never know what happened or why. The opportunity to talk about the death with others allows survivors to revise it in ways that make it more tolerable and to impose order on their experience, which is part of the healing process.

Many times there are warning signs of a person's intention to take his or her life. However, some individuals disguise or code their plans so that even trained professionals miss the clues. Occasionally there are no signs of suicide potential, and a person's decision becomes a puzzle that cannot be solved. Only as a survivor begins to accept the idea that the loved one's choice to kill himself or herself was that person's alone can the grip of the "what-ifs" of suicide begin to loosen.

Faith communities can play an important role in combating the stigma associated with the taking of one's life. Suicide is not a question of morality, but a psychological and medical issue. There is increasing evidence that both depression and suicide have a biological component—an imbalance in brain chemistry that significantly alters mood. Decreased levels of serotonin have repeatedly been found in the fluid that surrounds the brain and spinal cord of those who have attempted or committed suicide (Fawcett and Busch, 1993). Taking one's life must be understood similarly to addiction, which has moved in public understanding from being seen as a moral weakness into being recognized as the medical and psychological problem that it is. A person commits suicide because he or she feels so desperate that this fatal act is seen as the only way to relieve the depression and intense emotional pain.

Unfortunately, suicide is often viewed as evidence of personal and familial failure. Society's judgment may be that the family somehow provoked the death. Shame and stigmatization cause some family survivors of suicide to withdraw and isolate themselves. They may have difficulty sharing their feelings because of the fear of experiencing further pain and shame. Researchers have found that family members who lose a loved one to suicide are blamed and avoided more often than are the relatives of people who have died under other circumstances. This attitude may reinforce the guilt and self-blame that may already affect suicide survivors, increasing both their isolation and difficulty in talking about their feelings (Ness and Pfeffer, 1990).

Clergy are called upon to play a variety of roles as persons move through the grieving process. They are often anchors of hope for survivors. Pastors must be supportive, nurturing, and helpful in dealing with the survivors of grief. They also need a realistic and honest approach to the experience of loss as they help guide persons through this painful time.

There are special times when pastors and members of the faith community need to give particular attention to survivors, such as the anniversary of the death and during the major holidays, especially during the first year of mourning. Clergy can also invite bereaved parents to get together from time to time simply to talk and share feelings, and pastors can mobilize other caring people to surround survivors with supportive, loving relationships. Additionally, clergy can encourage bereaved parents to participate in grief support groups (Clark, 1993).

Pastors, lay leaders, and others can educate a congregation by providing factual information about teen depression and other mental health issues. There is considerable societal bias against those with mental illness, which is one of the reasons adults and young people are reluctant to admit being in distress or to seek help. Educating the faith community about adolescent depression can decrease bias and increase advocacy for mental health services for teens (Brent et al., 1993).

However, it must be emphasized that some of those who take their lives have been suffering from serious mental illness for a number of years. In a real sense, the factors over time that lead to taking one's life had been set in motion years before. Preventing suicide in an individual who has suffered for a long time from serious mental illness (such as depression) can be a bit like trying to stop a runaway train coming down a mountain. As the train reaches the bottom, it races at high speed, making the odds of stopping the tragedy very slim. Many therapists and clergy alike encounter suicidal people who have been in deep anguish for years. At times, despite the best efforts of family, friends, pastors, and mental health workers, such individuals do kill themselves.

It is not uncommon for bereaved parents to think about taking their own lives (Ness and Pfeffer, 1990). Although suicidal tendencies are not inherited, a suicide can have a profound influence on family members. Clergy and others need to encourage survivors to seek professional help and family counseling when necessary.

Indications for Referral

It is estimated that about seventy-five thousand parents are newly bereaved each year following the violent death of a child. Accidents, suicides, and homicides account for 80 percent of all deaths among youth and young adults in the United States (National Center for Health Statistics, 1992). High levels of alcohol consumption, anxiety, psychological trauma, and severe grief reactions can be the consequences of experiencing the death of a child (Murphy et al., 1999). Many bereaved parents will need professional help for these problems.

Treatment by Mental Health Specialist

Suicide rates among European Americans are higher than among African Americans at all ages, including the teen years. However, the rate for African American and other ethnic minority males has increased markedly since 1986. There has been no significant change in the suicide rate for either African American or European American females (Shaffer, Gould, and Hick, 1994).

Cross-Cultural Issues

—American Association of Suicidology; 4201 Connecticut Avenue, NW, Suite 408, Washington, DC 20008; (202) 237-2280; www.suicidology .org.

—American Foundation for Suicide Prevention; 120 Wall Street, 22nd Floor, New York, NY 10005; (888) 333-2377; www.afsp.org; provides up-to-date information on suicide prevention and related studies for the public, professionals, suicide survivors, and others.

—Centre for Suicide Prevention Training Programs; Suite 320, 1202 Centre Street, SE, Calgary, Alberta, Canada T2G 5A5; (403) 245-3900; www.suicideinfo.ca; provides information on suicide education and a suicide prevention training program.

Resources

—Compassionate Friends; P.O. Box 3696, Oak Brook, IL 60522; (877) 969-0010; www.compassionatefriends.org; is a group that gives support to parents who have lost a child.

—Friends for Survival; P.O. Box 214463, Sacramento, CA 95821; (916) 392-0664; www.friendsforsurvival.org; a nonprofit peer support group that provides direct services at no cost to those who have lost a loved one to suicide.

—Girls and Boys Town National Hotline: (800) 448-3000; 1410 Crawford Street, Boys Town, NE 68010; www.girlsandboystown.org; provides short-term counseling and referrals to local resources, including U.S. territories and Canada. Counsels on parent-child conflicts, suicide, depression, pregnancy, runaways, and abuse. Spanish-speaking operators are available. Operates twenty-four hours a day.

—National Depressive and Manic-Depressive Association; 730 North Franklin Street, Suite 501, Chicago, IL 60610; (800) 826-3632; www.ndmda.org.

—National Foundation for Depressive Illness; P.O. Box 2257, New York, NY 10116; (800) 239-1265; www.depression.org; a twenty-four-hour recorded message describes symptoms of depression and manic depression, gives an address for more information, and provides physician and support group referrals by state.

—National Mental Health Association; 2001 North Beauregard Street, 12th Floor, Alexandria, VA 22311; (800) 969-NMHA; www.nmha.org; provides information on clinical depression.

—National Suicide Foundation; 1045 Park Avenue, New York, NY 10028; (800) NSF-4042; provides state-by-state directories of survivor support groups for families and friends of a suicide.

—National Suicide Hotline: (800) SUICIDE.

—National Youth Crisis Hotline: (800) 448-4663; P.O. Box 178408, San Diego, CA 92177; www.1800hithome.com; provides counseling and referrals to local counseling services. Responds to youth dealing with pregnancy, molestation, suicide, depression, and child abuse. Operates twenty-four hours a day.

—Samaritans of Boston; 654 Beacon Street, 6th Floor, Boston, MA 02215; (617) 536-2460; www.samaritansofboston.org.

—Suicide Awareness Voices of Education; 7317 Cahill Road, Suite 207, Minneapolis, MN 55424-0507; (888) 511-SAVE; (952) 946-7998; www.save.org; an organization dedicated to educating the public about suicide prevention.

—Suicide Prevention Action Network USA; 5034 Odins Way, Marietta, GA 30068; (888) 649-1366; www.spanusa.org.

—Survivors Helping Survivors; 734 North Fourth Street, Suite 200, Milwaukee, WI 53201; (414) 276-3122; www.mhawilw.org; gives support to those who have lost loved ones to suicide.

—Yellow Ribbon Suicide Prevention Program; P.O. Box 644, Westminster, CO 80036-0644; (303) 429-3530; www.yellowribbon.org; provides a teen suicide prevention program.

Helpful Books

After Suicide (John Hewitt, Louisville: Westminster Press, 1980).

Clergy Response to Suicidal Persons and Their Family Members (David C. Clark, Chicago: Exploration Press, 1993).

Helping Your Depressed Teenager: A Guide for Parents and Caregivers (Gerald D. Oster and Sarah S. Montgomery, New York: John Wiley & Sons, 1995).

Lonely, Sad and Angry: A Parent's Guide to Depression in Children and Adolescents (Barbara D. Ingersoll and Sam Goldstein, New York: Doubleday, 1996).

The Minister As Crisis Counselor, rev. ed. (David K. Switzer, Nashville: Abingdon Press, 1985).

My Son . . . My Son: A Guide to Healing after Death, Loss or Suicide (Iris Bolton and Curtis Mitchell, Atlanta: Bolton Press, 1995).

No Time to Say Goodbye: Surviving the Suicide of a Loved One (Carla Fine, New York: Doubleday, 1996).

Suicide and Its Aftermath (Edward Dunne, John McIntosh, and Karen Dunne-Maxim, eds., New York: W. W. Norton and Co., 1987).

Suicide Survivor's Handbook: A Guide for the Bereaved and Those Who Wish to Help Them (Trudy Carlson, Minneapolis: Benline Press, 1995).

Suicide Survivors: A Guide for Those Left Behind (Adina Wrobleski, Minneapolis: Afterwords, 1994).

Surviving Suicide: Young People Speak Up (Susan Kuklin, New York: Putnam Publishing Group, 1994).

References

Brent, D. A., Perper, J. A., Allman, C. J., Moritz, G. M., Wartella, M. E., and Zelenak, J. P. (1991). The presence and accessibility of firearms in the homes of adolescent suicides: A case-control study. *Journal of the American Medical Association, 266(21)*, 2989-2995.

Brent, D. A., Poling, K., McKain, B., and Baugher, M. (1993). A psychoeducational program for families of affectively ill children and adolescents. *Journal of the American Academy of Child and Adolescent Psychiatry, 32*, 770-774.

Burstein, O. G., Brent, D. A., Perper, J. A., Moritz, G., Baugher, M., Schweers, J., Roth, C., and Balach, L. (1993). Risk factors for completed suicide among adolescents with a lifetime history of substance abuse. *Acta Psychiatrica Scandinavica, 88*, 403-408.

Clark, D. C. (1993). *Clergy's Response to Suicidal Persons and Their Family Members*. Chicago: Exploration Press.

Fawcett, J., and Busch, K. A. (1993). The psychobiology of suicide. *Clinical Neuroscience, 1,* 101.

Lehman, D. R., Lang, E. L., Wortman, C. B., and Sorenson, S. B. (1989). Long-term effects of sudden bereavement. *American Journal of Family Therapy, 2(3),* 344-367.

Murphy, S. A., Braun, T., Tillery, L., Cain, K. C., Johnson, L. C., and Beaton, R. D. (1999). PTSD among bereaved parents following the violent deaths of their 12- to 28-year-old children: A longitudinal prospective analysis. *Journal of Traumatic Stress, 12(2),* 273-291.

National Center for Health Statistics (1992). *Vital Statistics of the United States: Vol. 2, Mortality, Part A (1966–1988).* Washington, DC: U.S. Government Printing Office.

National Center for Health Statistics (1993). *Vital Statistics Report.* Hyattsville, MD: NCHS.

National Strategy for Suicide Prevention (2001). *National Strategy for Suicide Prevention, Summary 2001,* www.mentalhealth.org, retrieved September 5, 2001.

Ness, D., and Pfeffer, C. (1990). Sequelae of bereavement resulting from suicide. *American Journal of Psychiatry, 147(3),* 279-285.

Reynolds, W. M. (1995). Depression. In V. B. Van Hasselt and M. Hersen (Eds.), *Handbook of Adolescent Psychopathology* (pp. 297-348). New York: Lexington Books.

Shaffer, D., Gould, M., and Hick, R. (1994). Increasing rate of Black suicide in the U.S. *American Journal of Psychiatry, 151,* 1810-1812.

Childhood Cancer
"Chemotherapy made her very sick"

Jennifer Goodell and her family always attended church. Jennifer only missed when she played basketball, one of the things she most enjoyed. As the star player for her team, Jennifer was having one of her best games when she had a hard fall and broke her leg. It was later explained to her that the fall alone should not have caused the fracture—her leg broke because she had bone cancer. Jennifer cried when the doctor told her that this type of disease usually strikes teens and those in their early twenties. In another week she would be sixteen; cancer wasn't the kind of gift she had anticipated.

Jennifer celebrated her birthday in a hospital room that she shared with a young girl who cried for her grandmother the whole night. Jennifer was scared. She was given outpatient chemotherapy, and it made her feel terrible. There were nights she slept by the toilet because she was too sick to walk back and forth. When her hair fell out because of the chemotherapy, her mother assured her that it would grow back. Jennifer said she hated running her hand over her head and not feeling her once-abundant curly red hair.

While still in the hospital, she was told she would no longer be able to play sports, since she might develop complications that could worsen her condition. This put Jennifer in a morbid mood. There were days she would sit in bed and stare out the window, questioning her faith. The news got even worse when her physician told her that the chemotherapy was not working and that she would need to have a bone marrow transplant. The doctor explained that inside of human bones is marrow, where blood cells are made. Transplantation involves killing diseased marrow and replacing it with healthy bone marrow from a donor. The physician told her that the procedure was difficult, but it was her best chance for recovery. Jennifer and her family were experiencing a lot of pain, fear, and misery. It felt as if the whole world was falling apart. Their pastor, the Rev. James Hess, spent many hours with Jennifer and her family, listening and praying with them as they went through the ordeal of her treatments during the next months.

Almost a year after Jennifer first entered the hospital, the good news came from her doctor that she was in complete remission and could hope for a full recovery. There was great celebration in her family and church. Six months later, Jennifer's mother and father came to Pastor Hess with concerns. During the time since her recovery, Jennifer had become increasingly withdrawn, defensive, irritable, and fearful. She began having problems in school and had a hard time concentrating on her studies. Her sleep was difficult and restless. Pastor Hess knew that such symptoms could be a sign of psychological trauma in the aftermath of a grave illness such as cancer. Even normal reactions to the treatment of a life-threatening disease can include intrusive thoughts, separation from others and the world, sleep problems, and overexcitability. He recommended that the family consult with a psychologist he trusted.

Pastoral Care Assessment

Pastor Hess had worked with other families with members suffering from the difficulties of cancer. He knew that oncology patients commonly experience pain, weakness, nausea, and vomiting as they undergo painful and invasive procedures. Hospitalization can last for long periods of time, leading to feelings of isolation, loss of control, and helplessness, especially for those who have little social support.

The diagnosis of a life-threatening illness can cause feelings of extreme fear, helplessness, or horror and may trigger symptoms of post-traumatic stress disorder (PTSD) (Meeske et al., 2001). These responses include reexperiencing the trauma (nightmares, flashbacks, and interfering thoughts), avoiding reminders of the trauma (staying away from situations, responding less to others, showing little emotion), and being continuously excited (for example, having sleeping problems or being overly defensive, watchful, or irritable).

Rev. Hess also knew that cancer survivors can experience a sense of grief and anger for what they have lost. Jennifer was angry because she felt the cancer robbed her of a college basketball scholarship. She felt a sense of sadness for the prom she missed. Throughout many months, the pastor listened and empathized while feeling helpless that he could not do more for her. Yet his consistent presence offered Jennifer an embodiment of God's love for us even in difficult places.

Relevant History

Cancer develops when there is out-of-control growth of abnormal cells. The disease can occur anywhere in the human body, and there are over one hundred different types. When a cell becomes malignant, it loses the ability to regulate its own growth, control cell division, and correctly interpret messages from other cells. Each malignant tumor is believed to originate from a single cell gone awry.

The majority of adult cancer patients are treated in their own communities by family physicians, consulting surgeons, and medical oncologists or other specialists. However, children with cancer are rarely treated by family physicians or pediatricians. A child must be diagnosed precisely and treated by clinical and laboratory scientists who have expertise in the management of pediatric cancer. Such teams are found only in university medical centers, major children's hospitals, and cancer centers.

Diagnostic Criteria

Each year in the United States, approximately 1 in 330 children and adolescents is found to have cancer (National Institutes of Health, 1999), and frequently he or she has a more advanced stage of the disease when first diagnosed than do adults. Childhood malignancies are most often those of the white blood cells (leukemia), brain, bone, the lymphatic system, and tumors of the muscles, kidneys, and nervous system. About 2,300 children and teens die from cancer annually, which makes cancer the most common cause of disease-related death for Americans under twenty years of age (Fromer, 1998).

Fortunately, in the past thirty years, better treatment of childhood malignancies has resulted in increasing numbers of patients experiencing longer periods of disease-free survival. In 1970, the five-year survival rate was less than 30 percent, while today more than 75 percent of youngsters who are diagnosed with cancer are expected to survive the disease (Greenlee et al., 2001). By 2010, about 1 in every 250 Americans will be a survivor of childhood cancer (Keene, Hobbie, and Ruccione, 2000).

Being diagnosed with and treated for and surviving cancer can cause psychological problems, including PTSD (Meeske et al., 2001). The physical and mental shock of having a life-threatening disease, receiving treatment, and living with repeated threats to one's body and life can be traumatic experiences for patients. Symptoms of PTSD have also been identified in family members of cancer patients and survivors (Kazak et al., 1998). These responses may be due to family members having to face the patient's possible death as well as repeatedly witnessing treatments and side effects.

As many as 1 in 5 survivors of childhood cancer may have PTSD symptoms as he or she faces the challenges of adulthood (Hobbie et al., 2000). Additionally, they may have to cope with physical complications stemming from their original disease. Researchers conducted a study of 78 adults, aged eighteen to forty, who were survivors of childhood cancer. Twenty percent of them met the criteria for PTSD, exhibiting symptoms of avoidance, anxiety, and other psychological distress.

The researchers found that these young adults experienced frequent anxiety about their lives being in danger at reminders (such as going to hospitals and hospital smells), from new health challenges (such as infertility, neurocognitive deficits, cardiac impairments), and at memories of particularly intensive treatment of childhood cancer and/or recurrence of the disease (Hobbie et al., 2000). Besides PTSD limiting the quality of life for these persons, it can also threaten their physical health by causing them to avoid medical care.

One difficulty that mental health professionals have in determining if an oncology patient has PTSD is pinpointing the exact cause. Because the experience of having cancer involves so many upsetting events, it can be hard to single out the specific trigger of the psychological trauma. The stressful incident may be the initial diagnosis, realizing that the disease can be fatal, a long period of pain, a symptom that indicates the disease has returned, or a feared treatment procedure.

Response to Vignette

Dr. Mee Mei Choy is a clinical psychologist who had been of help to Pastor Hess in several pastoral counseling cases over the years. The pastor and Jennifer's parents explained their concerns. The psychologist agreed to see Jennifer and her family for a full assessment.

Dr. Choy found that both Jennifer and her parents were experiencing anxiety and depression related to their fear of the disease returning. Although their daughter had been given a clean bill of health from her physician, her parents continued to have deep fears about her dying. In family sessions it was revealed that the Goodells had had several tragic deaths resulting from cancer on both sides of their family. Post-traumatic stress symptoms are not uncommon in mothers and fathers of long-term survivors of childhood cancer, although not necessarily at the level of a clinical syndrome, and the responses are much higher than in families without serious illness (Kazak et al., 1998).

Jennifer was having trauma-related symptoms, which included avoiding certain situations, continuously thinking about her treatments, and being anxious. Her fears were triggered by such experiences as driving to a hospital or smells associated with her treatment. She also had difficulty going to sleep and staying asleep. When she slept, she had frightening nightmares about her cancer. Sometimes she would wake up in a cold sweat, feeling needles in her arms. Jennifer and her family agreed to enter therapy. Given their high motivation to work together in treatment and their openness to the process, they had a good prognosis.

Treatment Within the Faith Community

Caring for a sick child calls for truly unconditional love. Caregiving can be enormously stressful. There were many ways that church members were able to help the Goodell family as they dealt with Jennifer's cancer. Battling the disease can take one year or several, and a family needs practical and spiritual support throughout the course of treatment.

Members of the church realized that the family was often at the hospital, and the Goodells did not have time to keep up with housework.

Several people volunteered to help. Some mowed the lawn and picked up the mail and newspapers, while others looked after the care and feeding of the pets. The young adult group cooked a meal for the family on a regular basis and delivered it to them. Another church organization put together a food basket weekly that contained the items necessary to make a meal. The youth group held a fundraiser and donated the money to Jennifer's family to use for her care. Because the hospital was not close, several members gave prepaid phone cards to the Goodells so they could stay in touch with friends at home without a costly phone bill.

Through the ordeal, Jennifer and her family found that regularly keeping in contact by phone with their church friends was very important to them emotionally and spiritually. The sort of social support offered to the Goodells by the congregation has been shown to lower the risk of psychological distress after an emotional trauma and has many other valuable mental health benefits (National Advisory Mental Health Council Basic Behavioral Science Task Force, 1996).

In addition to offering the natural social support of community, faith can provide a suffering person with a framework for finding meaning and perspective through a source greater than self, and it can give a sense of control over feelings of helplessness (Flannelly, Flannelly, and Weaver, 2002). For example, fathers of children being treated for cancer in a hematology hospital clinic were asked about various methods of coping. Among twenty-nine separate coping strategies used, prayer was both the most common and the most helpful for the fathers (Cayse, 1994).

Indications for Referral

Rev. Hess was well prepared to help the Goodell family because he already had a working relationship with a mental health professional. He knew that in some cases good pastoral care means making an appropriate referral. It is important that clergy understand the limits of their training and know when to ask for help from specialists.

Most often when responding to a person with PTSD, a pastor's primary task is to identify the needs of the one seeking assistance and to connect him or her to a larger circle of specialized helpers.

Treatment by Mental Health Specialist

Because of the serious and sometimes chronic effects of its symptoms in some childhood cancer survivors and their families, PTSD should be identified and addressed promptly. Unfortunately, the avoidant responses that often appear with PTSD can keep persons from seeking help. The therapies used to treat cancer survivors are much the same as those available for other trauma victims and frequently involve more than one type of treatment.

The early stage of PTSD treatment focuses on reducing symptoms and returning a person to normal functioning. A therapist works with a survivor to solve problems, teach coping skills, and provide a supportive setting. Cognitive-behavioral methods have been shown to be very helpful (Foa, Keane, and Friedman, 2000). Some of these methods include helping a patient understand symptoms, teaching coping and stress management skills (such as relaxation training), reforming one's thinking, and trying to make a patient less sensitive to the symptoms.

Support groups may also help those who experience post-traumatic stress. In such settings, patients can receive emotional support, meet others with similar experiences and responses, and learn coping and management skills. Researchers have found that many parents are eager to talk about their cancer-related experiences and feel that they do not have others who understand their ongoing distress (Kazak et al., 1996). For patients with severe symptoms, medication may be needed, including antidepressants, antianxiety drugs, and, when necessary, antipsychotic medications.

Cross-Cultural Issues

African Americans are more likely to develop cancer and are less likely to survive it than any other racial or ethnic group. During the years 1992 to 1998, the cancer incidence rate per 100,000 was 445.3 among African Americans, 401.4 for European Americans, 283.4 in Asians/Pacific Islanders, 270.0 among Hispanic Americans, and 202.7 in American Indians/Native Alaskans (American Cancer Society, 2002).

Resources

—American Cancer Society; 1599 Clifton Road, NE, Atlanta, GA 30329-4251; (800) ACS-2345; www.cancer.org; is a nationwide, community-based voluntary health organization dedicated to eliminating cancer as a major health problem by preventing and diminishing suffering from cancer through research, education, advocacy, and service.

—Cancer Care; 275 Seventh Avenue, New York, NY 10001; (800) 813-4673; www.cancercare.org; provides professional one-to-one counseling, support groups, educational programs, workshops, and teleconferences to cancer patients and their families. It offers information on starting a cancer support group.

—Cancervive; 11636 Chayote Street, Los Angeles, CA 90049; (800) 4-TO-CURE; www.cancervive.org; is a national nonprofit organization, founded in 1985. Its mission is to assist those who have experienced cancer to assimilate the physical, emotional, and psychosocial changes brought about by the illness. It provides services for cancer patients, survivors, and family members as they deal with the aftermath of the disease.

—Candlelighters Childhood Cancer Foundation; P.O. Box 498, Kensington, MD 20895-0498; (800) 366-2223; www.candlelighters.org; was founded in 1970 as an international foundation with over four hundred groups. It offers support for parents of children and adolescents with cancer, their family members, and adult survivors of childhood cancer. Health and education professionals are also welcomed as members.

—Kidney Cancer Association; 1234 Sherman Avenue, Suite 203, Evanston, IL 60202; (800) 850-9132; www.nkca.org; was founded in 1990 and has eight affiliated groups. It provides information about kidney cancer to patients and doctors and advocates on behalf of patients. It offers information and referrals, literature, and conferences.

—Leukemia and Lymphoma Society of America, Family Support Group Program; 1311 Mamaroneck Avenue, White Plains, NY 10605; (800) 955-4572; (914) 949-5213; www.leukemia.org; is a national program of 125 professionally run groups, founded in 1949. It offers mutual support for patients, family members, and friends coping with leukemia, lymphoma, multiple myeloma, and Hodgkin's Disease.

—The MACC Fund, Midwest Athletes Against Childhood Cancer; 1200 North Mayfair Road, Suite 265, Milwaukee, WI 53226; (800) 248-8735; www.maccfund.org; is a charitable organization based in Milwaukee. It was created to support research into the effective treatment and cure of childhood cancer.

—National Cancer Institute, Pediatric Oncology Branch; Cancer Information Service, Suite 3036A, 6116 Executive Boulevard, MSC 8322, Bethesda, MD 20892; (877) 624-4878; home.ccr.cancer.gov/oncology /pediatric/; is part of the National Institutes of Health (NIH), the world's largest medical research institution, which is operated by the federal government. Patients who participate in clinical protocols are treated at the Clinical Center located on the NIH campus in Bethesda. The Internet home page provides patients, families, and physicians with an overview of the type of treatments available for children with cancer and of the research conducted by investigators at the Pediatric Oncology Branch.

—National Childhood Cancer Foundation; P.O. Box 60012, Arcadia, CA 91066-6012; (800) 458-6223; www.ncff.org.

—National Children's Cancer Society; 1015 Locust, Suite 600, St. Louis, MO 63101; (800) 532-6459; www.children-cancer.com; helps children with cancer through its nationwide programs and services. It offers financial and emotional support so that children and their families can more effectively deal with the difficulties of cancer treatment.

—National Coalition for Cancer Survivorship; 1010 Wayne Avenue, Suite 770, Silver Spring, MD 20910; www.canceradvocacy.org; (877) NCCS-YES; was founded in 1986 as a national grassroots network that works on behalf of persons with all types of cancer. Its mission is to strengthen and empower cancer survivors and advocate for policy issues. It provides information on employment and insurance issues, referrals, and publications.

Helpful Books

Caregiving: A Step-by-Step Resource for Caring for the Person with Cancer at Home (Peter S. Houts and Julia A. Bucher, eds., Atlanta: American Cancer Society, 2000).

Childhood Cancer: A Handbook from St. Jude Children's Research Hospital (Joseph Mirro and Grant Steen, eds., Boulder, CO: Perseus Books Group, 2000).

Childhood Cancer Survivors: A Practical Guide to Your Future (Nancy Keene, Wendy Hobbie, and Kathy Ruccione, Sebastopol, CA: O'Reilly & Associates, 2000).

Living with Childhood Cancer: A Practical Guide to Help Parents Cope (Leigh A. Woznick and Carol D. Goodheart, Washington, DC: American Psychological Association, 2001).

Supportive Care of Children with Cancer: Current Therapy and Guidelines from the Children's Cancer Group (Arthur R. Ablin, Baltimore: Johns Hopkins University Press, 1999).

Surviving Childhood Cancer: A Guide for Families (Margot Joan Fromer, Oakland, CA: New Harbinger Publishers, 1998).

References

American Cancer Society (2002). *Cancer Facts and Figures, 2002.* Atlanta, GA: American Cancer Society.

Cayse, L. N. (1994). Fathers of children with cancer: A descriptive study of the stressors and coping strategies. *Journal of Pediatric Oncology Nursing, 11(3),* 102-108.

Flannelly, L. T., Flannelly, K., and Weaver, A. J. (2002). Religious and spiritual variables in three major oncology nursing journals: 1990–1999. *Oncology Nursing Forum, 29(4),* 679-685.

Foa, E. B., Keane, T. M., and Friedman, M. J. (2000). *Effective Treatments for PTSD.* New York: Guilford Press.

Fromer, M. J. (1998). *Surviving Childhood Cancer: A Guide for Families.* Oakland, CA: New Harbinger Publishers.

Greenlee, R. T., Hill-Harmon, M. B., Murray, T., and Thun, M. (2001). Cancer statistics, 2001. *Cancer Journal for Clinicians, 51(1),* 15-36.

Hobbie, W. L., Stuber, M., Meeske, K., Wissler, K., Rourke, M. T., Ruccione, K., Hinkle, A., and Kazak, A. E. (2000). Symptoms of posttraumatic stress in young adult survivors of childhood cancer. *Journal of Clinical Oncology, 18(24),* 4060-4066.

Kazak, A. E., Stuber, M. L., Barakat, L. P., and Meeske, K. (1996). Assessing posttraumatic stress related to medical illness and treatment: The impact of Traumatic Stressors Interview Schedule (ITSIS). *Family Systems Health, 14,* 365-380.

Kazak, A. E., Stuber, M. L., Barakat, L. P., Meeske, K., Guthrie, D., and Meadows, A. T. (1998). Predicting posttraumatic stress symptoms in mothers and fathers of survivors of childhood cancers. *Journal of the Academy of Child and Adolescent Psychiatry, 37(8),* 823-831.

Keene, N., Hobbie, W., and Ruccione, K. (2000). *Childhood Cancer Survivors: A Practical Guide to Your Future.* Sebastopol, CA: O'Reilly and Associates.

Meeske, K. A., Ruccione, K., Globe, D. R., and Stuber, M. L. (2001). Posttraumatic stress, quality of life, and psychological distress in young adult survivors of childhood cancer. *Oncology Nursing Forum, 28(3)*, 481-489.

National Advisory Mental Health Council Basic Behavioral Science Task Force (1996). Basic behavioral science research for mental health: Family processes and social networks. *American Psychologist, 51(6)*, 622-630.

National Institutes of Health (1999). *Cancer Incidence and Survival Among Children and Adolescents: United States SEER Program 1975–1995*. NIH Publication 99-4649.

it has only been recognized recently by mental health researchers and clinicians).

Clergy are most often sought for counsel in situations associated with grief, such as the death of a spouse, family member, or close friend (Weaver, Revilla, and Koenig, 2001). In a national survey of more than 1,200 adults, 89 percent said that if they were facing their death, they would find comfort in "believing in [the] loving presence of God or [a] Higher Power," and 71 percent said they would be comforted by a visit from a clergyperson (Gallup, 1997). According to the National Funeral Directors Association, clergy officiate at an estimated 1.5 million funeral or memorial services annually in the United States (K. Walczak, personal communication, March 1, 2002). This means that each year, clergy interact with millions of Americans who are grieving the loss of a friend or family member.

Religious faith can help cushion the blow associated with the death of a loved one. Several studies in diverse populations have shown a positive relationship between religious involvement and adapting to the loss of a family member or close friend. In a study of 312 adults in Buffalo, New York, 77 percent said that their religious beliefs were of considerable help in their grief (Frantz, Trolley, and Johll, 1996). Researchers in California (Davis, Nolen-Hocksema, and Larson, 1998) and Great Britain (Walsh et al., 2002) who studied individuals grieving the death of a family member or close friend discovered that there is a strong link between one's ability to make sense of the loss through the practice of one's faith and positive psychological adjustment. People who profess stronger religious beliefs seem to resolve their grief more rapidly and completely after the death of someone close than do persons with none.

Intense anxiety symptoms following a loss, especially if sustained beyond a few weeks, clearly warrant mental health treatment. At times, a death provokes severe psychological symptoms in persons with preexisting vulnerability or mental illnesses, but such reactions can occur in otherwise emotionally healthy individuals. This should be explained to those experiencing traumatic bereavement. Furthermore, owing to the tenacity of the symptoms, such persons must be strongly encouraged to accept a referral to a mental health professional.

There are two compelling reasons for treating traumatic bereavement. The most obvious is to reduce or eliminate the disturbing symptoms. The second, however, is equally important. Complicated bereavement always interferes with the process of normal, healthy grieving. Thus, resolution of traumatic symptoms will open the door to productive grief work and eventual emotional healing.

Treatment Within the Faith Community

Indications for Referral

Treatment by a Mental Health Specialist

Treatment of traumatic bereavement often has three aspects. The first is psychotherapy designed to target intrusive symptoms; typically this involves exposure-based cognitive therapy (Foa, Keane, and Friedman, 2000). A second approach *may* include psychiatric medication. The only FDA-approved treatment for PTSD is the use of antidepressants (such as Zoloft, Prozac, Paxil, Celexa, Serzone, Effexor), which are often effective in reducing anxiety, intrusive memories, nightmares, and marked numbing/dissociation (in addition to depressive symptoms). These medications are generally well tolerated and non-habit-forming (Preston, O'Neal, and Talaga, 2001).

The final aspect of treatment is to help a person face the painful loss and continue to grieve.

Cross-Cultural Issues

A recent study in Ohio examined the role of unexpected death in the psychological symptoms of widows approximately six months after their husbands' deaths (Kitson, 2000). It focused on 276 African American and European American women aged nineteen to seventy-four whose spouses had died from homicide, suicide, or accidental death. Contrary to expectation, wives of the men who had died from long-term natural illnesses exhibited more distress than widows of those who had died from both violence and sudden natural deaths combined. Middle-aged and younger widows were more distressed than older ones. European American women reported more symptoms than their African American counterparts in violent but not in natural deaths.

Resources

—American Association of Retired Persons (AARP); Grief and Loss Programs, 601 E Street, NW, Washington, DC 20049; (800) 424-3410; www.aarp.org/griefandloss; provides a variety of bereavement programs that offer support to widows, widowers, and persons of all ages grieving the death of a parent, sibling, or other loved one. It offers services for all adult loss from death by providing publications, groups, courses, and one-to-one outreach. It gives assistance in starting and maintaining support groups and facilitates three online bereavement groups.

—American Counseling Association; 5999 Stevenson Avenue, Alexandria, VA 22304; (800) 347-6647; www.counseling.org.

—American Psychiatric Association; 1000 Wilson Boulevard, Arlington, VA 22209; (703) 907-7300; www.psych.org.

—American Psychological Association; 750 First Street, NE, Washington, DC 20002; (800) 374-2721; www.apa.org.

—GriefNet.org, www.griefnet.org, is an online discussion group for bereavement, which offers a group called the "Horrific Loss Support Group," specifically for those who lost a loved one on September 11, 2001. There is a small monthly fee required for each group joined.

—International Society for Traumatic Stress Studies, 60 Revere Drive, Suite 500, Northbrook, IL 60062; (847) 480-9028; www.istss.org.

—National Institute of Mental Health, 6001 Executive Boulevard, Room 8184, MSC 9663, Bethesda, MD 20892; (866) 615-NIMH; www.nimh.nih.gov/publicat/depressionmenu.cfm; provides free information and literature on depressive disorders, symptoms, treatment, and sources of help. Publications available in Spanish, Asian languages, and Russian.

—Rainbows, 2100 Gold Road #370, Rolling Meadows, IL 60008; (800) 266-3206; www.rainbows.org/rainbows.html; is an international organization with sixty-three hundred affiliated groups. Founded in 1983, it establishes peer support groups in churches, schools, and social agencies for children and adults who are grieving a divorce, death, or other painful change in their families. The groups are led by trained adults, and referrals are provided.

—Sidran Institute; 200 East Joppa Road, Suite 207, Towson, MD 21286; (410) 825-8888; www.sidran.org; focuses on education, advocacy, and research related to the early recognition and treatment of traumatic stress disorders.

—Stephen Ministries; 2045 Innerbelt Business Center Drive, St. Louis, MO 63114; (314) 428-2600; www.stephenministries.org; offers training in counseling skills for church members. Five thousand congregations worldwide offer this ministry.

—Young Widow, www.youngwidow.com, is an online support site for men and women who have lost their spouses. Founded by Lauren Raynor of Philadelphia after the September 11, 2001, tragedy, it offers a bulletin board, links to other online message boards, and lists of national support groups for young widowed persons.

Helpful Books

Good Grief: A Constructive Approach to the Problem of Loss (Granger E. Westberg, Minneapolis: Augsburg Fortress, 1983).

Grief Counseling and Grief Therapy: A Handbook for the Mental Health Professional (J. William Worden, New York: Springer Publishing, 2001).

A Grief Observed (C. S. Lewis, New York: Bantam Doubleday Dell, 1976).

Healing After Loss: Daily Meditations for Working Through Grief (Martha Whitmore Hickman, New York: William Morrow, 1994).

A Journal of Love and Healing: Transcending Grief (Sylvia Browne and Nancy Dufresne, Carlsbad, CA: Hay House, 2001).

You Can Beat Depression (John D. Preston, San Luis Obispo, CA: Impact Publishers, 1997).

References

American Psychiatric Association (2000). *Diagnostic and Statistical Manual of Mental Disorders* (Fourth Edition, Text Revised). Washington, DC: American Psychiatric Association.

Davis, C. G., Nolen-Hocksema, S., and Larson, J. (1998). Making sense of loss and benefiting from the experience: Two construals of meaning. *Journal of Personality and Social Psychology, 75(2)*, 561-574.

Foa, E. B., Keane, T. M., and Friedman, M. J. (2000). *Effective Treatments for PTSD*. New York: Guilford Press.

Frantz, T. T., Trolley, B. C., and Johll, M. P. (1996). Religious aspects of bereavement. *Pastoral Psychology, 44(3)*, 151-163.

Gallup, G. H. (1997). *Spiritual Beliefs and Dying Practices*. Princeton: George Gallup International Institute.

Horowitz, M. J. (1976). *Stress Response Syndromes*. New York: Jason Aronson.

Kitson, G. C. (2000). Adjustment to violent and natural deaths in later and earlier life for black and white widows. *Journal of Gerontology: Biological, Psychological, and Social Sciences, 55(6)*, 341-351.

Preston, J. D., O'Neal, J. H., and Talaga, M. C. (2001). *Handbook of Clinical Psychopharmacology for Therapists*. Oakland, CA: New Harbinger.

Walsh, K., King, M., Jones, L., Tookman, A., and Blizard, R. (2002). Spiritual beliefs may affect outcome of bereavement: Prospective study. *British Medical Journal, 324*, 1551-1554.

Weaver, A. J., Revilla, L. A., and Koenig, H. G. (2002). *Counseling Families Across the Stages of Life: A Handbook for Pastors and Other Helping Professionals*. Nashville: Abingdon Press.

Zisook, S., Chentsova-Dutton, Y., and Shuchter, S. R. (1999). PTSD following bereavement. *Annals of Clinical Psychiatry, 10(4)*, 157-163.

Pregnancy Loss

"She admitted being angry with God"

Chaplain Lawrence met Julie Bowen at the hospital's annual memorial service, Children Lost in Pregnancy. Julie had lost her first child at six months' gestation and had come to the service at a friend's suggestion. Julie was outgoing, able to talk about the loss, and very interested in joining the monthly support group led by the chaplain and a social worker. She participated in the group regularly, where she cried, complained, and laughed appropriately. She even brought a birthday cake and invited the group to join her in marking the due date of her deceased daughter. When Julie became pregnant again, she stayed with the group. She hadn't finished grieving her first child and needed support for her fears that the same thing might happen again. "Besides," she said, "coming to the group has helped me more than seeing my therapist one-on-one. It's comforting to know I am not alone."

When she lost her second pregnancy—twins, a boy and a girl—at five months, she looked to the group for support. The chaplain noticed that Julie now admitted to being angry with God, something not mentioned before. Three months after the loss of the twins, Julie was hospitalized for her first asthma attack. Julie called the chaplain, who went immediately to visit her.

Mary Lawrence is a chaplain with extensive experience with pregnancy loss patients. She and other staff members participate in a special bereavement protocol to help parents move toward healthy grieving when there is a pregnancy loss at the hospital. One of every five known pregnancies will end in loss (Lee and Slade, 1995). For most women, ectopic pregnancy, miscarriage, stillbirth, or new-born death has a major effect on their lives that can persist for a long time, regardless of the mother's age or the

Pastoral Care Assessment

presence of other children (Robinson, Stirtzinger, and Stewart, 1994). By its very nature, pregnancy loss creates difficulties for grieving. Often there is not a body to mourn, there are no memories of shared life experiences, death is sudden, there is a general lack of recognition of the depth or significance of the loss, and mourners may be subjected to insensitive attitudes or remarks. Suppressed or inhibited grief can have long-term, negative emotional consequences (Lee and Slade, 1995). Many hospitals now offer special guidance through this difficult territory, providing emotional and spiritual support and ways to create memories and mementos.

Until now, Julie had appeared to be experiencing normal grief reactions to her pregnancy losses. She had loving memories of her pregnancies and lost children; had sought opportunities for talking about her grief; cried; yearned for what was lost, been upset and angry at insensitive comments; felt sadness, emptiness, and loneliness; and looked for consolation from her spouse and others. She had held her babies, named them, engaged in rituals to honor their memory, and returned to normal routines.

Before going to visit, Chaplain Lawrence checked her notes. Julie's second pregnancy loss had occurred about three months ago, often a stress marker for grieving parents who are at the point that many obstetricians say they can try again (Lee and Slade, 1995). Both of Julie's pregnancies were the result of fertility interventions. The chaplain knows that depression is more frequent with assisted pregnancies, especially when there is a history of emotional problems (Nikcevic et al., 1999). She also recalls that new physical ailments can sometimes accompany unresolved emotional issues and grief. She will need to listen carefully to Julie during this hospital visit to see if Julie is grieving more deeply or is at risk for depression.

Diagnostic Criteria

Of all mental health problems, depression is the most common and the most treatable. In the general population, 1 in 10 individuals experiences a major depression at some time. For women who lose a pregnancy, the rate is much higher. They are 3.4 times more likely to be depressed than pregnant women and 4.3 times more likely than nonpregnant women (Neugebauer et al., 1992). Psychological signs of depression include dejection, self-pity, disappointing memories about the pregnancy, feelings of helplessness, hopelessness, inconsolability, withdrawal from personal relationships, feelings of worthlessness and shame, and a sense of personal responsibility or guilt for the loss. Physical symptoms include various bodily complaints, loss of appetite or weight, and sleep disturbances (Beutel et al., 1995).

Feelings of guilt are an unavoidable component of all grief. It is almost impossible not to wonder if one did or did not do something that contributed to the loss. When a child becomes ill or is injured, a loving parent automatically sorts through a mental list of what could have caused it and takes steps to put new controls in place to prevent it happening again. The majority of miscarriages are caused by chromosomal problems. Other known causes are insufficient progesterone, low thyroid hormones, uterine growths or structural abnormalities, bacterial or viral infections, autoimmune disorders, and prenatal tests (Tarkan, 1997). Most mothers report great relief in discovering the cause of their loss. Women who are unable to find a medical cause become vulnerable to self-blame, guilt, stress, and depression (Stirtzinger et al., 1999).

Self-esteem (feelings of self-worth and acceptance) also affects depressive levels. Mothers with low self-esteem may feel personally responsible for the loss, which discourages their interest in or hope of finding help and consolation from outside resources. Women who become pregnant through fertility treatments and lose a pregnancy more often experience lower self-esteem than those who became pregnant on their own, which puts them at higher risk for depression (Nikcevic et al., 1999). Also, a history of previous depression, a lack of social resources or an inability to access them, and an ambivalent attitude toward the fetus can trigger depression.

Some researchers are beginning to include pregnancy loss among those events that can trigger post-traumatic stress disorder (PTSD), particularly when a new pregnancy begins in less than twelve months. Miscarriage or stillbirth can be emotionally traumatic. The unexpected event with its sudden pain, loss of blood, hospitalization often with rapid surgery, and loss of life can induce great fear, helplessness, and horror (Turton et al., 2001). Women who are already vulnerable to restlessness, irritability, excessive fatigue, sleep disturbances, anxiety, startle reactions, depression, and concentration difficulties are especially at risk for PTSD after pregnancy loss.

Relevant History

Julie has no history of emotional problems prior to her pregnancy losses and no history of depression in her family. She continues to find the support group helpful and has a supportive husband. She had told the chaplain privately, soon after meeting her, that her first pregnancy loss had been a therapeutic abortion, not a spontaneous one. She and her husband are older, and they had agreed before beginning fertility treatments that if abnormalities were discovered, they would terminate the pregnancy. She had insisted that she felt fine about the decision and saw it as a protective gesture on their part, to spare their child who had not only Down's syndrome, but many additional abnormalities as well. Julie had held her daughter, who had died before being delivered, and she had seen the physical abnormalities her doctor had predicted.

Response to Vignette

When Chaplain Lawrence arrived, Julie's husband, Phil, was there. He had never come to the support group; Julie had said he was too reserved to talk about his feelings with people he didn't know. In this intimate setting, he talked freely and shared his fears about what would happen to them both if they had to go through another loss. "I have buried three children, and I can't do that again. Besides, I think Julie would fall apart completely if she had to go through this another time. It's just too traumatic." Julie agreed that another pregnancy loss might be unbearable, but she said, "Adopting is his idea. I'm not sure I am ready for that." Phil responded, "If we're going to have kids, we need to move on it now. We aren't getting any younger, especially me. I'm already forty-six." Although it was clear they needed to continue to work on which direction they would take next, it did not seem to Rev. Lawrence that this was an insurmountable subject for Julie or the source of her discomfort. Phil had to leave for work but said he would consider attending the next support group meeting with Julie.

After he was gone, the chaplain continued to look for signs of serious change in Julie's emotional state as she talked about her feelings. Julie explained that she had seen children with Down's syndrome several times lately and had begun to wonder if God was trying to tell her something. Slowly, she began to tell Rev. Lawrence that she thought God was punishing her by letting her twins die, that she wondered if God was angry because she and Phil had lived together before marriage and decided not to continue the first pregnancy. She accepted the idea that God would never forgive her, but she was depressed at the thought that God would punish her children for something she did. She could see no way out, because "what is done is done and can't be taken back. I just know I will burn in hell someday."

Julie explained that she and Phil had drifted away from church during their twenties but had called a pastor acquaintance when they were making the decision about their first child. She had been deeply hurt when he had insisted on praying first without spending any time listening to their concerns, telling them it would be an unpardonable sin if they decided to abort. He hadn't contacted her since then.

Phil and Julie made the decision to terminate the first pregnancy when they were told that their daughter would always need to be institutionalized if she lived. Julie became severely depressed after her baby's delivery. She lost interest in eating, could not sleep, and had no energy or interest in getting out of bed. She met with a psychiatrist several times but refused medication. She has not had such a severe episode since then, but she still has trouble sleeping, can fall into long periods of crying, and often must force herself out of bed. She promised the chaplain she would consider seeing a psychiatrist again, but only "if things got worse."

Meanwhile, Phil began attending the support group sessions with Julie, and they shared their religious concerns. Hearing that others were struggling with similar issues made it easier for Phil and Julie to decide to visit a church in their neighborhood. They connected with the pastor who had a "good listening ear" and a nonthreatening way of talking about God. He supported their plans for adoption by making several helpful referrals, and he kept in contact with them even before they became regular in their attendance.

Clergy and faith communities are in an excellent position to be helpful to those who experience grief and depression after losing a pregnancy. Including references to pregnancy loss in sermons and prayers is an excellent first step for creating a "safe environment" that encourages congregants to share what has happened with their pastor. Offering rituals of memorial, or funeral services when possible, helps mourners feel understood and supported by the larger community and better able to express their grief and eventually recover. Education events about depression and grief, dissemination of good mental health information, and distribution of flyers from groups addressing these topics all help remove the secrecy and stigma that have surrounded pregnancy loss and depression for far too long.

A National Institute of Health study found that a woman with a mental health problem is more likely to seek assistance from clergy than from a mental health specialist (Hohmann and Larson, 1993). Depression is not a benign condition, since 15 percent of those who go untreated for major depression commit suicide (Preston, 1997). Clergy and parishioner who recognize signs of depression and psychological trauma can be true lifesavers.

Information about community support groups should be made available to grieving parents, especially when they are feeling like they "are the only ones." Groups generally are of two kinds: drop-in groups that meet monthly and are open to bereaved parents at any stage of grieving, and closed groups that meet weekly for a set number of weeks with the same bereaved parents who have signed up for sessions in advance. A referral to a mental health specialist should be made for anyone who has not been able to return to normal routines, remains withdrawn from personal relationships, is preoccupied with thoughts about death, and continues to feel helpless and hopeless.

Many parents suffering from depression after a pregnancy loss find help from one or more of these interventions: psychotherapy, antidepressant medication, or psychological debriefing for PTSD.

In psychotherapy, a parent is encouraged to talk in detail about what happened, reviewing the memories and feelings of the loss in a safe relationship of trust. This may last for a few sessions or longer, depending on the circumstances. If there is evidence of "automatic thinking" or negative beliefs, the therapist may help a parent identify and modify such thoughts or beliefs in order to gain more self-esteem and a better sense of self-control.

Antidepressants restore to the brain the appropriate levels of chemicals that have been depleted by prolonged depression (Preston, 1997). Contrary to what many people believe, these medications are not

Treatment Within the Faith Community

Indications for Referral

Treatment by a Mental Health Specialist

addictive. However, it may take time to arrive at the correct dosage or to reach normal levels of chemical balance. The good news is that antidepressants are effective in 70 percent to 80 percent of cases (Reynolds et al., 1992).

Debriefing, sometimes called critical incident stress debriefing, may be beneficial for people who are suffering from psychological trauma. Through a series of stages, thoughts and expectations are discussed, along with feelings and other emotional reactions. This approach has been very helpful to survivors of disasters, witnesses of murders or suicides, and in situations involving the tragic death of children (Lee and Slade, 1995).

Cross-Cultural Issues

Men and women tend to grieve differently. Given the lack of social support for mourning pregnancy losses, it is helpful to assist couples in discussing their grief together or with a counselor who can facilitate their understanding of differing responses to the same event. Faith traditions vary widely in their attitudes toward the death of a child before birth. Thus, it is important to be aware of the religious backgrounds of the mourners, being sensitive to such issues as naming the child and burial or memorial practices.

Resources

—Depression and Bipolar Support Alliance; 730 North Franklin Street, Suite 501, Chicago, IL 60610; (800) 826-3632; www.dbsalliance.org.

—Growth House, an online community for end of life care, has a database of resources for pregnancy loss; www.growthhouse.org/natal.html.

—Hygeia: An Online Journal for Pregnancy and Neonatal Loss; www.hygeia.org.

—InterNational Council on Infertility Information Dissemination, The Miscarriage Manual; www.inciid.org/mismanl.html.

—National Foundation for Depressive Illness; P.O. Box 2257, New York, NY 10116; (800) 239-1265; www.depression.org. A twenty-four-hour recorded message describes symptoms of depression and gives addresses for more information; physician and support group referrals by state.

—National Institute of Mental Health, 6001 Executive Boulevard, Room 8184, MSC 9663, Bethesda, MD 20892; (866) 615-NIMH; www.nimh.nih.gov. It provides free information and literature on depressive disorders, symptoms, treatment, and sources of help. Publications available in Spanish, Asian languages, and Russian.

—SHARE, St. Joseph Health Center, 300 First Capitol Drive, St. Charles, MO 63301; www.nationalshareoffice.com; (800) 821-6819 or (636) 947-6164. An international support organization for parents who have lost children through miscarriage, stillbirth, or newborn death. SHARE has local chapters and a newsletter.

—Stephen Ministries; 2045 Innerbelt Business Center Drive, St. Louis, MO 63114; (314) 428-2600; www.stephenministries.org; offers training in counseling skills for local church members. Five thousand congregations worldwide offer this ministry.

—Subsequent Pregnancy After a Loss Support, www.spals.com, is a community of people who have experienced the loss of a child due to miscarriage, selective termination, stillbirth, neonatal death, sudden infant death, or accidental death. It is an active network, with about four hundred members sharing mutual support and information regarding subsequent pregnancy.

Helpful Books

Counseling Families Across the Stages of Life: A Handbook for Pastors and Other Helping Professionals (Andrew J. Weaver, Linda A. Revilla, and Harold G. Koenig, Nashville: Abingdon Press, 2001).

Empty Cradle, Broken Heart: Surviving the Death of Your Baby, rev. ed. (Deborah Davis, St. Paul: Fulcrum Publishers, 1999).

Help, Comfort, and Hope After Losing Your Baby in the First Year (H. Lothrop, Tucson: Fisher Books, 1997). Part One guides parents through bereavement, and Part Two provides specific information for caregivers. Includes an extensive resources section.

A Silent Sorrow: Pregnancy Loss, Guidance, and Support for You and Your Family, 2nd ed. (Ingrid Kohn and Perry-Lynn Moffitt, New York: Routledge, 2000). An excellent and reader-friendly encyclopedic approach.

You Can Beat Depression (John D. Preston, San Luis Obispo, CA: Impact Publishers, 1997).

References

Beutel, M., Deckardt, R., Von Rad, M., and Weiner, H. (1995). Grief and depression after miscarriage: Their separation, antecedents, and course. *Psychosomatic Medicine, 57,* 517-526.

Hohmann, A. A., and Larson, D. B. (1993). Psychiatric factors predicting use of clergy. In E. L. Worthington, Jr. (Ed.), *Psychotherapy and Religious Values* (pp. 71-84). Grand Rapids, MI: Baker Book House.

Lee, C., and Slade, P. (1995). Miscarriage as a traumatic event: A review of the literature and new implications for intervention. *Journal of Psychosomatic Research, 40(3),* 235-244.

Neugebauer, R., Kline, J., O'Connor, P., Johnson, J., Skodol, A., Wicks, J., and Susser, M. (1992). Determinants of depressive symptoms in the early weeks after miscarriage. *American Journal of Public Health, 82(10),* 1332-1339.

Nikcevic, A. V., Kucsmierczyk, A. R., and Nicolaides, K. H. (1998). Personal coping resources, responsibility, anxiety, and depression after early pregnancy loss. *Journal of Psychosomatic Obstetrics and Gynecology, 19,* 145-154.

Nikcevic, A. V., Tunkel, S. A., Kuczmierczyk, A. R., and Nicolaides, K. H. (1999). Investigation of the cause of miscarriage and its influence on women's psychological distress. *British Journal of Obstetrics and Gynecology, 106*, 808-813.

Preston, J. D. (1997). *You Can Beat Depression*. San Luis Obispo, CA: Impact Publishers.

Reynolds, C. F., Frank, E., Perel, J. M., Imber, S. B., Cornes, C., Morycz, R. K., Mazumdar, S., Miller, M. D., Pollock, B. G., and Rifai, A. H. (1992). Combination pharmacotherapy and psychotherapy in the acute and continuation treatment of elderly patients with current major depression: A preliminary report. *American Journal of Psychiatry, 149(12)*, 1687-1692.

Robinson, G. E., Stirtzinger, R., and Stewart, D. E. (1994). Psychological reactions in women followed for one year after miscarriage. *Journal of Reproductive and Infant Psychology, 12*, 31-36.

Stirtzinger, R. M., Robinson, G. E., Stewart, D. E., and Ralevski, E. (1999). Parameters of grieving in spontaneous abortion. *International Journal of Psychiatry in Medicine, 29(2)*, 235-249.

Tarkan, L. (1997). The pain of miscarriage. *Parents, 72(10)*, 120-122.

Turton, P., Hughes, P., Evans, C. D. H., and Fainman, D. (2001). Incidence, correlates, and predictors of post-traumatic stress disorder in the pregnancy after stillbirth. *British Journal of Psychiatry, 178*, 556-560.

Torture (Refugee)

"He was imprisoned, beaten, and tortured"

David Mutombo was twenty-one years of age and had been raised in a Christian home in Central Africa. His father was a Methodist pastor who spoke out for democracy in his country and was murdered for his convictions. David was imprisoned, beaten, and tortured with electric shock. He was forced to witness the execution of several church members he knew well and had been subjected to a mock execution by a group of soldiers. Through the efforts of Amnesty International and The United Methodist Church, David was released after several months in prison. He came to the U.S. with little more than the clothes on his back and a small photo of his mother and father who had both been murdered by a death squad.

The Rev. Rachel Haines was the senior pastor of the church that sponsored his coming to the United States. David worked for the church as a maintenance person while going to college part-time. Rev. Haines became concerned about David when he fell asleep at work several times. It was discovered that David was having a very difficult time sleeping at night and concentrating on his academic work.

When David first came to the church, Rev. Haines was surprised at how well he dealt with the dramatic changes in his life. He was a person of profound faith who was very bright and a hard worker. A family in the church took him into their home, where he lived while he continued his education in engineering. He appeared to cope well with his new environment and responded positively to people in the church. However, Rev. Haines and others in the church were aware of the need to "keep an eye on him" as he adjusted and to make sure he was continuing to cope.

Pastoral Care Assessment

Rev. Haines knew it would be good for him to see an experienced mental health specialist, given the nature of his displacement from his country and the death of his parents. The traumatic circumstances of his departure provided neither the time nor the resources for dealing with the psychological effects of events. However, he resisted the idea of counseling until Pastor Haines found him sleeping in a room in the church during his workday. He told the pastor that he could not sleep at night because of the terrible nightmares. That was the first time he told anyone about the maltreatment and torture he had experienced in prison. He told Rev. Haines that he was trying to work as hard as he could at his job and in school to keep his mind off the terrible memories he was having. With gentle guidance and pastoral care, Rev. Haines was able to persuade David to see an experienced pastoral counselor whom she knew and who shared his religious beliefs.

Relevant History

In the past two decades, there have been an increasing number of refugees globally, reflecting the political and economic instability in several regions of the world (Carter, French, and Salt, 1993). The breakdown of civil order has led to large-scale displacement and maltreatment of peoples. The nature of modern warfare puts entire populations at risk of trauma. From 1983 to 1990, Western countries received more than 2.2 million asylum applicants (Widgren, 1993). The traumatic circumstances that trigger a decision to leave one's home because of a well-founded fear of persecution are central to understanding the deep distress found in asylum seekers. In addition, many refugees that immigrate to North America and Europe have suffered severe maltreatment and torture (Mollica, 2000).

The Center for Victims of Torture (CVT) in Minneapolis estimates that 500,000 victims of torture now reside in the United States. CVT treats patients from across the globe—73.3 percent from Africa, 13.3 percent from the Middle East, 11.1 percent from Eastern Europe, and 2.2 percent from Asia. Less than 1 percent of their clients are U.S. citizens who were tortured abroad. An estimated two-thirds of their clients are seeking asylum from persecution at the time they first contact CVT.

Diagnostic Criteria

Many child and adult refugees are at risk for post-traumatic stress disorder (PTSD) and other severe mental health problems as a direct result of their exposure to war trauma, torture, and displacement from their homes (Goldstein, Wampler, and Wise, 1997). A study of 149 refugees from diverse areas of the globe, including the Middle East, Africa, Latin America, Eastern Europe, and Asia, revealed that almost 8 in 10 had PTSD and almost half of those were also suffering from depression (Ferrada-Noli et al., 1998).

Caught in the middle of a war zone, civilian refugees often experience greater brutality than combatants. In addition, war zones allow little opportunity to deal with the emotional pain, nor do they encourage expression of feelings. Refugees report experiencing a shattered sense of safety and stark vulnerability. The traumatic experiences of refugees may include experiencing or witnessing combat atrocities and mass killings. Executions may be witnessed and imprisonment is common.

PTSD is described as *acute* if symptoms last less than three months, *chronic* if symptoms last more than three months, and *delayed onset* if the symptoms start at least six months after the traumatic event. David probably has chronic and delayed-onset PTSD.

The American Psychiatric Association notes that "psychosocial and environmental problems may affect the diagnosis, treatment, and prognosis of mental disorders" (APA, 2000, p. 31). Many refugees experience these circumstances: problems with their primary support group, such as the death of a family member, family disruption, and physical abuse; problems related to the social environment, such as the death or loss of a friend, inadequate social support, acculturation problems, and discrimination; educational problems, including illiteracy and academic difficulties; occupational problems, including unemployment and stress at work; housing problems, such as inadequate housing, unsafe neighborhoods, or difficulties with neighbors; economic problems; problems of access to health services; problems related to the legal system; and other psychosocial and environmental problems, including exposure to disaster or war and the unavailability of social services. All of these (except difficulties related to the legal system) affect David's circumstances. The cumulative negative effects of these factors can increase the difficulty of resolving the mental health and other problems of many refugees.

Response to Vignette

David, like many survivors of torture, is reluctant to disclose information about his traumatic experiences. Survivors often suffer chronic pain, guilt, depression, anxiety, and symptoms of PTSD in silence. David is naturally suspicious and frightened, and he wants to forget about what has happened to him. Unfortunately these feelings discourage him from seeking the help he needs. Treatment for the psychological after-effects of torture requires a great deal of effort and sensitivity to develop trust on the part of pastors, mental health specialists, and others working with survivors. It is important to remember that torture survivors seeking mental health help are healthy people who have been subjected to brutality intended to destroy their sense of identity, their confidence, and their ability to function socially. Survivors often need assistance in understanding their experience and help in rebuilding their identity. In general, the whole story comes slowly and in stages.

Dr. Nina Summers was an experienced pastoral counselor and colleague of Rev. Haines who had specialized training in working with trauma survivors. Over the years, she had counseled many people who had experienced severe psychological trauma. She knew that grief is the normal response to loss, and it must be recognized and addressed in order to understand David's mental health. Dr. Summers was aware that trauma often resembles a grief reaction or, in David's case, a delayed grief reaction. Exploring and expressing feelings about the loss and trauma is vital to recovery. David was allowed to take the lead in deciding what was appropriate for discussion and when he was ready to deal with the loss. Through displacement and war, David lost his home, possessions, and parents. Any one of these might result in severe grief and be a source of chronic grief for him.

Over time David was able to begin to trust Dr. Summers. Their shared faith in Christ was an important factor in developing the trust that was needed to begin the healing process. He began to tell his story of the loss and trauma. She was skillful in helping clarify the details of his memory and separating what was real from what was not. She encouraged him over time to express and accept his sadness and emotional pain. She was sensitive to cultural and gender issues that affected his expression of feelings. After a time he was able to accept more of his negative emotions, such as his guilt, sadness, and anger. Working on, and, to some extent, through, these emotions can decrease distress and move David toward healing.

A Christian support group was especially helpful for him. The group and individual therapy helped him understand that his trauma was not his fault and that he had done the best he could. He was able to stop blaming himself and to accept God's love for him in a new way.

Treatment Within the Faith Community

Torture is a crime against humanity. It is usually used as a strategic tool of repression against people who are seeking political freedom. Its purpose is to control populations by destroying individual leaders and terrorizing entire communities. Amnesty International reports that systematic torture and other forms of maltreatment are practiced in 121 of the 205 nations of the world (Amnesty International, 1999). Torture inflicts spiritual as well as physical and psychological injury. Many refugees who survive torture and other forms of psychological trauma have sought and found help in religious communities (Lorenz, 1990).

Advocacy against torture is an important role that religious communities can play in the fight against this form of inhumanity. Amnesty International is one example of a worldwide group that works to promote human rights. It campaigns to free prisoners of conscience; ensure fair and prompt trials for political prisoners; abolish the death penalty, torture, and other cruel treatment of prisoners; end political killings and "disappearances"; and it opposes human rights abuses by opposition groups. It is one of several organizations that advocate for humane treatment and human rights that people of conscience can join.

Torture often cuts off survivors from the rest of society, exacerbating their problems. The Canadian Centre for Victims of Torture (see

Resources) helps concerned persons provide support to survivors through their Volunteer Friendship Program. Volunteers are trained in the effects of torture and the needs of survivors and then linked with a survivor in a one-on-one relationship. The volunteer acts as a friend, as well as a connection to the new community. These volunteers form part of a social network of personal support, helping survivors function well within their new community. Congregations could use such a friendship model to train their members to offer support to survivors of torture.

Refugees who have experienced torture and other forms of maltreatment and who have PTSD are at risk for suicide (Ferrada-Noli et al., 1998) and require screening by a mental health specialist. Suicide by trauma survivors is associated with having morbid nightmares, lack of social contact, pessimism about their future, and increased aggression. Other factors that increase the risk of suicide include alcoholism, depression or a history of it, unresolved grief, and a history of suicide attempts (Weaver and Koenig, 1996). Unrecognized physical and/or mental health problems further increase the risk.

Indications for Referral

Talking or hinting about suicide is the primary indication that a person is at risk for suicide. Retrospective studies of suicide often show that individuals made statements indicating despair and plans to resolve the despair by taking their life (Weaver and Koenig, 1996). Risk is increased if a person has specific and lethal plans. Someone who states when and how he or she will commit suicide is at very high risk; threats to take one's life with a gun are the highest risk. Pastors and others working with refugees who encounter a suicidal person should immediately get help from a suicide crisis center or other source of specialized services. Helping a person who is suicidal is not to be delayed or taken on alone.

There are increasing numbers of multidisciplinary professional networks in North America and Europe that provide medical and psychological evaluation and treatment for survivors of torture (see Resources).

Treatment by Mental Health Specialist

More than 150,00 Tibetans have fled into exile as a consequence of being persecuted by the Chinese government, and an estimated 15,000 have been tortured (Holtz, 1998). In one study, refugee Buddhist nuns and students who had been arrested and tortured in Tibet were compared with those who had not (Holtz, 1998). The results suggest that torture has long-term consequences on mental health over and above the effects of being uprooted, fleeing one's country, and living in exile as a refugee, although the additional effects were small. Political commitment and social support in exile fostered resilience against psychological problems. Buddhist spirituality played an active role in the development of protective coping mechanisms among these Tibetans.

Cross-Cultural Issues

Resources

—Advocates for Survivors of Torture and Trauma; 431 East Belvedere, Baltimore, MD 21212; (410) 464-9006; www.astt.org; is a nonprofit group of physicians, psychologists, social workers, ancillary health care providers, and human rights advocates who work together to help survivors of torture and trauma. It provides direct service to individuals who have experienced torture and assists survivors in establishing safety in the United States by aiding in the preparation of political asylum documents. It also seeks to educate the public regarding the world's human rights issues and the large number of torture survivors who seek or have obtained refuge or asylum in the U.S.

—Amnesty International USA, 322 Eighth Avenue, New York, NY 10001; www.amnestyusa.org; is a worldwide movement that works to promote all the human rights enshrined in the Universal Declaration of Human Rights. It has more than a million members and supporters in 162 countries and territories. Activities range from public demonstrations to letter-writing, human rights education, and individual appeals on a particular case to global campaigns on a particular issue.

—Canadian Centre for Victims of Torture; 194 Jarvis Street, 2nd Floor, Toronto, Ontario, Canada M5B 2B7; (416) 363-1066; www.icomm.ca/ccvt; is a nonprofit registered charitable organization, founded by medical doctors, lawyers, and social service professionals associated with Amnesty International. It was incorporated in 1983 and was the second such facility in the world established to treat survivors of torture. It has assisted approximately eleven thousand survivors from ninety-nine countries since its inception.

—Center for Victims of Torture; 717 East River Road, Minneapolis, MN 55455; (612) 436-4800; www.cvt.org; is a private, nonprofit organization founded in 1985 to provide direct care to survivors of politically motivated torture and members of their families. It was the first organization of its kind in the United States, pioneering a comprehensive assessment and care program. It works in research, training, and public policy initiatives designed to create new resources for torture survivors worldwide and new allies in the campaign to end the use of torture.

—Human Rights Watch; 350 Fifth Avenue, 34th Floor, New York, NY 10118-3299; (212) 290-4700; www.hrw.org; is an independent, non-governmental organization dedicated to protecting the human rights of people around the world. It seeks to prevent discrimination, to uphold political freedom, to protect people from inhumane conduct in wartime, and to bring offenders to justice. It challenges governments and those who hold power to end abusive practices and respect international human rights law. It works to enlist the public and the international community to support the cause of human rights.

—International Rehabilitation Council for Torture Victims; Borgergade 13, P.O. Box 9049, DK-1022 Copenhagen K, Denmark; 45-33-76-06-00;

www.irct.org; is an independent, international organization of health professionals, which promotes and supports the rehabilitation of torture victims and works for the prevention of torture worldwide. It seeks to promote and support new and existing rehabilitation centers and prevention programs and to initiate emergency intervention projects.

—Program for Torture Victims; 3655 South Grand Avenue, Suite 290, Los Angeles, CA 90007; (213) 747-4944; www.ptvla.org; was founded in 1980 to provide medical and psychological treatment for victims of torture and other human rights abuses. It offers referrals for social and legal assistance, as well as educational workshops on the consequences of torture and other human rights abuses.

—Survivors International; 703 Market Street, Suite 301, San Francisco, CA 94103; (415) 546-2080; www.survivorsintl.org; is a nonprofit organization made up of a multidisciplinary network of professionals dedicated to the treatment and support of survivors of torture. It also provides training programs for individuals and agencies working with refugees and immigrants to improve their understanding of the experience of torture and its psychological effect on persons, so that treatment interventions can be optimized.

—World Organization Against Torture USA; 1725 K Street, NW, Suite 610, Washington, DC 20006; (202) 296-5702; www.woatusa.org; is an international coalition of groups fighting against torture, summary executions, forced disappearances, and all other forms of cruel, inhuman, and degrading treatment in order to preserve human rights. It has an SOS Torture network consisting of some 240 nongovernmental organizations that act as sources of information. Its urgent interventions reach more than 90,000 governmental and intergovernmental institutions, nongovernmental associations, and pressure and interest groups daily.

Helpful Books

Caring for Victims of Torture (James Jarason and Michael Popkin, Washington, DC: American Psychiatric Press, 1998).

The Mental Health Consequences of Torture (Ellen Gerrity, Terence Keane, and Farris Tuma, New York: Kluwer Academic/Plenum Publishers, 2001).

Torture and Its Consequences: Current Treatment Approaches (Metin Basoglu, Cambridge: Cambridge University Press, 1999).

Unspeakable Acts, Ordinary People: The Dynamics of Torture (John Conroy, New York: Knopf, 2000).

References

American Psychiatric Association (2000). *Diagnostic and Statistical Manual of Mental Disorders* (Fourth Edition, Text Revised). Washington, DC: APA.

Amnesty International (1999). *Amnesty International Report 1999*. London: Amnesty International.

Carter, F. W., French, R. A., and Salt, J. (1993). International migration between East and West in Europe. *Ethnic and Racial Studies*, 16, 401-421.

Ferrada-Noli, M., Asberg, M., Ormstad, K., Lundin, T., and Sundbom, E. (1998). Suicidal behavior after severe trauma. Part 1: PTSD diagnoses, psychiatric comorbidity, and assessments of suicidal behavior. *Journal of Traumatic Stress*, 11(1), 103-112.

Goldstein, R. D., Wampler, N. S., and Wise, P. H. (1997). War experiences and distress symptoms of Bosnian children. *Pediatrics*, 100(5), 873-878.

Holtz, T. H. (1998). Refugee trauma versus torture trauma: A retrospective controlled cohort study of Tibetan refugees. *The Journal of Nervous and Mental Disease*, 186(1), 24-34.

Lorenz, W. (1990). For we are strangers before Thee and sojourners—2 Chronicles 29:15. *American Baptist Quarterly*, 9(4), 268-280.

Mollica, R. F. (2000). Waging a new kind of war: Invisible wounds. *Scientific American*, 282(60), 54-57.

Weaver, A. J., and Koenig, H. G. (1996). Elderly suicide, mental health professionals and the clergy: A need for collaboration, training and research. *Death Studies*, 20(5), 495-508.

Widgren, J. (1993). Movements of refugees and asylum seekers: Recent trends in a comparative perspective. In Organization for Economic Cooperation and Development, *The Changing Course of International Migration* (pp. 87-95). Paris, France: OECD.

Rape

"I took myself away in my mind when they raped me"

Judy, age twenty-six, was accosted at knifepoint at night in a shopping mall parking lot and forced by two strangers into a car. They drove her to a rural area, raped and stabbed her, and left her for dead. Although seriously injured, she survived. Her rabbi, Bonita Oppenheimer, came to the hospital to see her as soon as she heard of the attack. She spent time listening to her and being supportive. Judy had great medical care and made a rapid recovery from her physical wounds.

After Judy left the hospital, she continued to have difficulty sleeping; she would wake up at night and experience anxiety attacks. Every time she lay down, she kept recounting the events of the night of the rape. She would get a picture of the attack in her mind, which created an enormous amount of fear. Judy kept feeling the presence of the rapists. She was unable to stay alone; she could not tolerate the dark. She could drive in a car only if the doors were locked and the windows closed. Judy could not watch television programs with violence or read her favorite mystery books. Although she was able to resume work activities, there was a deterioration in her motivation and drive to excel. She had difficulty concentrating. Physically, her back ached.

Judy had a marked change in the quality of her relationship with her boyfriend. There was a disruption in feelings of intimacy and a lack of sexual interest. In general, there was a feeling of estrangement from others, a diminished interest and decline in enjoyment of previously experienced activities, and an increasing distrust of people. Her recovery was prolonged.

Survivors of rape frequently experience changes in their overall mental health. Sleep disorders such as insomnia or eating disorders often occur

**Pastoral
Care
Assessment**

following rape or sexual assault. Some women experience nightmares and flashbacks. Others encounter body aches, headaches, and fatigue. Post-traumatic stress disorder (PTSD) is the most common disorder seen in victims of rape or sexual assault. Rape victims sometimes experience anxiety, depression, self-injury, and suicide attempts, as well as other emotional disorders.

Rape survivors often have problems in their intimate and family relationships or close friendships. Sexual problems can be among the most long-standing difficulties experienced by women who are the victims of sexual assault. Women can experience fear and avoidance of any sexual activity and an overall decrease in sexual interest and desire. Marriage partners, friends, or family members may feel hurt, alienated, or discouraged, and then become angry or distant toward the survivor.

Most rape survivors have feelings of shame related to the assault. Sexual activities are a private matter, and rape is a violent invasion of that privacy. Most individuals express embarrassment at having to repeat the details of the assault to medical or legal officials and embarrassment that such a horrific thing could happen to her or him. They sometimes try to cope with their feelings by taking alcohol or drugs. Research has linked sexual assault with psychological trauma and increased risk for substance abuse (Polusny and Follette, 1996).

Many times those who have been raped face an enormous uphill emotional struggle to regain self-respect, self-esteem, self-assurance, and self-control. It is a struggle that can be won with the help of caring and supportive friends, family, counselors, physicians, and clergy.

Relevant History

Sexual assault has widespread effects on women's psychological and physical health (Koss, 1993), and as a result, rape victims may contact several community agencies for assistance, including the legal, medical, and mental health systems (Campbell, 1998). The services provided by these systems can be difficult to access and potentially stressful for rape survivors, and the help they do receive may even leave them feeling revictimized (Campbell, 1998). More than 50 percent of female rape victims are not advised about pregnancy testing and prevention, and only 40 percent are given information about the risk of sexually transmitted diseases, including HIV/AIDS (Campbell and Bybee, 1997). These negative experiences have been called the second victimization. This is part of the reason that rape remains the most underreported violent crime in the United States, with less than 50 percent ever reported (Bureau of Justice Statistics, 2000).

Diagnostic Criteria

Sexual assault is the most rapidly growing violent crime in the U.S., with 261,000 victims of rape, attempted rape, or sexual assault in the year 2000. Rape is not sex. Rape is an expression of power and control in which a person uses a sexual act as a means of violence. For women younger than thirty-five years of age and living in cities, rape is feared more than murder (Warr, 1985). The National Women's Study (Resnick et al., 1993) estimated that 12.1 million (12.7 percent) of adult American women have experienced a completed rape at some point in their lives. Approximately 43 percent of victims are raped by a friend or acquaintance, 34 percent by a stranger, 17 percent by an intimate partner, and 2 percent by another relative (Bureau of Justice Statistics, 2000). About 40 percent of sexual assaults take place at the victim's own home, while 20 percent take place in the home of a friend, neighbor, or relative. One in ten takes place outside, away from home, with about 1 in 12 in a parking garage. Only 1 in 4 of reported rapes is accepted for prosecution, 12 percent of defendants are actually found guilty, and 7 percent of all cases result in a prison term (Frazier and Haney, 1996).

Researchers found that very high numbers of women suffer from PTSD as a result of rape. In one study, 94 percent of women had PTSD one week after the attack, 65 percent at four weeks after the attack and 47 percent at twelve weeks after the attack (Rothbaum et al., 1992). Other studies have discovered significant improvement in a large number of women during the first few months after a rape (Foa and Rothbaum, 1998). However, for the remaining women who do not improve during the first months after a rape, chronic PTSD can persist for years. Women who attribute blame for the rape to their own character or behavior experience higher rates of emotional distress for longer periods of time than those who do not (Frazier and Schauben, 1994).

Response to Vignette

Rape victims experience a broad range of powerful emotions; a compassionate clergyperson can help by allowing the survivor to express these feelings. A woman who has been assaulted needs to vent her feelings about the traumatic events. It is helpful to reassure a rape survivor of the normalcy of her reactions and of the necessity of expressing her feelings to enhance recovery. Rabbi Bonita Oppenheimer knew it was also important to reassure Judy that her claims were not doubted and to stress that she is not to blame for the assault. The rabbi was able to establish trust and rapport with Judy by listening and validating her feelings. Any physical intimacy, even hugs or supportive hand-holding, are usually unwanted and resisted.

The rabbi helped her make changes in her life that made her feel safer. Rape victims often feel unsure of themselves and their ability to make decisions. Rabbi Oppenheimer pointed out to Judy her strengths and how she had overcome difficult problems in the past with the help of her friends, family, and faith. The rabbi advocated for her when she needed help facing the medical and legal systems. She let Judy know that she believed in her and that she knew Judy had the strength to heal and survive. These responses, in addition to counseling by a mental health specialist experienced in treating rape victims, helped Judy come to terms with her traumatic experience.

Treatment Within the Faith Community

Research has found that avoidant reactions among rape survivors, such as dropping away from friends and activities, are associated with negative psychological consequences (Santello and Leitenberg, 1993). Encouraging a survivor to stay active in her community and religious congregation appears to have benefits for women who have been traumatized by sexual assault. Based upon recent research at Boston University School of Public Health, an active faith can be an important element in healing and recovery. Using a national sample of 3,543 female victims, the scientists found that frequent religious worship attendance was a source of strength and comfort for rape survivors, buffering the negative effects of sexual assault on their mental health (Chang, Skinner, and Boehmer, 2001).

The typical socialization of men and women in the United States fosters attitudes that women should be passive and dependent and not experiment with their sexuality. Men are socialized to be aggressive and competitive, to have strong sexual feelings, and to experiment with them. These social conventions encourage men to dominate and abuse women (Berkowitz, 1992). Churches, synagogues, and mosques can be of great value in the efforts to decrease sexual assault by conducting educational programs to raise awareness regarding myths about sexual assault, helping implement prevention strategies, and fostering better communication between genders on sexual and power issues.

Indications for Referral

A major depressive disorder is a common reaction following sexual assault. Symptoms of a major depression can include depressed mood, inability to enjoy activities previously enjoyed, difficulty sleeping, changes in patterns of sleeping and eating, problems in concentration and decision making, feelings of guilt, hopelessness, and decreased self-esteem. Research suggests that about 1 in 3 rape victims has at least one period of major depression in her or his lifetime (Foa and Rothbaum, 1998). And for many of these women, the depression can last for a long period of time. Thoughts about suicide are common. Studies estimate that one-third of rape survivors contemplate suicide and that 17 percent actually attempt suicide (Foa and Rothbaum, 1998). Crisis issues in rape trauma survivors, such as major depression or suicidal thinking, extreme panic or disorganized thinking, or a need for drug or alcohol detoxification, will require a referral to a mental health specialist.

Treatment by Mental Health Specialist

A variety of successful mental health treatments have been beneficial to rape survivors (Foa and Rothbaum, 1998). The type of treatment an individual will receive depends on the symptoms she or he is experiencing and should be tailored to meet the needs of the individual. Treatment for rape survivors with PTSD begins with a detailed evaluation, followed by the development of a treatment plan that is designed for the unique needs of the survivor.

It is important the mental health specialists educate trauma survivors and their families about how individuals acquire PTSD and how it affects survivors and their loved ones. It is also important to inform survivors of how other problems such as depression and substance abuse are often related to PTSD. Understanding that PTSD is a recognized anxiety disorder that occurs in normal individuals under extremely stressful conditions is essential for effective treatment.

Many therapies assist survivors of rape trauma by helping them talk about the assault so that memories and pain associated with the assault can be reduced. Therapy can also involve learning skills to cope with the symptoms associated with the trauma. Exposure to the event through imagery allows the survivor to reexperience the event in a safe, controlled environment, while carefully examining his or her reactions and beliefs in relation to that event (Foa and Rothbaum, 1998). The survivor will need to be taught to cope with traumatic memories and feelings without becoming overwhelmed or emotionally numb. Trauma memories usually do not go away entirely as a result of therapy but can become manageable with new coping skills. Examining and resolving strong feelings such as anger, shame, or guilt, which are common among survivors of trauma, will be important (Foa and Rothbaum, 1998). Medications can reduce the anxiety, depression, and insomnia often experienced with PTSD and in some cases may help relieve the distress and emotional numbness caused by trauma memories (Preston, O'Neal, and Talaga, 2001). Finally, an able therapist understands the need to help survivors reestablish the meaning in their lives that has been shattered by the traumatic experience.

Cross-Cultural Issues

Rape survivors belong to both sexes, all races and ethnic groups, all economic backgrounds, and all ages. However, African Americans are about 10 percent more likely to be attacked than European Americans. In 2000, there were 1.1 victimizations per 1,000 European Americans, and 1.2 victimizations per 1,000 African Americans (Bureau of Justice Statistics, 2000).

Cultural attitudes can be a significant factor when counseling rape victims. A study of African American, Hispanic, and European American females found that Hispanic women may be particularly traumatized by rape because of the greater tendency to believe themselves culpable and tainted by sexual assault. Rape victims who experience shame and self-blame are more likely to avoid treatment than those who do not (Lefley et al., 1993).

Resources

—Center for the Prevention of Sexual and Domestic Violence, 2400 North Forty-fifth Street #10, Seattle, WA 98103; (206) 634-1903;

www.cpsdv.org; offers training, consultation, videos, and publications for clergy, laity, seminary faculty, and students.

—Incest Survivors Anonymous; P.O. Box 17245, Long Beach, CA 90807; (562) 428-5599; www.lafn.org/medical/isa/; is an international association based on the twelve-step approach. Women, men, and teens meet to share experiences, strength, and hope so they recover peace of mind. Send a self-addressed stamped envelope for information, if you are a survivor.

—Incest Survivors Resource Network International; P.O. Box 7375, Las Cruces, NM 88006; (505) 521-4260.

—Interfaith Sexual Trauma Institute, St. John's Abbey and University, Collegeville, MN 56321; (320) 363-2011; www.csbsju.edu/isti.

—Male Survivor; PMB 103, 5505 Connecticut Avenue, NW, Washington, DC 20015; (800) 738-4181; www.malesurvivor.org; is an organization of diverse individuals committed through research, education, advocacy, and activism to the prevention, treatment, and elimination of all forms of sexual victimization of boys and men.

—Men Can Stop Rape; P.O. Box 57144, Washington, DC 20037; (202) 265-6530; www.mencanstoprape.org.

—National Clearinghouse on Marital and Date Rape; 2325 Oak Street, Berkeley, CA 94708; www.members.aol.com/ncmd.

—National Coalition Against Sexual Assault; 125 North Enola Drive, Enola, PA 17025; (717) 728-9764; www.dreamingdesigns.com/other/indexncasa.html; is a membership organization committed to the prevention of sexual violence through intervention, education, and public policy.

—National Organization for Victim Assistance; 1730 Park Road, NW, Washington, DC 20010; (800) TRY-NOVA; www.try-nova.org; founded in 1975, provides support, referrals, and advocacy for victims of violent crimes and disasters.

—Rape, Abuse & Incest National Network; 635-B Pennsylvania Avenue, SE, Washington, DC 20003; (800) 656-HOPE; www.rainn.org.

—Survivor Connections; 52 Lyndon Road, Cranston, RI 02905; (401) 941-2548; members.cox.net/survivorconnections; is a grassroots activist organization for survivors of sexual assault.

—VOICES in Action; 8041 Hosbrook, Suite 236, Cincinnati, OH 45236; (800) 7-VOICE-8; www.voices-action.org.

—Women Against a Violent Environment; P.O. Box 93196, Rochester, NY 14692; (716) 234-7019; www.rochesternow.org/wave.html.

Helpful Books

The Gift of Fear: Survival Signals That Protect Us from Violence (Gavin De Becker, New York: Dell Publishing, 1998).

If You Are Raped: What Every Woman Needs to Know (Kathryn M. Johnson, Holmes Beach, FL: Learning Publications, 1985).

Rape Victim: Clinical and Community Interventions (Mary P. Koss and Mary R. Harvey, New York: Sage Publications, 1991).

Recovering from Rape, 2nd ed. (Linda E. Ledray, New York: Henry Holt and Co., 1994).

Recovery: How to Survive Sexual Assault for Women, Men, Teenagers, and Their Friends and Families (Helen Benedict and Susan Brison, New York: Columbia University Press, 1994).

Sexual Violence: The Unmentionable Sin (Marie M. Fortune, Cleveland: Pilgrim Press, 1994).

Stopping Rape: Successful Survival Strategies (Pauline B. Bart and Patricia H. O'Brian, New York: Pergamon Press, 1993).

Trauma and Recovery: The Aftermath of Violence from Domestic Abuse to Political Terror (Judith L. Herman, New York: Basic Books, 1997).

References

Berkowitz, A. (1992). College men as perpetrators of acquaintance rape and sexual assault: A review of recent research. *Journal of American College Health, 40,* 175-180.

Bureau of Justice Statistics (2000). *National Crime Victimization Survey (2000).* Washington, DC: U.S. Department of Justice.

Campbell, R. (1998). The community response to rape: Victims' experiences with the legal, medical, and mental health systems. *American Journal of Community Psychology, 26,* 355-379.

Campbell, R., and Bybee, D. (1997). Emergency medical services for rape victims: Detecting the cracks in service delivery. *Women's Health: Research on Gender, Behavior and Policy, 3,* 75-101.

Chang, B. H., Skinner, K. M., and Boehmer, U. (2001). Religion and mental health among women veterans with sexual assault experience. *International Journal of Psychiatry in Medicine, 31(1),* 77-95.

Foa, E. B., and Rothbaum, B. O. (1998). *Treating the Trauma of Rape.* New York: Guilford Press.

Frazier, P., and Schauben, L. (1994). Causal attributions and recovery from rape and other stressful life events. *Journal of Social and Clinical Psychology, 13,* 1-14.

Frazier, P. A., and Haney, B. (1996). Sexual assault cases in the legal system: Police, prosecutor, and victim perspectives. *Law and Human Behavior, 20,* 607-628.

Koss, M. P. (1993). Rape: Scope, impact, interventions, and public policy responses. *American Psychologist, 48,* 1062-1069.

Lefley, H. P., Scott, C. S., Llabre, M., and Hicks, D. (1993). Cultural beliefs about rape and victims' response in three ethnic groups. *American Journal of Orthopsychiatry, 63(4),* 623-632.

Polusny, M., and Follette, V. (1996). Remembering childhood sexual abuse: A national survey of psychologists' clinical practices, beliefs, and personal experiences. *Professional Psychology: Research and Practice, 27(1)*, 41-52.

Preston, J. D., O'Neal, J. H., and Talaga, M. (2001). *Handbook of Clinical Psychopharmacology for Therapists.* Oakland, CA: New Harbinger

Resnick, H. R., Kilpatrick, D. G., Dansky, B. S., Saunders, B. E., and Best, C. B. (1993). Prevalence of civilian trauma and post-traumatic stress disorder in a representative national sample of women. *Journal of Consulting and Clinical Psychology, 61*, 984-991.

Rothbaum, B. O., Foa, E. B., Riggs, D. S., Murdock, T., and Walsh, W. (1992). A prospective examination of post-traumatic stress disorder in rape victims. *Journal of Traumatic Stress, 5*, 455-475.

Santello, M. D., and Leitenberg, H. (1993). Sexual aggression by an aquaintance: Methods of coping and later psychological adjustment. *Violence and Victims, 8(2)*, 91-104.

Warr, M. (1985). Fear of rape among urban women. *Social Problems, 32*, 239-250.

Common Date Rape Drugs

Rohypnol is a brand name for flunitrazepam (a benzodiazepine), a very potent tranquilizer similar to Valium (diazepam), but many times stronger. The drug produces a sedative effect, amnesia, muscle relaxation, and a slowing of psychomotor responses. Sedation occurs twenty to thirty minutes after administration and lasts for several hours. The drug is often distributed on the street in its original "bubble packaging," which adds an air of legitimacy and makes it appear legal. The drug is not commonly used by physicians in the United States and is not listed in the widely used *Physician's Desk Reference*.

Gamma-hydroxybutryate, GHB ("liquid X" or "g-juice"), is also being used to incapacitate victims in order to sexually abuse them. GHB was once sold in health food stores to bodybuilders because it was believed to help stimulate muscle growth but was pulled off the market in 1990 because of its negative side effects. The effects of GHB are similar to those of Rohypnol: dizziness, confusion, and memory loss. GHB is also colorless and odorless and is most commonly found in liquid form. This drug is inexpensive and easy to obtain, making it a frighteningly powerful weapon in the hands of potential rapists.

Hate Crime

"He saw the church burning and heard shots"

The local paper told the story. Bruce Andersen, 22, and two sixteen-year-old boys were charged with assault with a deadly weapon, arson, and criminal damage to property at the Thurman Memorial African Methodist Episcopal Church. One week earlier, three masked males had torched the educational building and defaced the church bus with graffiti, including a swastika, a threatening racial epithet, and the words "Go back where you belong or we'll kill you." (This was particularly ironic, as many members of the church had Native American ancestors.) Although no one was hurt by the fire, it left the church in financial need since the congregation is not wealthy.

The county sheriff began investigating the suspects after officers were at Andersen's home on an unrelated call a few days later and saw Nazi and white supremacist posters on the walls. After obtaining a warrant, during a search of the residence, police found two AK-47 assault rifles, a MAC-11 assault weapon, a 12-gauge shotgun, two handguns, white supremacist literature, Nazi flags, and photos of the three males together. The defendants were arrested and formally charged.

Church member A. O. Sumner, seventy-three, a widower and Korean War combat veteran, witnessed the church fire from his house across the street. When he went out to investigate, several gunshots were fired in his direction from the masked arsonists, striking close to where he stood. He had been emotionally distraught ever since. Mr. Sumner experienced fears and anger related to the hate crime, difficulty sleeping, and increased watchfulness of his environment, and he was easily startled.

With the increasing diversity in U.S. society has come a resurgence of hate crime. Victims of such violence are more likely to sustain severe

Pastoral Care Assessment

physical and psychological injury than are victims of other forms of violent crime (Perry, 2001). Hate crimes are less likely than non-bias-motivated crimes to have been reported to police (Herek, Cogan, and Gillis, 2002). The effect of such violence can affect a whole community.

Survivors of hate crimes are often left with strong emotional reactions, which can include terror, rage, or anger at the perpetrators; intense fear for themselves or their families; depression about the incident; a feeling of powerlessness; a deep suspicion of others; and diminished self-confidence (Barnes and Ephross, 1994). Other reactions can include irritability, difficulty sleeping, fatigue, palpitations, headaches, and intensified startle reactions. Survivors may also experience avoidance responses, which can include moving out of their neighborhood, increasing their home security, and adding further safety precautions for themselves and their families (Barnes and Ephross, 1994). Many victims stay away from community activities that previously were a part of their lives. Others may seek revenge for their victimization. Some who are victims of hate crime violence search for reasons other than their race, ethnicity, or sexual orientation to explain the attack, since these human characteristics are impossible to change.

Hate violence not only affects an individual, but also has repercussions on the whole community, particularly upon the group that the victim represents (Perry, 2001). Hate crimes can cause a whole group to feel angry, isolated, vulnerable, intimidated, unprotected, and fearful of future attacks. The group may wonder how widespread the bigotry is and how many others would be willing to commit this type of violence. The larger community may also become afraid that the victimized group will seek revenge. Clearly, hate crime violence can have a damaging influence on an entire community, leading to mistrust, the loss of a sense of safety, and substantial injury to its cohesiveness. It is important that victims not fall into the common trap of self-blame, but recognize that their personal identity did not lead to the attack—rather, it was a premeditated act aimed at their community.

Relevant History

The federal Church Arson Prevention Act of 1996 was enacted in response to a disturbing rash of fires at houses of worship, which disproportionately victimized African American churches. According to Justice Department officials, 658 investigations of suspicious fires, bombings, and attempted bombings between January 1, 1995, and August 18, 1998, have been pursued. Of the 658 attacks on houses of worship, 220 were against predominantly African American institutions (National Criminal Justice Reference Service, 2002).

Diagnostic Criteria

Hate crimes are violent acts resulting from intolerance and bigotry, intended to hurt and intimidate someone because of race, ethnicity, national origin, religion, sexual orientation, or disability. They can include physical attacks, rapes, bombings, murders, and terroristic threats. In 2000, there were 8,063 hate crime incidents reported to the Federal Bureau of Investigation, which involved 9,924 victims and 7,530 known offenders. Of the total reported incidents, 4,337 were motivated by racial bias; 1,472 by religious bias; 1,299 by sexual orientation bias; and 911 by ethnicity/national origin bias (Summary of Hate Crime Statistics, 2000).

Hate crimes are particularly devastating to the survivors because the only motive is the person's own identity in a particular group. Compared with other victims, hate crime survivors manifested significantly more symptoms of depression, anger, anxiety, and post-traumatic stress (Herek, Gillis, and Cogan, 1999). They also displayed more crime-related fears than do victims of nonbias violence. Researchers found that some victims have required as long as five years to overcome the hate crime, while survivors of nonbias crimes experienced a decrease in their psychological problems within two years of the incident (Herek, Cogan, and Gillis, 1997).

Hate crimes are often more violent than other types of personal crimes and tend to be committed by people with a history of antisocial behavior (Perry, 2001). In approximately half of the assaults related to hate violence, a weapon is involved. As a result of the unpredictable and sometimes brutal nature of these crimes, victims often develop symptoms of post-traumatic stress disorder (PTSD). Survivors of such violence may experience fears related to the trauma and reminders of the incident; increased watchfulness of their environment; changes in their relationships with others; difficulty sleeping; and flashbacks. Like others with post-traumatic stress, hate crime victims may heal more quickly when appropriate support and resources are made available soon after the incident occurs.

Response to Vignette

Hate is an intense hostility and emotional aversion to someone or something, and it is frightening to be the object of the behavior it provokes. Even though Mr. Sumner had survived combat in Korea and race riots as a child in Tulsa, Oklahoma, he was nevertheless in emotional shock that human beings could be so intentionally cruel and vicious. The Rev. Janet Murray, his pastor, knew it was important to provide immediate pastoral care and that Mr. Sumner, like all survivors of hate crimes, should not be allowed to become isolated and lonely. Pastor Murray knew the importance of a caring pastoral presence in difficult times as well as the value of church solidarity with survivors of violence. She and others in the congregation spent time listening to his story and praying with him. Several members of the church brought him "good home cooking." He was able to process some of his emotions by telling his story of the events to various friends from the congregation.

Rev. Murray also recognized the urgency of responding to the needs of all her parishioners. She held a special prayer and healing service in which members supported one another, and they were advised of the mental health benefits of debriefing sessions that could help defuse their emotions. A synagogue nearby took the leadership role in organizing an interfaith rally followed by a prayer service. The interfaith group took a public stand against hate violence, speaking out against it and encouraging the community to protest the fires and the hatred that caused them. They organized workshops, forums, discussion groups, and other events in the community designed to encourage racial and ethnic tolerance. Volunteers formed "Faith Watch" patrols to guard houses of worship located in isolated parts of the county.

Mr. Sumner was uplifted in spirit as the church and the community gathered in solidarity with him and in resistance to hate violence. Rev. Murray was inspired to deliver a powerful series of sermons on the words of Jesus, "Fear not for I am with you." Mr. Sumner's fears decreased, and his anger found an empowering outlet through work with a task force on combating hate violence formed by the interfaith coalition. His nightmares about the event ceased, and he began to sleep more restfully. Mr. Sumner found new meaning in his faith through the experience. The church began to work on raising funds for a new educational building with help from the National Council of Churches.

Treatment Within the Faith Community

Faith communities need to be well informed about hate group activity in the nation and in their region. It is a mistake to underestimate the strength of the bigotry and violence within these groups. The membership in hate groups in the United States is difficult to document exactly. A conservative estimate is that 25,000 are actively involved in such organizations, with an additional 150,000 "armchair sympathizers" who receive literature and possibly attend rallies (Southern Poverty Law Center, 2002).

The Southern Poverty Law Center has found that the number of hate groups operating in the United States jumped by almost 12 percent in 2001. The latest increase was mostly accounted for by higher numbers of neo-Nazi organizations (Southern Poverty Law Center, 2002).

The Internet has been a boon to hate groups. Online hate grew 70 percent from November 2000 to November 2001 (Ladd, 2001). At the end of 2001, the number of Web pages on the Internet related to hate was more than 373,000. Such organizations use the Web's global reach to transmit their message, often anonymously, to a network of followers.

It is important that faith communities band together to develop leadership to combat hate groups and their toxic messages. This outreach is particularly needed in ministry to youth. Reacting against positive social changes brought by the civil rights movement, new hate organizations have formed, including the Aryan Nation, the Christian Identity Church, the White Aryan Resistance, and the neo-Nazis. They use manipulative magazines, cable TV, radio talk shows, comic books, and the Internet to promote their message of hate and violence, especially to young people. Many of their recruits are alienated youth who would have responded to the efforts of pastors and congregations that expressed love and concern for them. Within faith communities are young people who, if encouraged and trained, would lead or take part in efforts to counter hate violence.

Congregations need to build strong interfaith relationships. Churches must take the lead in doing this since Christians represent the vast majority (87 percent) of those in faith communities in the United States (Gallup and Lindsay, 1999), and much hate violence is done by individuals who misuse Christian scripture in an attempt to justify their actions. Persons in congregations and the community must be taught that the church stands strongly in the prophetic tradition of Jesus that teaches love and acceptance, not hate and fear.

A strong interfaith presence can act as a deterrent to hate violence. Working to find common ground by establishing an ongoing ecumenical and interfaith dialogue about the issues that divide people of faith is vital to countering the messengers of hate. It is valuable to develop educational efforts aimed at dispelling stereotypes, reducing hostility among groups, and encouraging intercultural understanding and appreciation. Hate groups seek to exploit diversity as an evil and to pit groups against one another. Diverse people of faith working together exert a moral force that can resist hate.

Indications for Referral

When individuals have survived hate violence, they may find their views of themselves, others, and the world have changed. Survivors can experience symptoms such as irritability, anger, fear, anxiety, depression, intrusive thoughts and sensations, and increased watchfulness. They may also avoid activities, people, and places they had enjoyed in the past and might find they are jumpier than usual. Other common symptoms include substance abuse, addictions, and self-harming behaviors. Treatment can be of benefit to those who feel distressed by these responses or who find that their lives have been changed because of their overwhelming experiences. Pastors need the skill to recognize when a person is in need of a mental health specialist in order to make an effective referral.

Treatment by Mental Health Specialist

Because of the excellent support Mr. Sumner received from his church and his natural resilience, he was able to rebound quickly from the psychological trauma he experienced. Many people will not recover as quickly and will suffer a much more severe aftermath, requiring professional treatment.

The most effective mental health treatment for persons suffering from acute stress disorder or PTSD involves an integration of cognitive, behavioral, psychodynamic, and psychopharmacological interventions (Friedman, Keane, and Foa, 2000). Cognitive Processing Therapy may be particularly helpful to survivors of hate crimes who tend to self-blame or have low self-esteem (Resick and Schnicke, 1992).

Cross-Cultural Issues

The chief reason for hate crimes is racial bias, with African Americans at the greatest risk. In 2000, of the 8,063 such crimes reported to the FBI, 54 percent (4,337) were race related, two-thirds of which targeted African Americans. The types of crimes committed against African Americans include bombing and vandalizing churches, burning crosses on home lawns, and murder. Among the other racially motivated crimes reported, about 20 percent were committed against European Americans, 6 percent against Asian/Pacific Islanders, and 1 percent against Native Americans and Alaskan Natives (Summary of Hate Crime Statistics, 2000).

Resources

—Anti-Defamation League; 823 United Nations Plaza, New York, NY 10017; (212) 490-2525; www.adl.org.

—Arab American Institute; 1600 K Street, NW, Suite 601, Washington, DC 20006; (202) 429-9210; www.aaiusa.org.

—Bureau of Justice Assistance; 810 Seventh Street, NW, Fourth Floor, Washington, DC 20531; (202) 616-6500; www.ojp.usdoj.gov/bja.

—Community Relations Service (CRS), U.S. Department of Justice; 600 E Street, NW, Suite 6000, Washington, DC 20530; (202) 305-2935; www.usdoj.gov/crs. This is the only federal agency whose primary task is to help communities respond appropriately to organized hate groups. CRS helps prevent and resolve community-wide conflict stemming from race, color, and national origin. Its staff provides mediation and conciliation, technical assistance, training for law enforcement personnel, public education and awareness, and contingency planning for potentially provocative events. In 1996, the agency helped resolve eight hundred cases of conflict in all fifty states.

—Federal Bureau of Investigation, Criminal Justice Information Services Division; 1000 Custer Hollow Road, Clarksburg, WV 26306; (304) 625-2000; www.fbi.gov/ucr/ucr.htm.

—Human Rights Campaign; 1640 Rhode Island Avenue, NW, Washington, DC 20036; (202) 628-4160; www.hrc.org.

—Ministries in the Midst of Hate and Violence, Women's Division, General Board of Global Ministries, The United Methodist Church; 475 Riverside Drive, Room 1502, New York, NY 10115; gbgm-umc.org /umw/antihate/.

—National Asian Pacific American Legal Consortium; 1140 Connecticut Avenue, NW, Suite 1200, Washington, DC 20036; (202) 296-2300; www.napalc.org.

—National Conference for Community and Justice; 475 Park Avenue South, 19th Floor, New York, NY 10016; (212) 545-1300; www.nccj.org. This organization was formerly known as the National Conference of Christians and Jews.

—National Congress of American Indians; 1301 Connecticut Avenue, NW, Suite 200, Washington, DC 20036; (202) 466-7767; www.ncai.org.

—National Council of La Raza; 1111 Nineteenth Street, NW, Suite 1000, Washington, DC 20036; (202) 785-1670; www.nclr.org.

—National Criminal Justice Association; 720 Seventh Street, NW, Third Floor, Washington, DC 20001; (202) 628-8550; www.ncja.org.

—National Gay and Lesbian Task Force; 1325 Massachusetts Avenue, NW, Suite 600, Washington, DC 20005; (202) 393-5177; www.ngltf.org.

—National Partnership for Women and Families; 1875 Connecticut Avenue, NW, Suite 650, Washington, DC 20009; (202) 986-2600; www.nationalpartnership.org.

—National Women's Law Center; 11 Dupont Circle, NW, Suite 800, Washington, DC 20036; (202) 588-5180; www.nwlc.org.

—Office of Juvenile Justice and Delinquency Prevention; 810 Seventh Street, NW, Washington, DC 20531; (202) 307-5911; www.ojjdp.ncjrs.org.

—Office for Victims of Crime; 810 Seventh Street, NW, Washington, DC 20531; (202) 307-5983; www.ojp.usdoj.gov/ovc.

—Political Research Associates; 1310 Broadway, Suite 201, Somerville, MA 02144; (617) 666-5300; www.publiceye.org.

—Simon Wiesenthal Center; 1399 South Roxbury Drive, Los Angeles, CA 90035; (310) 553-9036; (800) 900-9036; www.wiensenthal.com.

—Southern Poverty Law Center; 400 Washington Avenue, Montgomery, AL 36104; (334) 956-8200; www.splcenter.org.

—U.S. Commission on Civil Rights; 624 Ninth Street, NW, Washington, DC 20425; (202) 376-8317; www.usccr.gov.

—U.S. Department of Justice, Civil Rights Division, Criminal Section; 950 Pennsylvania Avenue, Washington, DC 20530; (202) 514-3204; www.usdoj.gov.

—Violence Against Women Office; 810 Seventh Street, NW, Washington, DC 20531; (202) 307-6026; www.ojp.usdoj.gov/vawo.

Helpful Books

American Skinheads: The Criminology and Control of Hate Crimes (Mark Hamm, Westport, CT: Praeger Publishers, 1993).

Hate Crime: The Story of a Dragging in Jasper, Texas (Joyce King, New York: Pantheon, 2002).

Hate Crimes: Confronting Violence Against Lesbians and Gay Men (Gregory M. Herek and Kevin T. Berrill, eds., Newbury Park, CA: Sage Publications, 1992).

Hate Crimes: New Social Movements and the Politics of Violence (Valerie Jenness and Kendal Broad, New York: Aldine de Gruyter, 1997).

Hate Crimes: The Rising Tide of Bigotry and Bloodshed (Jack Levin and Jack McDevitt, New York: Plenum Press, 1993).

In the Name of Hate: Understanding Hate Crimes (Barbara Perry, New York: Routledge, 2001).

When Hate Groups Come to Town: A Handbook of Effective Community Responses (Atlanta: Center for Democratic Renewal, 1992).

References

Barnes, A., and Ephross, P. H. (1994). The impact of hate violence on victims: Emotional and behavioral responses to attacks. *Social Work, 39(3)*, 247-251.

Gallup, G. H., and Lindsay, D. M. (1999). *Surveying the Religious Landscape: Trends in U.S. Beliefs.* Harrisburg, PA: Morehouse Publishing.

Herek, G. M., Cogan, J. C., and Gillis, J. R. (1997, November). *The Impact of Hate Crime Victimization.* Paper presented at a congressional briefing co-sponsored by the American Psychological Association and the Society for the Psychological Study of Social Issues, Washington, DC.

Herek, G. M., Cogan, J. C., and Gillis, J. R. (2002). Victim experiences in hate crimes based on sexual orientation. *Journal of Social Issues, 58(2)*, 319-339.

Herek, G. M., Gillis, J. R., and Cogan, J. C. (1999). Psychological sequelae of hate-crime victimization among lesbian, gay, and bisexual adults. *Journal of Consulting and Clinical Psychology, 67(6)*, 945-951.

Ladd, T. (2001, November 30). *The Web of Online Hate Is Growing, Warns Websense Inc.* Retrieved March 29, 2002, from http://www.websense.com/company/news/pr/01/112901.cfm.

National Criminal Justice Reference Service. (2002, Spring). *Church Arson Prevention Act of 1996.* Retrieved March 29, 2002, from http://www.ncjrs.org/hate_crimes/legislation.html#cap1996.

Perry, B. (2001). *In the Name of Hate: Understanding Hate Crimes.* New York: Routledge.

Resick, P. A., and Schnicke, M. K. (1992). Cognitive processing therapy for sexual assault victims. *Journal of Consulting and Clinical Psychology, 60(5)*, 748-756.

Southern Poverty Law Center (2002). *The Year in Hate.* Retrieved March 29, 2002, from http://www.splcenter.org/intelligenceproject/ip-4u1.html.

Summary of Hate Crime Statistics (2000). Retrieved March 29, 2002, from www.infoplease.com/ipa/A0004885.html.

Police Officer

"A gun went off"

Katherine Murphy and her husband, Kevin, have been involved in church and parochial school activities for the past nine years. He coaches the soccer team, and she volunteers for parent-teacher projects. After a recent game, Father Donovan approached Kevin and casually inquired about Katherine. The priest mentioned that he hadn't seen her for the past two months, even though school groups were busy at this time of year.

Kevin said that he was very concerned about his wife, a ten-year veteran of the police force. He explained that Katherine had become increasingly withdrawn from the family and activities she used to enjoy. She had once loved cooking and frequently tried out new recipes. She had always made sure the family had a weekly movie night, either going to a theater or renting a video. Now, she goes to work, comes home, has a few cocktails, and that's it—she does not even talk about her job anymore. After a few drinks, Katherine falls asleep on the couch, awaking after three or four hours and unable to return to sleep. She says that she feels tired all the time. Kevin has assumed responsibility for most of the parenting and household chores for the past two months because Katherine has become increasingly impatient with their children, Danny (seven years old) and Eileen (five years old). According to Kevin, she is quick to scold the youngsters for little things and often lashes out at people for no reason. The family feels as if they must walk on eggshells when they are around her.

Two months ago, Katherine and her partner responded to a domestic dispute in progress. She immediately recognized the address because she had responded to incidents at the same place in the past. On previous occasions, neighbors had called the police to complain about loud arguing coming from the residence where a couple lived with their three children. There was no history of physical violence, although both parents were known to abuse alcohol. All was quiet when Katherine and her partner arrived at the home. A neighbor approached them and reported that she thought somebody might be seriously injured this time because the arguing ended with terrified screaming by the wife. When Katherine and her partner knocked and announced themselves, a male voice responded, "Get out of here! I have a gun and I'll use it." Concerned about the welfare of the woman and children, Katherine insisted that the man open the door. A gun went off and the bullet lodged just inches from where her partner was standing. She immediately ran to the car and called for backup. A police negotiator was sent to the scene and coaxed the father from the building within fifteen minutes. When Katherine entered the residence, she found the three children—aged six, ten, and fourteen years—unhurt. The mother was severely intoxicated.

Pastoral Care Assessment

Father Donovan's immediate concerns were the drastic changes in Katherine's behavior and their effects on her family's everyday functioning. Her absence from church activities that were once important to her was alarming, indicating a need for attention from Mrs. Mackey, the parish nurse. When the priest talked with Mrs. Mackey, she recognized that Katherine exhibited possible symptoms of post-traumatic stress disorder (PTSD). Years ago when the parish nurse's brother, a police officer, witnessed the shooting death of his partner, he had had similar behavior. And one year after the incident, Mrs. Mackey's brother attempted suicide while he was intoxicated. By the end of their conversation, the priest and the parish nurse prioritized their concerns for Katherine as: (1) symptoms of depression with a potential for suicide, (2) alcohol abuse, and (3) social withdrawal from family, friends, and church groups.

Relevant History

According to the American Psychiatric Association (2000), the lifetime prevalence rate for PTSD is approximately 8 percent of the adult population in the U.S. Unfortunately, the authors of that manual did not include studies of law enforcement officers as a population at risk for PTSD. Police can experience frequent, repetitive, and cumulative exposure to trauma and be at much greater risk of PTSD than the general public (Carlier, Lamberts, and Gersons, 1997).

Diagnostic Criteria

Katherine Murphy will satisfy the diagnostic criteria for PTSD if her symptoms persist for three months or longer (APA, 2000). Exposure to an extremely traumatic stressor in which a person experienced, witnessed, or was confronted with an event involving actual or threatened death or serious injury to self or others is necessary for a diagnosis. Additionally, the response to that incident must involve intense fear, feelings of helplessness, or horror. Both aspects are necessary to make a diagnosis of PTSD (APA, 2000).

Police often encounter situations that jeopardize their physical safety as well as the lives of civilians and fellow officers (Kates, 1999). In Katherine's case, the domestic dispute presented the potential for injury to everyone and was the impetus for her demand that the father open the door. Unfortunately, he responded by shooting near where her partner was standing, and the bullet could have killed her or him. Katherine later realized that her concern for the safety of the mother and children clouded her decision making. Instead of immediately assessing it as a potential hostage situation requiring assistance, her intense fear prompted her to demand the man come to the front door. According to Katherine, the shooting might have been avoided if she had first called for assistance. Knowing that her action had agitated the father, she and her partner felt a sense of helplessness as they waited for assistance to arrive, hoping that no other shots would be fired.

Although the police negotiator resolved the situation within fifteen minutes, Katherine's efforts to retrieve the children turned out to be more difficult than she expected. They were unharmed but very frightened. When she saw the youngsters, she thought of her own children and was almost overcome with emotion.

The characteristic symptoms that follow exposure to extreme trauma include persistent reexperiencing of the event, continuing avoidance of stimuli associated with it, numbing of general responsiveness, and increased anxiety. Katherine's experiences of recurrent images of dead children, her inability to stop thinking about the incident, and her continuing nightmares of the event meet the criteria for PTSD. Her inability to remember important aspects of the situation, her diminished participation in church and family activities, and her belief that her career as a police officer is finished are also significant. Katherine's difficulty falling and staying asleep, irritability with her children, and difficulty concentrating on job tasks are evidence of her increased anxiety. It is not uncommon for a person with PTSD to exhibit symptoms of one or more concurrent mental health problems, such as depression or substance abuse.

Katherine might meet the criteria for a diagnosis of a major depressive episode in which at least five symptoms—such as sad mood, fatigue, lack of pleasure, or significant change in sleep or eating patterns—have occurred during the same two-week period, representing a change from previous functioning (APA, 2000). Either a depressed mood or a loss of interest in pleasure must be a pattern. Katherine admitted to feeling depressed, and her husband's observations revealed that she has been so since the traumatic event. She showed a markedly diminished interest in school and church activities as well as other things that were once a source of pleasure (movies, cooking). Katherine has insomnia, characterized by early awakening and an inability to return to sleep. Feeling tired all of the time demonstrates that she is experiencing fatigue.

Since Katherine denied excessive drinking during the initial assessment, there was no way for Mrs. Mackey to determine whether it is a concurrent problem. Alcohol use and abuse is a common coping method among law enforcement officers, especially Americans who are descendants of Northern Europeans. Alcohol is a central nervous system depressant, and by virtue of its effects, it has the potential to trigger many of the symptoms associated with PTSD and depressive disorders (APA, 2000). If Katherine avoids drinking at night, she will have a better chance of experiencing a restful sleep that will allow her insomnia, energy level, and concentration to improve. With the cessation of alcohol use, Katherine could have more energy to participate in household, church, and other activities. Her irritability with the children and her angry outbursts might disappear.

Response to Vignette

As part of a Healthy Living Program, the parish nurse offers free health screenings to parishioners, so she used this ministry as an opportunity to contact Katherine. After a chat about the church, Mrs. Mackey made an appointment to screen Katherine and the children. While at the home, the parish nurse took Katherine's vital signs and asked some general questions about her health patterns (sleeping, eating habits). Katherine was surprised to learn that her blood pressure was elevated, and she admitted that she had not had a physical exam in more than a year. The nurse's nonthreatening questions about physical concerns seemed to relax Katherine and open the door for Mrs. Mackey to assess mental health problems.

Katherine confirmed most of the information that her husband had reported to Father Donovan. She said that she couldn't stop thinking about how her actions might have caused the deaths of others. She often had mental images of the children lying dead at the scene, and her nightmares of the experience persisted. Katherine declared that her career as a police officer was finished. She reported that after the incident, her superiors had become impatient when she had trouble remembering important details of the event. In fact, she experienced difficulty concentrating on the day-to-day tasks of her job. Katherine admitted to feeling depressed but denied thoughts of suicide. She also stated that there had been no excessive intake of alcohol.

Treatment Within the Faith Community

Religious faith is a primary coping method for those suffering from psychological trauma—one-half to three-quarters of PTSD sufferers indicated that their religion helped them to cope (Weaver, Koenig, and Ochberg, 1996). Attention to a person's strengths are noted as part of an assessment and included in a plan of treatment. Katherine's long-standing participation in church and school activities is an asset to be acknowledged and encouraged. Religious organizations provide social relationships that can be nurturing, supportive, and healing to those suffering from a traumatic event (Pargament, 1997).

Pastors, rabbis, imams, and parish nurses have both formal and informal contacts with members of their congregations, presenting many opportunities to become aware of problems. If a community of faith includes police and rescue workers, a needs assessment might be conducted to ascertain the situations of these helpers and their families. Internet and local resources can be used to develop peer support groups for them. A church, synagogue, or mosque also might open its doors for meetings of self-help groups, such as Alcoholics Anonymous, Al-Anon, and Alateen.

There are several risk factors for suicide that are unique to law enforcement personnel. Peace officers have continuous access to firearms, one of the most lethal means of attempting to end one's life. According to Clark and White (2000), police use guns to commit suicide 86 percent of the time—a much higher rate than the national average of 59 percent. Alcohol abuse is often associated with attempts on one's life. In a summary of nine research studies on police suicide, 35 percent of them involved alcohol (Clark and White, 2000). Although police appear to have a camaraderie not seen in many occupational groups, their solidarity does not necessarily include sharing psychological concerns. Internal investigations of critical incidents and other matters that threaten an officer's employment are a source of stress and anxiety. For many, police work is their whole identity rather than just an occupation. Finally, the frequent exposure to human problems and suffering can have a cumulative effect on an officer's view of humanity and on the meaning of being a peace officer.

In a review of the empirical literature on religion and mental health, Gartner (1996) reported that religious beliefs and affiliation served as a buffer against suicide. But there are times when suffering can become so overwhelming that faith is no longer of comfort. Shafranske (2000) warns clinicians and clergy that a dramatic loss of faith is an indicator of suicide risk and should be assessed.

Katherine's depression and the potential for suicide must be evaluated to see if she should be referred to a mental health professional. There are three questions that clergy and other caregivers need to ask of anyone who might be suffering from depression:

1. Have you thought about hurting or killing yourself?
2. If so, how would you do it (what would you use, when, where)?
3. Do you have the means to do it (e.g., gun with bullets, pills)?

If a person has a suicide plan and a lethal means, a mental health specialist needs to be involved to assist the religious professional (Weaver, 1993). The ability to recognize one's limitations is essential, and clergy

Indications for Referral

must develop skill in knowing when to seek consultation with and referral to mental health professionals.

Treatment by Mental Health Specialist

The best treatment for PTSD involves an integration of cognitive, behavioral, psychotherapeutic, and psychopharmacological interventions (Foa, Keane, and Friedman, 2000). One study reported that a form of brief psychotherapy has been successfully used with police officers with psychological trauma (Gersons et al., 2000).

PTSD is frequently associated with other mental health problems, such as depression and substance abuse. The use of alcohol or drugs for self-medication is often a pattern among people with poor coping skills and high addictive potential. A mental health professional will use questions such as these to evaluate the need for alcohol or drug treatment: How much is the person in denial about his or her substance abuse problem? Does he or she minimize the drug or alcohol abuse? How much insight does the person have into his or her problem?

Depression has been linked to abnormal levels of neurotransmitters in the brain, and treatment using medications seeks to correct the imbalance. There are several groups of drugs available to treat depression, and they can affect individuals differently (Preston, O'Neal, and Talaga, 2001). It is important for patients to work with their physicians to find the most beneficial choice. Medication for depression is usually prescribed in conjunction with psychotherapy or cognitive behavioral therapy, which help a person learn techniques to better manage undesirable behavior patterns (Preston, O'Neal, and Talaga, 2001).

Cross-Cultural Issues

Roman Catholicism, the largest Christian denomination in the U.S., has a diverse membership of over sixty million. Described by Dolan (1992) as the immigrant church, Catholicism has a long tradition of helping waves of those from other countries become acculturated while maintaining their ethnic identity. Parishes have been the hub of community activities, often in neighborhoods defined by ethnicity. As time passes and immigrants become assimilated, some congregations reflect culturally diverse neighborhoods while others retain their ethnic distinctions.

Americans of Irish ancestry have had a long presence in public safety occupations such as law enforcement and firefighting. The Emerald Society is the largest Irish-American organization in the United States outside the Ancient Order of Hibernians. Prominent at St. Patrick's Day parades, members of the Emerald Society's pipe band are often called upon to assist in the funeral services of police who have died in the line of duty. Irish-American Catholics of the nineteenth and twentieth centuries survived immigration and assimilation with the help of their parish and its priest. Their legacy includes fraternal organizations, magazines, publishing houses, parochial schools, and higher education institutions. Later generations inherited their ancestors' ways of living as Irish-American Catholics. Many embraced the role of parishioner, learned the life of the public safety officer, and integrated the two as part of their culture.

—Alcoholics Anonymous; General Service Office, P.O. Box 459, Grand Central Station, New York, NY 10163; www.alcoholics-anonymous.org; (212) 870-3400; is an international organization that provides a self-test for alcoholism and a description of what AA offers, such as anonymity and a twelve-step program.

—International Association of Women Police; 731 North Deer Isle Road, Deer Isle, ME 04627; (207) 348-6976; www.iawp.org; provides a network of international and regional contacts, employment opportunities, training options, conference announcements, and a chaplain's corner. Its purpose is to further the just and equitable treatment of policewomen working in criminal justice systems internationally.

—International Critical Incident Stress Foundation; 3290 Pine Orchard Lane, Suite 106, Ellicott City, MD 21042; (410) 750-9600; www.icisf.org; works to manage emergency services stress, including that of police officers, and is used by law enforcement agencies around the world.

—Internet Depression Resources List; www.execpc.com/~corbeau; contains a list of sites as well as a catalog of newsgroups.

—Membership Assistance Program; New York City Police Department, 40 Fulton Street, 3rd Floor, New York, NY 10038-1850; (212) 298-9111; is a union-initiated program in which working police who are trained to provide peer support function independently from their employer and ensure confidentiality. Other departments can receive assistance to create their own programs.

—Peer Support Training Institute; Manhattan Counseling and Psychotherapy Associates, LLC, 61 West Ninth Street, New York, NY 10011; (212) 477-8050; www.peersupport.com; provides training for peer support counselors of the Membership Assistance Program in New York. Plans for the future include training opportunities for other departments in the U.S. wanting to develop similar programs.

—Police Families; www.policefamilies.com; provides information and referral for spouses, children, and parents of police officers. The website has chat rooms, games, and activities for children and teens, and online educational workshops and reading lists.

—Police and PTSD; www.policeptsd.freeservers.com; is a comprehensive website for police and the general public that contains basic information about the recognition and treatment of PTSD. It provides first-hand accounts of the stressors encountered by law enforcement officers and offers links to other police websites with stress-related themes (including suicide), as well as counseling referral services for fire and police workers.

—Police Stress Unit; www.policestressunit.org; provides confidential support including peer counseling, referral services, a twenty-four-hour hotline, and information about PTSD, depression, divorce, and family crises.

Helpful Books

Cops Don't Cry: A Book of Help and Hope for Police Families (Vali Stone, Ontario, Canada: Creative Bound, 1999).

CopShock: Surviving Posttraumatic Stress Disorder (PTSD) (Allen R. Kates, Tucson: Holbrook Street Press, 2001).

Danger, Duty, and Disillusion: The Worldview of Los Angeles Police Officers (Joan C. Barker, Prospect Heights, IL: Waveland Press, 1998).

Force Under Pressure: How Cops Live and Why They Die (Lawrence Blum, New York: Lantern Books, 2000).

Forces of Deviance: Understanding the Dark Side of Policing (Victor E. Kappeler, Richard D. Sleeder, and Geoffrey P. Alpert, Prospect Heights, IL: Waveland Press, 1998).

I Love a Cop (Ellen Kirschman, New York: Guilford Press, 1997).

References

American Psychiatric Association (2000). *Diagnostic and Statistical Manual of Mental Disorders* (Fourth Edition, Text Revised). Washington, DC: American Psychiatric Association.

Carlier, I. E. V., Lamberts, R. D., and Gersons, B. P. R. (1997). Risk factors for posttraumatic stress symptomatology in police officers: A prospective analysis. *Journal of Nervous and Mental Disease, 185(3)*, 498-506.

Clark, D. W., and White, E. K. (2000, April). *Exploring Law Enforcement Suicide: An Inside Look.* Paper presented at the meeting of the American Association of Suicidology, Los Angeles, CA.

Dolan, J. P. (1992). *The American Catholic Experience.* Notre Dame, IN: University of Notre Dame Press.

Foa, E. B., Keane, T. M., and Friedman, M. J. (2000). *Effective Treatments for PTSD.* New York: Guilford Press.

Gartner, J. (1996). Religious commitment, mental health, and prosocial behavior: A review of the empirical literature. In E. P. Shafranske, *Religion and the Clinical Practice of Psychology* (pp. 187-214). Washington, DC: American Psychological Association.

Gersons, B. P. R., Carlier, I. V. E., Lamberts, R. D., and van der Kolk, B. A. (2000). Randomized clinical trial of brief eclectic psychotherapy for police officers with posttraumatic stress disorder. *Journal of Traumatic Stress, 13(2)*, 333-347.

Kates, A. R. (1999). *Cop Shock: Surviving Posttraumatic Stress Disorder (PTSD).* Tucson: Holbrook Street Press.

Pargament, K. I. (1997). *The Psychology of Religion and Coping: Theory, Research, Practice*. New York: Guilford Press.

Preston, J. D., O'Neal, J. H., and Talaga, M. (2001). *Handbook of Clinical Psychopharmacology for Therapists*. Oakland, CA: New Harbinger.

Shafranske, E. P. (2000). Psychotherapy with Roman Catholics. In P. S. Richards and A. Bergin (Eds.), *Handbook of Psychotherapy and Religious Diversity* (pp. 59-88). Washington, DC: American Psychological Association.

Weaver, A. J. (1993). Suicide prevention: What clergy need to know. *Journal of Psychology and Christianity, 12(1)*, 70-79.

Weaver, A. J., Koenig, H. G., and Ochberg, F. M. (1996). Posttraumatic stress, mental health professionals and the clergy: A need for collaboration, training and research. *Journal of Traumatic Stress, 9(2)*, 861-870.

Combat Veteran

"The attack brought back memories of combat in Vietnam"

Peter came from a long line of Presbyterian clergy. He was admitted to graduate school at Harvard on a full scholarship to study Arabic, but before the term began he was drafted. He served as a medic in Vietnam and was exposed to combat missions in enemy territory, encountered ambushes and firefights, was attacked by snipers and rockets, witnessed many deaths, and responded to the terrible injuries of others. With a small dose of medical knowledge and large amounts of courage and determination, Peter saved many lives. Nevertheless, a number of the soldiers he tried to save died. Many of these casualties were beyond all medical help, yet Peter continued to suffer extremely painful memories for several years, blaming his "incompetence" for these deaths.

It took him a long time to adjust when he returned home. His faith in a loving God and the caring members of his church were the keys to his recovery. Nevertheless, he did not marry, lives alone, and tends to isolate himself. His pastor, Walter Harding, who also served in Vietnam, is a friend. Peter went to see Rev. Harding after the September 11, 2001, terrorist attacks. Those events triggered memories of the war in Vietnam. Peter found himself feeling and acting as if the combat trauma were happening again. He felt angry, panicked, in danger, and a need to escape.

Persons most likely to be affected by a catastrophic event like a terrorist attack are those who were close to the victims. However, such horrifying actions have effects that are likely to be experienced widely. For previously traumatized individuals like Peter, one possible result is the feeling that one is reexperiencing the earlier trauma. Catastrophic events can reignite intense fears, vulnerability, and other PTSD-related symptoms. Peter is wise to make time to talk with his old friend. He understands the long-term effects of PTSD in his life and the need to get help. Peter went to see his pastor to find support and Christian fellowship, to quell his anxieties, and to talk about his feelings.

Pastoral Care Assessment

Imagine that you are driving home after church one Sunday. On the way, you witness a terrible plane crash involving hundreds of victims. Bodies litter the fields, blood and gore are everywhere, and you instinctively stop to help. You apply your Red Cross training and attempt to stop the bleeding. There is moaning, dying, screaming, moments of hell. Mercifully, it ends. You get back in your car and drive home as though nothing unusual occurred. You do not talk about what happened because everyone wants to forget it. That is analogous to the experience of most Vietnam combat veterans from the U.S.

The saying "war is hell," only begins to describe how horrible it has been for hundreds of thousands of veterans. War is a life-threatening experience that involves witnessing and engaging in terrifying and gruesome acts of violence. It is also, for most military personnel, a patriotic response in order to protect and defend their country, loved ones, values, and way of life. The trauma of war is a shocking confrontation with death, devastation, and violence. It is normal for human beings to react to war's psychic trauma with profound feelings of fear, anger, grief, repulsion, helplessness, and horror, as well as with emotional numbness and disbelief.

Many veterans are psychologically unable to leave behind the trauma of war and return home. They struggle with a variety of severe problems that neither they nor their families, friends, or communities know how to address or understand. Even experienced military personnel may never become fully desensitized to exposure to violent death, and they remain particularly vulnerable when victims include children.

Because many veterans have not been taught how surviving trauma can affect persons, they may have trouble understanding what is happening to them. They may think it is their fault that the trauma happened, that they are going crazy, or that there is something wrong with them since others who were at the same place do not seem to have the same problems. They may use drugs or alcohol to escape their feelings. They may turn away from friends and family who seem not to understand. Because thinking about a trauma and feeling endangered is upsetting, people who have experienced combat generally want to avoid all reminders. Sometimes survivors are aware of this and avoid such triggers intentionally, but they may do so without realizing it. Survivors may not know what to do to get better.

Relevant History

Psychological problems after exposure to war were described as "soldier's heart" in the Civil War, "shell shock" in World War I, and "combat fatigue" in World War II. After World War II, mental health specialists began to recognize these difficulties were not hereditarily predisposed mental illnesses such as schizophrenia or manic depressive illness, but a different form of psychological problem resulting from too much exposure to extreme stress in a war zone. As one might expect, the most important risk factor for PTSD among veterans is the level of exposure to traumatic events during war (Foy, 1992).

Recently efforts have been made to understand the long-term psychological effects of military combat that may persist into the later years of life. Those surveying veterans almost twenty years after the conflict in the National Vietnam Veterans Readjustment Study estimated that over 30 percent of the 2.8 million who served in Southeast Asia have suffered a lifetime history of PTSD (Kulka et al., 1990). What is especially problematic is that this was America's first primarily teenaged war—the average age of combatants was close to twenty (Wilson, 1989). That is a developmental period during which young people need time to establish a stable and enduring personality structure and sense of self. For many Vietnam veterans, this was disrupted by the violence of war.

It also appears that combat exposure is a significant risk factor for PTSD in the nearly 1 in 4 U.S. men aged sixty-five or older who served in World War II or the Korean conflict (Spiro, Schnurr, and Aldwin, 1994). World War II veterans exposed to moderate or heavy combat were found to be at much greater risk of PTSD symptoms when measured more than four decades later, compared to noncombat veterans. Blake and colleagues (1990) found current PTSD in 19 percent of World War II veterans and 30 percent of Korean conflict veterans seeking psychiatric treatment.

Diagnostic Criteria

Participation in hazardous duty can result in significant and enduring stress reactions. There are times when the experience is so extreme and unanticipated (for example, seeing and smelling decaying bodies) that everyone involved is at risk for psychological trauma. Stress reactions can create sleep disturbances, irritability, intrusive painful reexperiencing of events, restricted emotional capacity, and impairments of memory and problem-solving capabilities (APA, 2000). Long-term stress reactions may include depression, chronic anxiety, and the symptoms of PTSD, which include reexperiencing the events (nightmares, intrusive thoughts), avoidance (staying away from situations that remind the veteran of what happened), restriction in the capacity to experience and express feelings, and a variety of indications of hyperarousal (sleep disturbance, exaggerated startle, irritability). One response is to self-medicate with alcohol or drugs to counter distressing feelings and thoughts, as well as guilt over having survived when others died. Perhaps the most perplexing symptom for relatives and friends to understand is psychological numbness: a withdrawal of affection and avoidance of close emotional ties with family members, friends, and colleagues. These responses can cause or exacerbate marital, vocational, or substance abuse problems (Matsakis, 1996).

Response to Vignette

Rev. Harding had a special interest in working with Vietnam veterans because of his own experience. He knew it was important to offer Peter support and reassurance to help defuse his anxiety. Compassionate listening, as well as offering information and practical help, may assist Peter in coping with the emotional isolation that often accompanies traumatic experiences. Reassurance about normal responses to an event may decrease self-criticism and worry. Information about common reactions and stress management strategies may lower anxiety and help Peter cope with feelings of helplessness or loss of control. It is important to assess Peter's support system to determine his coping resources. Helping him recall previously successful coping strategies may also be useful.

Rev. Harding talked to Peter about joining a group of other combat veterans who met at a nearby church. A group provides a setting in which he can interact with others and decrease the tendency to isolate himself. It can also help remove the fear prevalent among veterans that they are the only individuals with these symptoms. It offers a forum in which those troubled by their combat experiences can talk about their feelings with others who have had similar experiences.

As group members achieve increased understanding of their trauma, they often feel more confident and able to trust. As they discuss and share their coping strategies for shame, guilt, rage, fear, doubt, and self-condemnation, they prepare themselves to focus on the present rather than the past. Telling their stories and directly facing the grief, anxiety, and guilt related to their trauma enable many survivors to cope with their symptoms, memories, and other aspects of their lives. Such groups serve to direct the energy of survivors toward providing mutual support as well as addressing practical problems and common concerns. In addition, many of the veterans form close supportive friendships outside of the meetings and help one another through particularly problematic episodes.

Treatment Within the Faith Community

Faith communities can provide an important service by offering space to support groups for those suffering from psychological trauma. One of the ways trauma survivors can reestablish their sense of control is through the formation of community-based self-help groups. These are often an ideal healing environment because survivors are able to risk sharing traumatic material surrounded by the safety and empathy of other survivors.

Clergy and the religious community can also play an important role in combat veterans' healing processes by developing commemorative rituals. Those who witnessed widespread destruction may benefit from ceremonies that help reestablish comfort in social equilibrium. For some survivors, rituals may provide a sense of place in the universe, the world, their communities, and their families. Formal and informal commemorations allow the powerful emotions associated with these debilitating effects to be directed into activities that unify veterans with one another, with their branch of service, and, in some instances, with the nation itself.

Scholars have written about the healing value of ritual in the treatment of PTSD for Vietnam veterans, using insights gained from both Western and Native American spirituality. In Veterans Affairs (VA) medical centers in Pennsylvania (Obenchain and Silver, 1992) and Connecticut (Johnson et al., 1995), clinicians reported that the ceremonies were highly effective in accessing and managing intense emotions that fostered therapeutic work. One ritual, "Ceremony for the Dead," used religious images and included the words, "It is now the time to release the souls of the dead to God and to the earth." The rituals enhanced social bonds within the veterans groups and with their families and staff. At discharge, veterans reported that the commemorations and rituals were the most therapeutically valuable of any treatment offered, including group treatment, individual therapy, and medication (Johnson et al., 1995).

Indications for Referral

The fear, distress, and confusion that some combat veterans experience can result in intense feelings of isolation, alienation, and aggression. Veterans with serious homicidal or suicidal thoughts must be handled in a crisis-oriented setting until the crisis is resolved. Refer these persons to an appropriate mental health setting or hospital.

Treatment by Mental Health Specialist

VA medical centers provide a network of more than one hundred specialized programs for persons with PTSD, working closely with the centers operated by VA Readjustment Counseling Service (see resources). Each specialized PTSD program offers education, evaluation, and treatment conducted by mental health professionals from a variety of disciplines, such as psychiatry, psychology, social work, and nursing. Outpatient programs include three types of clinics in which veterans meet with a PTSD specialist for regularly scheduled appointments. PTSD clinical teams provide group and one-to-one evaluation, education, counseling, and psychotherapy. Substance use PTSD teams offer out-patient education, evaluation, and counseling for the combined problems of PTSD and substance abuse. Women's stress disorder treatment teams provide women veterans with group and one-to-one evaluation, counseling, and psychotherapy.

A common issue associated with stress reactions is disturbances within interpersonal relationships. PTSD and other stress-related problems can affect an entire family. Many times family or couple therapy can help a family cope with a veteran's stress-related problems. These types of treatment may include stress reduction and relaxation techniques that can help all members of the family with the healing process. Therapy might also address the structure of the family and the way members interact (Figley, 1989).

Cross-Cultural Issues

The American Indian Vietnam Veterans Project surveyed a group of veterans residing in the Southwest and Northern plains (Friedman, 1998). The researchers found that exposure to war zone stress and other military dangers placed these veterans at risk for PTSD several decades after military service. Native American veterans of Vietnam had both high levels of exposure to war zone stress and late-onset PTSD. More than half of them experienced war-related trauma in Vietnam, in part, because they were proportionately more likely than any other ethnic group to serve in the Marines. About 1 in 3 Native American veterans suffered from full or partial PTSD at the time of the study, a quarter century or more after the Vietnam conflict. These rates of PTSD were more than twice as high as those for veterans of European American or Japanese American ancestry. Furthermore, more than 7 in 10 Native American veterans of Vietnam were found to have serious problems with alcohol overuse or dependence, which was twice as many as in any other group studied.

Resources

—American Counseling Association; 5999 Stevenson Avenue, Alexandria, VA 22304; (800) 347-6647; www.counseling.org.

—American Psychiatric Association; 1000 Wilson Boulevard, Arlington, VA 22209; (703) 907-7300; www.psych.org.

—American Psychological Association; 750 First Street, NE, Washington, DC 20002; (800) 374-2721; www.apa.org.

—Anxiety Disorders Association of America; 8730 Georgia Avenue, Suite 600, Silver Spring, MD 20910; (240) 485-1001; www.adaa.org.

—Department of Veterans Affairs (VA), www.va.gov, website is a resource that provides information on VA programs, veterans' benefits, and VA facilities worldwide. The VA is the parent organization of the National Center for PTSD.

—Gift from Within; 16 Cobb Hill Road, Camden, ME 04843; (207) 236-8858; www.giftfromwithin.org; is a nonprofit organization dedicated to helping those who suffer from PTSD. It maintains a roster of trauma survivors who participate in a national network for peer support.

—International Society for Traumatic Stress Studies, 60 Revere Drive, Suite 500, Northbrook, IL 60062; (847) 480-9028; www.istss.org.

—National Center for Post-Traumatic Stress Disorder; VA Medical Center, 215 North Main Street, White River Junction, VT 05009; (802) 295-9363; www.ncptsd.org.

—National Conference of Vietnam Veteran Ministers is composed of clergy who served in Vietnam as chaplains and former enlisted personnel who later were ordained to ministry or entered full-time religious service. It offers spiritual care to Vietnam veterans and their families; www.vietnamveteranministers.com.

—Posttraumatic Stress Disorder Alliance; www.ptsdalliance.org; (877) 507-PTSD; is a multidisciplinary group that provides educational resources to health care professionals and those diagnosed with PTSD.

—Sidran Institute; 200 East Joppa Road, Suite 207, Towson, MD 21286; (410) 825-8888; www.sidran.org; focuses on education, advocacy, and research related to the early recognition and treatment of traumatic stress disorders.

—U.S. Department of Veteran Affairs (VA), www.va.gov, website is a resource that provides information on VA programs, veterans' benefits, and VA facilities worldwide. The VA is the parent organization of the National Center for PTSD.

Helpful Books

Coping with Trauma: A Guide to Self-Understanding (Jon Allen, Washington, DC: American Psychiatric Press, 1995).

I Can't Get Over It: A Handbook for Trauma Survivors (Aphrodite Matsakis, Oakland, CA: New Harbinger Publications, 1992).

Recovering from the War: A Woman's Guide to Helping Your Vietnam Vet, Your Family, and Yourself (Patience H. C. Mason, New York: Viking, 1990).

Soldiers' Heart: Survivors' Views of Combat Trauma (Sarah Hansel, Ann Steidle, Grace Zaczek, and Ron Zaczek, Lutherville, MD: Sidran Press, 1994).

Trauma and Recovery (J. L. Herman, New York: Basic Books, 1992).

Trauma and the Vietnam War Generation: Report of Findings from the National Vietnam Veterans Readjustment Study (Richard A. Kulka, John A. Fairbank, Kathleen Jordan, Dani Weiss, and Alan Cranston, New York: Brunner/Mazel, 1990).

Vietnam Wives: Facing the Challenges of Life with Veterans Suffering Post Traumatic Stress (Aphrodite Matsakis, Towson, MD: Sidran Press, 1996).

References

American Psychiatric Association. (2000). *Diagnostic and Statistical Manual of Mental Disorders* (Fourth Edition, Text Revised). Washington, DC: APA.

Blake, D. D., Keane, T. M., Wine, P. R., Mora, C., Taylor, K. L., and Lyons, J. A. (1990). Prevalence of PTSD symptoms in combat veterans seeking treatment. *Journal of Traumatic Stress, 3,* 15-27.

Figley, C. R. (1989). *Helping the Traumatized Family.* San Francisco: Jossey-Bass.

Foy, D. W. (Ed.) (1992). *Treating Post-traumatic Stress Disorder: Cognitive-Behavioral Strategies.* New York: Guilford Press.

Friedman, M. J. (1998). The Matsunaga Vietnam Veterans Project. *PTSD Research Quarterly, 9(4),* 7.

Johnson, D. R., Feldman, S. C., Lubin, H., and Southwick, M. (1995). The therapeutic use of ritual and ceremony in the treatment of post-traumatic stress. *Journal of Traumatic Stress, 8(2)*, 283-298.

Kulka, R. A., Schlenger, W. E., Fairbank, J. A., Hough, R. L., Jordan, B. K., Marmar, C. R., and Weiss, D. S. (1990). *Trauma and the Vietnam War Generation: Report of Findings from the National Vietnam Veterans Readjustment Study*. New York: Brunner/Mazel.

Matsakis, A. (1996). *I Can't Get Over It: A Handbook for Trauma Survivors* (2nd ed). Oakland, CA: New Harbinger Publications.

Obenchain, J. V., and Silver, S. M. (1992). Symbolic recognition: Ceremony in a treatment of post-traumatic stress disorder. *Journal of Traumatic Stress, 5(1)*, 37-43.

Spiro, A., Schnurr, P. P., and Aldwin, C. M. (1994). Combat-related posttraumatic stress disorder symptoms in older men. *Psychology and Aging, 9*, 17-26.

Wilson, J. P. (1989). *Trauma, Transformation, and Healing: An Integrative Approach to Theory, Research, and Post-Traumatic Therapy*. New York: Brunner/Mazel.

Burn Survivor

"She was burned on her face"

Paula Furlong was a fifty-two-year-old bright, attractive, and cheerful woman who worked as a church secretary. She suffered second-degree burns on 20 percent of her face and hands from a kitchen stove fire, and her husband received minor injuries extinguishing it. Paula stayed in the hospital for ten days. She experienced support from her husband, grown children, and Pastor Marilyn Hanson, but she was depressed when she went home. Two months later, her plastic surgeon ordered a psychiatric evaluation for Paula. This previously active and independent woman could no longer concentrate on simple tasks and had become withdrawn. She experienced vivid intrusive memories of the accident, nightmares of being burned, fears of being in a room with an open flame, mood swings, general anxiety, and fatigue.

Burn injuries are painful and frightening, and anyone who is hurt seriously enough to require hospitalization is at risk for emotional difficulties. Psychological complications can persist for a prolonged period after surviving such a serious injury. Advances in medicine have increased the survival rates for even the severely burned, which means that pastors and hospital chaplains will work with increasing numbers of individuals and their loved ones in the aftermath of fires.

If burns cause disfigurement, a survivor can experience serious damage to self-esteem and body image that complicates recovery (Bryant, 1996). In a study conducted at Cornell Medical Center, researchers found that 4 in 10 patients experienced post-traumatic stress disorder (PTSD) six months after a serious burn injury (Perry et al., 1992). Rizzone and colleagues reported in 1994 that about half of the mothers of burned children developed PTSD.

Pastoral Care Assessment

Clergy can play an important role in helping focus patients' religious beliefs on the healing process. Spirituality increases the emotional well-being of a survivor, which can translate into faster physical and psychological recovery (Koenig and Cohen, 2001). Research shows that when burn patients are given the opportunity to talk about what helps them cope, they frequently credit their religious faith or God (Sherrill and Larson, 1988). A pastor or chaplain can help medical staff understand the relationship between patients' religious beliefs and their ability to deal with the stress of a traumatic injury.

Relevant History

The U.S. has one of the highest fire injury and death rates in the industrialized world (Istre et al., 2001). Each year, fires kill more Americans than all natural disasters combined. In the year 2000, firefighters responded to more than 1.7 million blazes involving 4,045 deaths and 22,350 injuries, over 80 percent of which occurred in residences. Fire is the third leading cause of accidental death in the home, and direct property loss due to it is estimated at $8.6 billion annually (Karter, 2001).

Diagnostic Criteria

PTSD occurs when persons repeatedly experience a distressing event, such as intrusive memories of a fire. Survivors also tend to avoid situations that remind them of the trauma, become emotionally numb, and develop fears that impair normal living. If these symptoms continue for at least a month, PTSD can be diagnosed (APA, 2000).

The chief indicator of PTSD is the intrusive memory of a traumatic event—often vivid and occasionally so real that it is called a flashback. Survivors of a residential blaze may feel a burning sensation, revisualizing the moment of the conflagration. They may begin to fear that they are crazy because their mind and body uncontrollably return to the awful incident. Emotional numbing can protect persons from overwhelming distress between memories, but it also robs them of the very feelings that make life worth living. The other symptom of PTSD is a lowered threshold for anxious arousal, which is both physiological and automatic. For example, unexpected flashes of light can cause a burn survivor to have an exaggerated startle response.

Facial injuries are common in fires, often accompanied by psychological difficulties (Bryant, 1996). Scar disfigurement of exposed parts of the body resulting from burns can dramatically change the way persons see themselves (Fauerbach et al., 2002). There are many significant rehabilitation challenges for survivors with lasting facial disfigurement. The most fundamental difficulty is dealing with the social response. Maintaining a sense of self-esteem despite negative reactions by others to their disfigurement can be a major problem. Additionally, depression and the loss of hope of ever again looking normal frequently lead patients to severe social withdrawal.

Pain control is often an important treatment issue because burn pain is intense and can cause great suffering. Anxiety and pain are closely related for patients with burns. Researchers found that the more survivors suffered from PTSD, the more anxious they were before, during, and after painful medical procedures (Taal and Faber, 1997). Clearly, management of PTSD is critical to the physical recovery of a burn patient.

Response to Vignette

It has been demonstrated that the encouragement of family members is important (Thompson et al., 1999). If loved ones can contribute their emotional support, the chances for an optimal recovery are increased. To help in the healing of a burn patient, it is vital for clergy and medical staff to assist, educate, and encourage families so that they can carry out a supportive role. The most stressful ordeals for loved ones were found to be the times of uncertainty of prognosis and waiting (Thompson et al., 1999). Family members revealed that prayer and the use of social support were the most helpful aids in getting them through the hospitalization of a loved one. Patient support groups can also be useful in lessening serious psychological problems for burn survivors (Cooper and Burnside, 1996).

Treatment Within the Faith Community

The religious community can play an important educational role in fire prevention. Older adults, children, and the poor have the greatest likelihood of burn injury and death (Istre et al., 2001). Adults aged sixty-five and older face a risk twice the average, while people aged eighty-five and older are in almost four-and-a-half times more danger than the average. The elderly, children younger than five years, and residents of substandard housing or mobile homes are at the highest risk for fire-related deaths.

Residential fires are most frequently started by cooking or heating equipment (Hall, 1998). Smoking is the second most common origin of home fires and the leading cause of deaths. The vast majority of residential burn injuries and deaths can be prevented. Working smoke alarms in every room can reduce the risk of death in a home blaze by as much as half (Marshall et al., 1998). The Center for Disease Control suggests using alarms with lithium-powered batteries that can last up to ten years and a hush button that allows one quickly to stop nuisance ringing.

Indications for Referral

PTSD can significantly impair recovery in patients with burns, resulting in their failure to return to work quickly, an increased economic impact, and social withdrawal. It can also impose a serious burden on a survivor's family. Therefore, early diagnosis of PTSD is important. Pastors and hospital chaplains can be crucial in early detection by recognizing the symptoms of PTSD and helping a burn survivor seek specialized help.

Treatment by Mental Health Specialist

Integrative therapy with the use of both psychodynamic and cognitive-behavioral approaches can be effective for patients with PTSD (Foa,

Keane, and Friedman, 2000). This treatment includes normalization of the symptoms, mobilization of coping skills, reinforcement of self-respect, permission to express anger, and emotional support for family members. Every effort should be made to involve loved ones in the active coping of a burn survivor because familial support is crucial in successful rehabilitation. Both psychological interventions and medication are valuable in assisting burn patients who develop PTSD (Preston, O'Neal, and Talaga, 2001).

When a person suffers from PTSD, anxiety management techniques can be used to reduce the intensity of symptoms and the distress they create. A mental health specialist can help a survivor learn effective ways to deal with anxiety, typically teaching several skills that will help in coping with PTSD, but they must be practiced until they can be employed easily and automatically. There are several anxiety management techniques such as: breathing training, relaxation, assertiveness training, positive thinking and self-talk, and thought-stopping (Foa, Keane, and Friedman, 2000).

Cross-Cultural Issues

African Americans and Native Americans have significantly higher death rates per capita from fires than the national average. Although African Americans comprise 13 percent of the population, they account for 26 percent of fire deaths (U.S. Fire Administration, 2000). The southern U.S. has the highest death rate from fires per capita, with 18.4 civilian deaths per million population. Men die or are injured in fires almost twice as often as women.

Resources

—Alisa Ann Ruch Burn Foundation; 3600 Ocean View Boulevard #1, Glendale, CA 91208; (818) 249-2230; Survivor Assistance: (800) 242-BURN; www.aarbf.org; was founded in 1971. It works in partnership with firefighters, educators, and burn care professionals to develop innovative programs and services. Recognizing that education is essential to avoid burn injuries, it has produced a variety of prevention materials that are distributed around the world. Its survivor assistance programs are designed to relieve emotional suffering, create opportunities for socializing, and help build the skills necessary to cope in a society that highly values physical appearance.

—American Burn Association; ABA Central Office—Chicago; 625 North Michigan Avenue, Suite 1530, Chicago, IL 60611; (312) 642-9260; www.ameriburn.org; was founded in 1967. It has more than 3,500 members in the U.S., Canada, Europe, Asia, and Latin America, which include physicians, nurses, occupational and physical therapists, researchers, social workers, firefighters, and hospitals with burn centers. It is dedicated to stimulating and supporting burn-related research, education, care, rehabilitation, and prevention. To advance these goals, it sponsors a variety of educational programs, fellowships, research projects, and publications.

—American Red Cross; National Headquarters, 431 Eighteenth Street, NW, Washington, DC 20006; (202) 303-4498; www.redcross.org; is not a government agency, although its authority to provide disaster relief was given by Congress in 1905. Currently operating on a budget of $2.7 billion, it responds to more than 67,000 disasters, including residential fires (the majority of disaster responses), hurricanes, floods, earthquakes, tornadoes, hazardous materials spills, transportation accidents, explosions, and other natural and human-caused disasters.

—National Center for Injury Prevention and Control; Mailstop K65, 4770 Buford Highway, NE, Atlanta, GA 30341-3724; (770) 488-1506; www.cdc.gov/ncipc.

—National Fire Protection Agency; 1 Batterymarch Park, P.O. Box 9101, Quincy, MA 02269-9101; (617) 770-3000; www.nfpa.org; is an international nonprofit organization founded in 1896 as the National Fire Protection Association. With more than 75,000 members representing nearly 100 nations and 320 employees around the world, it serves as a leading advocate of fire prevention. Its mission is to reduce the burden of fire and other hazards through research, training, and education.

—National SAFE KIDS Campaign; 1301 Pennsylvania Avenue, NW, Suite 1000, Washington, DC 20004; (202) 662-0600; www.safekids.org; is a nonprofit organization dedicated solely to the prevention of unintentional childhood injury—the number one killer of children aged fourteen and under. More than three hundred state and local SAFE KIDS coalitions in all fifty states, the District of Columbia, and Puerto Rico comprise the Campaign, which is chaired by former U.S. Surgeon General C. Everett Koop.

—The Shrine of North America; Shriners International Headquarters, 2900 Rocky Point Drive, Tampa, FL 33607-1460; (813) 281-0300; www.shrinershq.org/shrine/index.html; is an international fraternity of approximately 500,000 members. Its official philanthropy is Shriners Hospitals for Children, a network of twenty-two institutions that provide free expert orthopedic and burn treatment to those under the age of eighteen. If there is a child that they might be able to help, call (800) 237-5055 in the U.S. or (800) 361-7256 in Canada. Shriners Hospitals in Boston, Cincinnati, Galveston, and Sacramento treat children with acute, fresh burns; youngsters needing plastic, reconstructive, or restorative surgery as a result of "healed" burns; those with severe scarring, resulting in interference with mobility of the limbs; and children with facial scarring and deformity.

—U.S. Fire Administration (USFA); 16825 South Seton Avenue, Emmitsburg, MD 21727; (301) 447-1000; www.usfa.fema.gov. As an entity of the Federal Emergency Management Agency, the USFA's mission is to reduce life and economic losses due to fire and related emergencies through leadership, advocacy, coordination, and support.

Helpful Books

Burns Sourcebook: Basic Consumer Health Information About Various Types of Burns and Scalds, Including Flame, Heat, Cold, Electrical, and Chemical (Allan R. Cook, ed., Holmes, PA: Omnigraphics, 1999).

Coping Strategies for Burn Survivors and Their Families (Norman R. Bernstein, Alan Jeffry Breslau, and Jean Ann Graham, eds., Tempe, AZ: Greenwood Publishing Group, 1988).

Journeys Through Hell: Stories of Burn Survivors' Reconstruction of Self and Identity (Dennis J. Stouffer, Lanham, MD: Rowman and Littlefield, 1994).

Rising from the Flames: The Experience of the Severely Burned (Albert Howard Carter and Jane A. Petro, Philadelphia: University of Pennsylvania Press, 1998).

References

American Psychiatric Association (2000). *Diagnostic and Statistical Manual of Mental Disorders* (Fourth Edition, Text Revised). Washington, DC: American Psychiatric Association.

Bryant, R. A. (1996). Predictors of post-traumatic stress disorder following burns injury. *Burns, 22(2)*, 89-92.

Cooper, R., and Burnside, I. (1996). Three years of an adult burns support group: An analysis. *Burns, 22(1)*, 65-68.

Fauerbach, J. A., Heinberg, L. J., Lawrence, J. W., Bryant, A. G., Richter, L., and Spence, R. J. (2002). Coping with body image changes following a disfiguring burn injury. *Health Psychology, 221(2)*, 115-121.

Foa, E. B., Keane, T. M., and Friedman, M. J. (2000). *Effective Treatments for PTSD*. New York: Guilford Press.

Hall, J. R. (1998). *The U.S. Fire Problem and Overview Report: Leading Causes and Other Patterns and Trends*. Quincy, MA: National Fire Protection Association, Fire Analysis and Research Division.

Istre, G. R., McCoy, M. A., Osborn, L., Barnard, J. J., and Bolton, A. (2001). Death and injuries from house fires. *New England Journal of Medicine, 344(25)*, 1911-1916.

Karter, M. J. (2001). *United States Fire Loss*. Quincy, MA: National Fire Protection Administration.

Koenig, H. G., and Cohen, H. J. (2001). *The Link Between Religion and Health: Psychoneuroimmunology and the Faith Factor*. Oxford: Oxford University Press.

Marshall, S., Runyan, C. W., Bangdiwala, S. I., Linzer, M. A., Sacks, J. J., and Butts, J. D. (1998). Fatal residential fires: Who dies and who survives? *Journal of the American Medical Association, 279*, 1633-1637.

Perry, S., Difede, J., Musngi, G., Frances, A. J., and Jacobsberg, L. (1992). Predictors of posttraumatic stress disorder after burn injury. *American Journal of Psychiatry, 149(7)*, 931-935.

Preston, J. D., O'Neal, J. H., and Talaga, M. (2001). *Handbook of Clinical Psychopharmacology for Therapists*. Oakland, CA: New Harbinger.

Rizzone, L. P., Stoddard, F. J., Murphy, J. M., and Kruger, L. J. (1994). Posttraumatic stress disorder in mothers of children and adolescents with burns. *Journal of Burn Care Rehabilitation, 15(2)*, 158-163.

Sherrill, K. A., and Larson, D. B. (1988). Adult burn patients: The role of religion in recovery. *Southern Medicine Journal, 81(7)*, 821-825.

Taal, L. A., and Faber, A. W. (1997). Post-traumatic stress, pain, and anxiety in adult burn victims. *Burns, 23(7-8)*, 545-549.

Tompson, R., Boyle, D., Teel, C., Wambach, K., and Cramer, A. (1999). A qualitative analysis of family member needs and concerns in the population of patients with burns. *Journal of Burn Care and Rehabilitation, 20(6)*, 487-496.

U.S. Fire Administration (2000). *Facts on Fire*. Retrieved March 10, 2000, from the National Fire Protection Association in 1998, Fire Loss in the U.S., and Fire in the United States, 1987-1996, 11th ed.

Elder Abuse

"Larger bruises were found on her legs"

Mrs. Wilson, an eighty-five-year-old widow who lives with her disabled daughter and unemployed son-in-law, suffers from arthritis, hypertension, and dementia. She can no longer drive and has to use a cane to get around. Mrs. Wilson was dropped off at the hospital clinic by her son-in-law for an appointment with her physician. She had to walk fifty yards in the cold in slippers to get to the waiting room. The patient, who is thin, was wearing a badly stained dress and had lost ten pounds in the preceding two months. She appeared to be in considerable pain while waiting to be seen. When her doctor inquired about her pain, Mrs. Wilson insisted that she was all right and that Jesus would look after her. She adamantly refused to be admitted to the hospital for overnight observation.

Her physician asked Chaplain Rose Alejandro to come talk with his patient, a fellow Baptist. Mrs. Wilson began to tell the chaplain about her fears, describing how her son-in-law became angry when he drank. She said he gave her money to her daughter, who was not happy with her mother and scolded her a lot. Rev. Alejandro was very patient and listened to the story. Mrs. Wilson said that she had had a difficult time sleeping lately and had bad nightmares. When the chaplain suggested it would be good to have the doctor observe her overnight, Mrs. Wilson said she would agree to it only if Rev. Alejandro would stay and pray for her. During a medical examination in the hospital, large bruises were found on Mrs. Wilson's legs, which were clear evidence of a severe beating. A report was made to Adult Protective Services (APS).

There is general agreement among experts that at least 3 percent of elderly people are maltreated by those who care for them (Pillemer and

Pastoral Care Assessment

Finkelhor, 1988). It is important for chaplains and pastors to know which caregivers are most at risk for maltreating a senior. They include persons who are responsible for dependent adults over seventy-five years old, are isolated and continuously living with an elderly person, lack experience, or are unwilling caregivers (Reay and Brown, 2001). Many of those who are potentially abusive also have relationships marked by conflict and threatening behavior. Drug or alcohol abuse, mental health problems, a family history of violence, and high levels of personal stress also increase the risk (Reay and Brown, 2001). Research has shown that the more risk factors present in a family, the greater the likelihood of elderly maltreatment (Pillemer and Finkelhor, 1988).

Relevant History

Most neglect and abuse of elders takes place in the home. The great majority of older adults live on their own or with spouses, children, siblings, or other relatives—not in institutional settings (Quinn and Tomita, 1997). When maltreatment occurs, family, other household members, or paid caregivers are usually the perpetrators. Because most abuse happens in homes, a concerted effort to educate the public about the special needs and problems of the elderly and the risk factors for mistreatment is needed.

Diagnostic Criteria

As the number of adults aged sixty-five and over has increased, so has the hidden problem of elder abuse. Each year, hundreds of thousands of seniors are neglected, abused, and exploited. A national study conducted in 1996 found that more than a half-million older adults were victims of neglect or abuse in a twelve-month period (Quinn and Tomita, 1997). Almost four times as many occurrences of elder maltreatment were not reported to authorities as were reported. Those aged eighty and older were at the greatest risk of mistreatment. Many victims are frail, vulnerable, and dependent on others to meet their basic needs. In 9 of 10 cases, the perpetrator is a family member and two-thirds of those are adult children or spouses. All fifty states have enacted elder abuse prevention laws and have established reporting systems. Generally, APS agencies receive and investigate reports of suspected neglect or abuse of seniors.

There are five categories of elder maltreatment (Quinn and Tomita, 1997):

- Physical abuse is the willful infliction of bodily pain or injury, including beating, pinching, burning, kicking, slapping, sexually molesting, or unreasonable physical restraint.
- Sexual abuse is the infliction of nonconsensual sexual contact of any kind.
- Psychological abuse is the willful infliction of mental suffering by a person in a position of trust, including verbal assaults, threats, instilling fear, humiliation, intimidation, or isolation.

- Financial or material exploitation is any theft or misuse of a person's money or personal property for another's benefit.
- Neglect is the failure of a caretaker to provide goods or services necessary to avoid physical harm, emotional anguish, or mental illness as a result of abandonment, denial of food, or withholding health-related services.

Response to Vignette

Professionals who work with victims of elder abuse know about the grave psychological distress that many of them experience, often well after the actions have ended. Some have noted that these emotional effects can cause post-traumatic stress disorder (PTSD), an anxiety disorder that can develop after exposure to terrifying events (Ruskin and Talbot, 1996). Understanding how elderly victims of maltreatment respond to trauma is a critical first step in helping them heal. When persons are overwhelmed by abuse, they may not be able to cope with the acute stress. They may either try to block the experience from their minds or review it repeatedly. A key symptom of PTSD is the alternation between avoidance and intrusion of thoughts about a traumatic event. Another characteristic is "numbing," or pulling away from the outside world, which is evidenced by a lack of emotion and a loss of spontaneity. With older adults, a new traumatic experience may also reawaken memories of psychological trauma that happened years earlier.

Elder abuse, like all domestic violence, is extremely complex. Generally a combination of psychological and social factors contribute to this form of maltreatment. Some families are more prone to the use of violence than others because abusiveness is a learned behavior that is transmitted from one generation to another. In such families, violent acts are a normal reaction to tension or conflict since these persons have not learned any other way to respond.

Caregiver stress is a significant risk factor for abuse and neglect (Quinn and Tomita, 1997). When thrust into the demands of daily care without appropriate training and information about balancing the requirements of an older person with their own needs, caregivers frequently experience intense frustration and anger that can lead to abusive behavior. The risk of elder maltreatment increases when the person providing care is responsible for an older person who is physically or mentally impaired (Moon and Williams, 1993). Caregivers in such stressful situations often feel trapped and are unaware of available resources. If they have limited skills for managing difficult behavior, those who provide care can find themselves using physical force.

Treatment Within the Faith Community

The population of the United States is aging rapidly. About 1 in 8 Americans is now sixty-five years of age or over—a figure that will increase to about 1 in 5 by 2030 (Koenig and Weaver, 1997). The membership of churches and synagogues is aging even more rapidly than the general population. In the year 2000, about half the members of faith communities were over the age of sixty, and the percentage is growing (Koenig and Weaver, 1997). Congregations generally do well at providing programs and services for the elderly. According to a recent Gallup poll, 80 percent of older adults say they are members of a church or synagogue, and 52 percent of seniors attend worship services weekly (Gallup and Lindsay, 1999).

Clergy are in a particularly useful position to counsel troubled older adults and their families and to assist them in finding the specialized care they require. A study by the National Institute of Mental Health found that those aged sixty-five or over with a mental health problem are more likely to approach clergypersons than mental health specialists for help (Hohmann and Larson, 1993). Clergy are among the few, and perhaps the only, professionals whose responsibilities regularly take them into homes and care facilities. Persons in no other occupations are in a better position to observe the signs of abuse and neglect by a caretaker and to do something to protect a victim.

In a study assessing stress, those who provide care to seniors stated that the single most valuable assistance would be a support group where they could discuss their problems and find emotional support (Steinmetz, 1988). These caregivers also indicated that short-term respite—having someone else relieve them, even for a few hours each week—and help with basic household chores would make it much easier to cope with the high stress of continually providing care.

Every person needs time alone, free from the responsibility of looking after someone else's needs. Respite care is especially important for caregivers of adults suffering from Alzheimer's or other forms of dementia or those who are severely disabled. When people from one's church, synagogue, or mosque are part of the social network, tensions are less likely to reach unmanageable levels. Having persons from one's faith community with whom to talk is a vital aspect of relieving stress.

When caregivers of those with serious illnesses were followed for two years to determine which characteristics predicted faster adjustment to their role, only the number of social contacts and support received from personal faith predicted better adaptation over time (Rabins et al., 1990). Thus, having support from one's religion appears to be one of the most important factors for successful coping with the stress of caregiving. Religious teachings foster an ethos of compassion and responsibility that is an important resource for those facing the work of providing long-term care. Furthermore, those who have an active faith tend to have a better relationship with their care recipients than do nonreligious persons, reducing the caregivers' risk of depression (Chang, Noonan, and Tennstedt, 1998).

An additional element in preventing elder abuse is the significant religious value that teaches no one should be subjected to abusive or neglectful behavior. When older adults are regarded as disposable, society fails to recognize the importance of assuring dignified and respectful living situations for all. In addition to promoting positive social attitudes toward seniors, faith communities can take positive steps to educate people about elder maltreatment and to encourage interventions that help families cope with problems that contribute to abuse.

Every state has an organization designated to investigate allegations of elder abuse and neglect. Even if such an agency determines that there is only the potential for abuse, it will make referrals for counseling (call the Eldercare locator at 800-677-1116). It is important not to increase an older person's vulnerability by confronting an abuser yourself, unless you have permission and are in a position immediately to help by moving the victim to a safe place. If a pastor sees that someone is being neglected or abused, a good strategy is to talk to a physician or mental health professional about the situation. Both medical doctors and mental health specialists have a legal obligation to report abuse and can help clergypersons with the reporting process.

In most states, the APS agency is the primary office responsible for both investigating reports of elder abuse and providing victims and their families with treatment and protective services. In many jurisdictions, county departments of social services maintain an APS unit that serves the need of local communities.

An experienced mental health professional will first try to bring symptoms of PTSD under control with medication or relaxation training, thereby redirecting a survivor's attention away from the traumatic memory and lowering the anxiety level. This would accompany psychological therapy to help integrate the traumatic experiences so that they become events in the past instead of overwhelming, destructive forces ever in the present. Also, a therapist will explore what the trauma means to a person and the effect it has had on him or her. Mental health professionals will provide pragmatic support, which may include giving a victim of abuse practical advice, referrals, and education about the criminal justice system.

In a large five-year study of abused seniors living in Texas communities, Hispanic elders accounted for 20.6 percent of all cases reported to APS (Otiniano and Herrera, 1999). A 10 percent to 20 percent annual increase was seen over each of the five years. Self-neglect was the most frequently identified problem (63.2 percent). The most common perpetrators were adult children (44.6 percent). Women were twice as likely as men to suffer abuse of any kind. The reluctance of victims to become involved in services to help their situation was a major barrier to effective intervention. There is evidence of differences of perception regarding

Indications for Referral

Treatment by Mental Health Specialist

Cross-Cultural Issues

elder abuse and help-seeking in several ethnic groups (Moon and Williams, 1993).

Resources   —Administration on Aging (AOA); U.S. Department of Health and Human Services, Washington, DC 20201; (202) 619-0724; www.aoa.gov; Eldercare Locator: (800) 677-1116, Monday–Friday, 9 A.M. to 8 P.M. Eastern time. AOA is the only federal agency dedicated to policy development, planning, and the delivery of supportive home and community-based services to our nation's diverse population of older persons and their caregivers. It provides critical information, assistance, and programs that protect the rights of vulnerable, at-risk older persons through the national aging network.

—American Association of Retired Persons (AARP); 601 E Street, NW, Washington, DC 20049; (800) 424-3410; www.aarp.org; is the nation's leading organization for people over the age of fifty. Several of its divisions have services related to elder abuse. These include the Fraud Fighters Program Kit, Abused Elders or Older Battered Women Report on the AARP Forum, and Survey of Services for Older Battered. AARP also assists communities interested in setting up money management and volunteer guardianship programs.

—Association for Protection of the Elderly; 1047 Barr Road, Lexington, SC 29072; (800) 569-7345; www.apeape.org; a national nonprofit corporation, seeks to ensure civil and criminal liability for all offenses committed against America's elders and vulnerable adults, especially for those who reside in institutional settings.

—Clearinghouse on Abuse and Neglect of the Elderly; University of Delaware, Department of Consumer Studies, Alison Hall West, Room 211; Newark, DE 19716; (302) 831-3525; www.elderabusecenter.org/clearing/. Karen.Stein@mvs.udel.edu operates the Clearinghouse. It is the nation's largest and most used computerized collection of elder abuse materials and resources.

—Commission on Legal Problems of the Elderly; American Bar Association, 740 Fifteenth Street, NW, Washington, DC 20005; (202) 662-8694; operates the National Center of Elder Abuse's listserv, which provides a twenty-four-hour, seven-day-a-week online connection to others working on elder abuse issues. Subscribers E-mail questions, announcements, or discussion topics, and their messages are automatically distributed to the subscribers list. This service is for practitioners, administrators, educators, health professionals, researchers, law enforcement personnel, advocates, the legal profession, and policy makers. Subscribe by contacting the list manager: lstiegel@staff.abanet.org.

—Interfaith Caregivers Alliance; 112 West Ninth, Suite 600, Kansas City, MO 64105; (816) 931-5442; has existed since 1987 to develop and support interfaith volunteer caregiving programs across the U.S. Members work in their communities to provide care and services for those in need of help due to age, illness, frailty, or because they are alone. Most of the members' programs draw upon the compassion of trained volunteers from churches, synagogues, temples, and mosques. Though it is nondenominational, the Alliance recognizes the nation's heritage of faith-based caregiving programs. Its purpose is to support the development and increase the success of any volunteer caregiving program.

—National Association of Adult Protective Services Administrators; 960 Lincoln Place, Boulder, CO 80302; (720) 565-0906; is a membership organization established in the mid-1980s. Its mission is to improve the quality and availability of services for disabled and at-risk adults and elderly persons who are abused, neglected, or exploited, and other vulnerable adults who are unable to protect their own interests. This is accomplished through advocacy at the national level and by assisting state and local administrators to secure technical assistance, develop resources, and educate the public and legislative bodies about the needs of dependent adults.

—National Association of Bunco Investigators (NABI); P.O. Box 287; Maryland Line, MD 21105; is a nonprofit organization of law enforcement and associated professionals dedicated to the investigation and apprehension of con artists and transient criminals. Members have developed extensive knowledge in the investigation of Bunco crimes. NABI facilitates the continuous exchange of resources by publishing a bulletin that provides up-to-date information on criminals. It also provides a forum for the dissemination of data on suspects wanted by law enforcement agencies around the country. To date, the information disseminated through NABI has helped in the identification of over two thousand criminal suspects.

—National Center on Elder Abuse; 1201 Fifteenth Street, NW, Suite 350, Washington, DC 20005; (202) 898-2586; www.elderabusecenter.org; is funded by the Administration on Aging as a resource for public and private agencies, professionals, service providers, and individuals interested in elder abuse prevention information, training, technical assistance, and research. The website includes a state-by-state listing of relevant toll-free telephone numbers.

—National Center for Victims of Crime; 2000 M Street, NW, Suite 480, Washington, DC 20036; (202) 467-8700; www.ncvc.org; is a resource and advocacy center for victims of crime. Among the issues it has advocated for is greater attention to victims of financial crimes and abuse.

—National Clearinghouse on Domestic Violence in Later Life; a resource center operated by the Wisconsin Coalition Against Domestic Violence, 307 South Paterson, Suite #1, Madison, WI 53703; (608) 255-0539; provides materials and technical assistance on domestic violence in later life.

—National Long Term Care Ombudsman Resource Center; c/o National Citizens' Coalition for Nursing Home Reform, 1424 Sixteenth

Street, NW, Suite 202, Washington, DC 20036; (202) 332-2275; www.nccnhr.org; supports the development and operation of long-term care ombudsman programs across the country through technical assistance, consultation, and information dissemination. It also facilitates communication about timely issues, program needs, and resources among state ombudsman programs and assists states in promoting public awareness about these programs.

—National Organization of Triads, Inc. (NATI); 1450 Duke Street, Alexandria, VA 22314; www.sheriffs.org/defaults/defaults_s_triad.htm; (703) 836-7827; provides advice, support, technical assistance, and training to local Triads. Created in 1988 as a partnership between the American Association of Retired Persons, the International Association of Chiefs of Police, and the National Sheriffs' Association, it is a network of local programs that promotes collaboration between senior volunteers and law enforcement. NATI hosts training events and a national conference, manages a speakers' bureau, and produces a quarterly newsletter. It distributes guidebooks, information packets, and an informational video on getting started.

Helpful Books

Abuse, Neglect, and Exploitation of Older Persons: Strategies for Assessment and Intervention (L. A. Baumhover and S. C. Beall, eds., Baltimore: Health Professions Press, 1996).

Abuse and Neglect of Older Canadians: Strategies for Change (M. J. MacLean, ed., Ottawa: Thompson Educational Publishers, 1995).

The Dimensions of Elder Abuse: Perspectives for Practitioners (G. Bennett, P. Kingston, and B. Penhale, London: Macmillan Press, 1997).

Elder Abuse: International and Cross-Cultural Perspectives (J. I. Kosberg and J. L. Garcia, eds., Binghamton, NY: Haworth Press, 1995).

Elder Abuse and Neglect: Causes, Diagnosis, and Intervention Strategies (2nd ed.) (M. J. Quinn and S. K. Tomita, New York: Springer Publishing, 1997).

Elder Abuse and Neglect in Residential Settings (F. Glendennning and P. Kingston, eds., Binghamton, NY: Haworth Press, 1999).

Elder Abuse in Perspective (S. Biggs, C. Phillipson, and P. Kingston, London: Open University Press, 1995).

Elder Abuse Work: Best Practice in Britain and Canada (J. Pritchard, London: Jessica Kingsley, 1999).

Elder Mistreatment: Ethical Issues, Dilemmas, and Decisions (T. F. Johnson, Binghamton, NY: Haworth Press, 1995).

Gender Issues in Elder Abuse (L. Aitken and G. Griffin, Thousand Oaks, CA: Sage Publications, 1996).

National Elder Abuse Incidence Study: Final Report (National Center on Elder Abuse, Washington, DC: American Public Human Services Association in collaboration with Westat, Inc., 1998).

Self-Neglect: Challengers for Helping Professions (J. O'Brien, ed., Binghamton, NY: Haworth Press, 1999).

Understanding Elder Abuse in Minority Populations (T. Tatara, Philadelphia: Taylor and Francis, 1999).

References

Chang, B., Noonan, A. E., and Tennstedt, S. L. (1998). The role of religion/spirituality in coping with caregiving for disabled elders. *The Gerontologist, 38(4),* 463-470.

Gallup, G. H., and Lindsay, D. M. (1999). *Surveying the Religious Landscape: Trends in U.S. Beliefs.* Harrisburg, PA: Morehouse Publishing.

Hohmann, A. A., and Larson, D. B. (1993). Psychiatric factors predicting use of clergy. In E. L. Worthington Jr. (Ed.), *Psychotherapy and Religious Values* (pp. 71-84). Grand Rapids, MI: Baker Book House.

Koenig, H. G., and Weaver, A. J. (1997). *Counseling Troubled Older Adults: A Handbook for Pastors and Religious Caregivers.* Nashville: Abingdon Press.

Moon, A., and Williams, O. (1993). Perceptions of elder abuse and help-seeking patterns among African American, Caucasian American and Korean American elderly women. *The Gerontologist, 33(3),* 386-395.

Otiniano, M. E., and Herrera, C. R. (1999). Abuse of Hispanic elders. *Texas Medicine, 95(3),* 68-71.

Pillemer, K., and Finkelhor, D. (1988). The prevalence of elder abuse: A random sample survey. *The Gerontologist, 28,* 51-57.

Quinn, M. J., and Tomita, S. K. (1997). *Elder Abuse and Neglect: Causes, Diagnosis, and Intervention Strategies* (2nd ed.). New York: Springer Publishing.

Rabins, P. V., Fitting, M. D., Eastham, J., and Zabora, J. (1990). Emotional adaptation over time in caregivers for chronically ill elderly people. *Age and Ageing, 19,* 185-190.

Reay, A. M., and Brown, K. D. (2001). Risk factor characteristics in carers who physically abuse or neglect their elderly dependents. *Aging & Mental Health, 5(1),* 56-62.

Ruskin, P. E., and Talbott, J. A. (Eds.) (1996). *Aging and Posttraumatic Stress Disorder.* Washington, DC: American Psychiatric Press.

Steinmetz, S. K. (1988). Elder abuse by family caregivers: Processes and intervention strategies. *Contemporary Family Therapy, 10(4),* 256-271.

Compassion Fatigue in a Pastor

"He became overwhelmed and exhausted"

Just before 4:00 A.M. one April morning, a monster tornado swept into a small North Carolina community. It cut a path a mile wide and ten miles long, right through the town. It sounded like a freight train coming through, destroying everything in its wake. In all, twenty-five structures were completely destroyed, and sixty-five were severely damaged as it hurled trees, smashed homes, and inflicted severe injuries. Coloring the trees the next morning were not cherry blossoms but tufts of pink insulation from the ravaged homes in the community.

The United Methodist church that the Rev. Wesley Cunningham served was damaged, and several homes of members were demolished. A half-dozen parishioners were seriously injured; two very active church members and their two small children were killed. There were months of grieving and emotional pain over the losses in the small town. Rev. Cunningham found himself working within a community in crisis, not only helping others manage their fears and stress, but also dealing with his own emotional trauma.

Rev. Cunningham, a volunteer firefighter in the small community, was involved in recovering the bodies of the two small children. He helped in the rescue of several families and became "confessor" and confidant for many of the firefighters in the area. After weeks of this high stress, Rev. Cunningham began to find himself feeling disconnected from his sense of identity, isolating himself and feeling mistrustful of others. He became aware of the changes in his perspective and behavior through the observations of friends and colleagues who began saying things such as, "You used to be such a caring person," "You used to be so trusting," "You always think the worst," "You seem so worried and irritable," and "You're so isolated, you only talk about work."

Pastoral Care Assessment

Mental health specialists have recognized that those who help trauma survivors are themselves exposed to a form of traumatic stress. These people include clergy, mental health professionals, emergency workers, physicians, firefighters, and police. These professionals are at risk for secondary *traumatization*, also called *compassion fatigue* or *vicarious traumatization*. The symptoms are usually less severe than those of post-traumatic stress disorder (PTSD) experienced by survivors of a severe trauma, although the distress can affect a person's ability to enjoy life and work (Figley, 1995).

Vicarious traumatization is a state of tension and preoccupation with a traumatized person or traumatic event. Secondary exposure to trauma can lead to the development of a chronic condition in which work seems to take over a person's sense of self. In some respects, this is similar to the concept of burnout. However, burnout takes on a special quality when it is combined with exposure to secondary traumatic stress. All professional helpers, including clergy, carry a vulnerability to living out the traumatic experience of those they assist (Stamm, 1999).

One way an individual can recognize the effect of secondary trauma is by experiencing a significant change in outlook. Just as a trauma survivor becomes aware of dangers that he or she previously ignored or denied, those who repeatedly listen to painful stories can begin to see the world differently. Over a period of time, a person can lose a balanced sense of perspective and enter the world of the traumatized. This outlook is accompanied by a state in which a person stays constantly on guard, anticipating danger at every turn.

Working with the traumatized can be emotionally draining, especially if the survivor's trauma reverberates with a person's own experience (Pearlman and Mac Ian, 1995). Paradoxically, working with traumatized persons can cause a professional to feel emotionally drained, even while experiencing increased physical arousal. Clergy and other helpers can reach a state in which they are exhausted yet cannot slow down. At such times, an individual is especially vulnerable to the distressing thoughts and perceptions that can come from working with trauma survivors, whose sense of safety and living in a predictable world has been shattered (Stamm, 1999).

Diagnostic Criteria

There is a cost for helping and caring for traumatized people. Compassion fatigue is the emotional cost of exposure to working with those suffering from the consequences of traumatic events. The *Diagnostic and Statistical Manual* for mental illness defines acute stress disorder and PTSD as existing in anyone who has "witnessed or has been directly confronted with an event that involves actual or threatened death or serious injury, or is a threat to the physical integrity of oneself or others" (APA, 2000). Research indicates that the risk of trauma also exists for those who are exposed to trauma through their relationship to a person who was directly exposed to an event (Stamm, 1999). There are three major risk factors for secondary traumatization: exposure to the stories of multiple disaster victims, a person's empathic vulnerability to the suffering of others, and unresolved emotional issues that relate to the suffering of the survivors.

Relevant History

The tornado is nature's most violent wind. It is an intense, rotating column of air extending from the base of a thundercloud to the ground. An average tornado will be four hundred to five hundred feet wide and travel four to five miles on the ground, lasting only a few minutes. Generally, tornadoes move across the earth at 20 to 50 mph, but some race faster than 70 mph. A few huge tornadoes are a mile or more wide and can last for an hour or more. The United States is the world capital of tornadoes. An average of eight hundred of these vortices spin up beneath thunderstorms year round in the U.S. and can generate wind speeds faster than 250 mph, at times devastating whole communities.

Response to Vignette

Rev. Cunningham's District Superintendent (supervising pastor) became concerned for his well-being and talked to him about the need to seek some counseling and take time off from his duties. Rev. Cunningham sought help from the United Methodist Counseling Center in his region, which works with clergy and their families. The services were provided without cost as a benefit for those serving in that region of The United Methodist Church.

Dr. Long, the staff psychologist at the counseling center, assessed Rev. Cunningham and recognized his burnout, depression, and secondary posttraumatic stress. The pastor was suffering from emotional exhaustion, and, as a result of his depleted emotional state, he had begun to develop a negative attitude toward those seeking his care. He had low energy, feelings of helplessness, lowered motivation to engage in work, and negative attitudes toward himself, his ministry, and others. Rev. Cunningham was continuing to have nightmares about the small children who had died in the disaster and was suffering from sleep deprivation and survivor's guilt. He also had a physical reaction to the stress in the form of a severe skin rash. The pastor began individual psychotherapy with Dr. Long and was referred to a psychiatrist for a medication consultation and to a medical specialist to examine his severe skin rash.

Pastoral Care Assessment

During individual therapy, Rev. Cunningham had a chance to begin talking about how he was feeling. He saw the therapist twice a week. He began to feel some of his hurt, anger, and grief instead of pushing it away or hiding the emotions. The pastor was able to cry for the first time since the tornado. He began to talk about how overwhelming and shocking it was for him to be a part of the recovery of the two dead children from his

175

church and how difficult holding their funeral services had been. Rev. Cunningham realized later that he had moved through the crisis period with a feeling of detachment from himself. In his therapy, he worked on relaxation techniques and stress management skills. He began to keep a journal. His skin rash subsided as his stress decreased. He was soon able to stop taking medications for sleep.

Over the next several weeks, Rev. Cunningham took a respite from his duties at his church with the support of his District Superintendent who continued to encourage him to be self-nurturing. Rev. Cunningham began to make sure that he got enough rest and sleep. He started eating healthier foods and took time to walk, swim, and relax. He allowed himself to do things just because they felt good, such as taking a warm bath or sitting in the sun. He spent time with his family and friends having fun. Increasingly, he became aware of his need for connection to his body, his feelings, God, and other people to give him strength. The pastor spent time praying and reflecting on how this experience had changed his life. He made a two-week spiritual retreat at a nearby Benedictine monastery.

Treatment Within the Faith Community

Fortunately, Rev. Cunningham took clinical pastoral education in seminary and had continuing education in pastoral care while serving his parish. Clergy with pastoral care training have more tools than do most other individuals to cope with and recover from emotional distress, including psychological trauma. Trained pastors can also have knowledge of the ways in which trauma affects them and others. Clergy with good pastoral counseling skills can use them to help soothe and process feelings related to their distress. In addition, pastors have one another, a support system with the potential to help maintain perspective and find understanding during difficult times. And most important, they have their faith that fosters resilience and sustains community.

One of the primary sources of support for clergy is a professional peer group. The effects of secondary exposure to trauma are mitigated by supportive listeners. A clergy peer group has the power to buffer the impact of secondary traumatic stress, to normalize the disturbing reactions, and to help pastors maintain connections with those they serve, despite their personal upheaval. Consulting with colleagues can help in determining whether one's perspective has become distorted. Pastors who do not have the opportu-nity to consult with peers run the risk of losing their sense of perspective.

In a national survey of United Methodist clergy, 85 percent believed that religious bodies should provide opportunities for clergy and their families to receive private, confidential, low-cost counseling (Orthner, 1986). One excellent model of how this can be implemented is found in the East Ohio Conference of The United Methodist Church. Since 1968, the conference has provided pastoral counselors whose services are available as a resource to clergy, full-time church professionals, and their families. The conference recognizes that because of their position, clergy are frequently asked to be caregivers by those facing spiritual and personal crisis. The Pastoral Care Program has counselors with training to integrate the resources of faith and behavioral sciences (East Ohio Conference of The United Methodist Church, 2002).

Indications for Referral

Clergy are exposed to painful stories on a regular basis; but when working with trauma survivors, clergy need to take explicit steps to protect themselves at the first sign of problems. Secondary traumatization is a normal reaction resulting from empathic interactions with survivors of trauma. It can have an effect on a person's sense of self, worldview, faith in God, and interpersonal relationships. It is not a reflection of inadequacy on the part of a clergyperson to seek psychological help.

Pastors need to acknowledge that what is good for their parishioners is good for them. Psychotherapists understand the need for therapy for their emotional self-care and so should clergy. In a study of 467 psychologists, 85.7 percent found their own therapy to be very or extremely helpful in reducing distressing emotions such as anxiety or depression or in helping with difficult relationships (Pope and Tabachnick, 1994). Many reported positive changes in self-understanding, self-esteem, and self-confidence.

Treatment by Mental Health Specialist

Secondary traumatic stress is the natural and treatable consequence of working with suffering people. Most intervention programs combine several methods of treatment, including relaxation techniques, cognitive stress management, attitude change, and time management (Pines and Aronson, 1988). The treatment for symptoms of PTSD involves an integration of cognitive, behavioral, psychodynamic, and psychopharmacological interventions (Foa, Keane, and Friedman, 2000).

Cross-Cultural Issues

Clergy working in inner-city areas may be exposed to high numbers of persons who are suffering from psychological trauma. In a study of African American and European American adolescents and young adults (aged fourteen through twenty-three) in Detroit, Michigan, 42 percent had seen someone shot or stabbed and 22 percent had seen someone killed. Nine percent had seen more than one person killed (Shubiner, Scott, and Tzelepis, 1993). Researchers surveyed African American pastors in ninety-nine churches in urban areas of Connecticut and found that ninety-four of the churches offered community outreach programs for those in need (Williams et al., 1999). Most of the programs offered services to persons who suffered from conditions that placed them at risk for PTSD, including substance abuse, child abuse, domestic violence, AIDS, imprisonment, homelessness, and hunger.

Resources   —American Association of Pastoral Counselors; 9504A Lee Highway, Fairfax, VA 22031; (703) 385-6967; www.aapc.org; provides information on qualified pastoral counselors and church-related counseling centers.

—American Psychiatric Association; 1000 Wilson Boulevard, Arlington, VA 22209; (703) 907-7300; www.psych.org.

—American Psychological Association; 750 First Street, NE, Washington, DC 20002-4242; (800) 374-2721; www.apa.org; provides online services for professionals and the general public.

—International Society for Traumatic Stress Studies; 60 Revere Drive, Suite 500, Northbrook, IL 60062; (847) 480-9028; www.istss.org.

—National Center for Post-Traumatic Stress Disorder; VA Medical Center, 215 North Main Street, White River Junction, VT 05009; (802) 295-9363; www.ncptsd.org.

—Posttraumatic Stress Disorder Alliance; www.ptsdalliance.org; (877) 507-PTSD; is a multidisciplinary group that provides educational resources to health care professionals and those diagnosed with PTSD.

—Sidran Institute; 200 East Joppa Road, Suite 207, Towson, MD 21286; (410) 825-8888; www.sidran.org; focuses on education, advocacy, and research related to the early recognition and treatment of traumatic stress disorders.

Helpful Books

Compassion Fatigue: Coping with Secondary Traumatic Stress Disorder in Those Who Treat the Traumatized (C. R. Figley, ed., New York: Brunner/Mazel, 1995).

Secondary Traumatic Stress: Self-care Issues for Clinicians, Researchers, and Educators, 2nd ed. (B. H. Stamm, Lutherville, MD: Sidran Press, 1999).

Shattered Assumptions: Towards a New Psychology of Trauma (R. Janoff-Bulman, New York: Basic Books, 1992).

Transforming the Pain: A Workbook on Vicarious Traumatization (K. W. Saakvitne, L. A. Pearlman, and the Staff of the Traumatic Stress Institute, New York: W. W. Norton, 1996).

References   American Psychological Association (2000). *Diagnostic and Statistical Manual of Mental Disorders* (Fourth Edition, Text Revised). Washington, DC: American Psychological Association.

East Ohio Conference of The United Methodist Church (2002). *Caring for the Pastoral Community and Their Families.* Retrieved March 5, 2002, from www.eocumc.com/pastcare.html.

Figley, C. R. (Ed). (1995). *Compassion Fatigue: Coping with Secondary Traumatic Stress Disorder in Those Who Treat the Traumatized.* New York: Brunner/Mazel.

Foa, E. B., Keane, T. M., and Friedman, M. J. (2000). *Effective Treatments for PTSD*. New York: Guilford Press.

Orthner, D. K. (1986). *Pastoral Counseling: Caring and Caregivers in The United Methodist Church*. Nashville: The General Board of Higher Education and Ministry of The United Methodist Church.

Pearlman, L. A., and Mac Ian, P. S. (1995). Vicarious traumatization: An empirical study of the effects of trauma work on trauma therapists. *Professional Psychology: Research and Practice, 26(6)*, 558-565.

Pines, A., and Aronson, E. (1988). *Career Burnout: Causes and Cures*. New York: Free Press.

Pope, K. S., and Tabachnick, B. G. (1994). Therapists as patients: A national survey of psychologists' experiences, problems, and beliefs. *Professional Psychology: Research & Practice, 25(3)*, 247-258.

Shubiner, H., Scott, R., and Tzelepis, A. (1993). Exposure to violence among inner-city youth. *Journal of Adolescent Health, 14(3)*, 214-219.

Stamm, B. H. (Ed). (1999). *Secondary Traumatic Stress: Self-Care Issues for Clinicians, Researchers, and Educators* (2nd ed). Lutherville, MD: Sidran Press.

Williams, D. R., Griffins, E. H., Young, J. L., Collins, C., and Dobson, J. (1999). Structure and provision of services in Black churches in New Haven, Connecticut. *Cultural Diversity and Ethnic Minority Psychology, 5(2)*, 118-133.

Although not all pastors have all the benefits of care available that Rev. Cunningham did, there are several ways clergy can find help through difficult places.

1. Telephone or Internet support from others is helpful for persons who are in isolated areas. Colleagues can provide pastoral care to one another from a distance in difficult times.
2. A personal retreat removed from one's professional setting can be helpful. Find a place such as a monastery or retreat center where you can have some time for personal reflection and healing.
3. Find a spiritual director or wise mentor who may not have a mental health license, but who can give sound counsel when a therapist is not available.
4. Clergy can organize an ecumenical or interfaith support group in a region, which can meet to provide pastoral care and support to one another.

PART THREE

Summary

Responding to a Crisis: Clergy's Unique Advantages

Survivors of traumatic events are born out of crises. It is important to understand the nature of different types of crisis situations and how to respond to them. This chapter will provide guidance in those areas. Crisis situations offer pastors, priests, imams, and rabbis opportunities to foster spiritual, mental, and physical well-being. Slaikeu (1990) outlines several characteristics that give them unique advantages when they encounter crises, including the following:

1. Clergy are often the first persons sought for help before someone in crisis contacts a mental health professional.
2. Clergy have more freedom than most mental health professionals to "reach out" in a nonthreatening manner because they are expected to "go where the people are" instead of waiting for persons to come to them and because of the varied contexts in which members of a congregation gather.
3. Pastors, priests, imams, and rabbis conduct religious rites associated with life transitions. Rituals such as circumcision, baptism, bar/bat mitzvah, confirmation, weddings, and funerals often serve to reduce anxiety associated with these changes.
4. Clergy who have had continuing contacts with members who are in crisis are able to assess progress because they know the baseline functioning of these persons.
5. Clergy can mobilize networks of support using their contacts within and outside of the congregation. They can call upon teachers in religious schools and others to assist in working through certain crisis situations.
6. Pastors, priests, imams, and rabbis offer religious faith as a resource for individuals in crisis, who often experience anxiety, helplessness, hopelessness, depression, and feelings of worthlessness. Clergy can work with a person's faith to counteract negative emotions and move toward an attitude of hopefulness and problem-solving.

Definition

It is worth noting that in the Chinese language, two characters are used to make the ideogram *crisis*; one means "danger" and the other means "opportunity" (Slaikeu, 1990). A crisis is an acute, time-limited state of emotional upset and psychological disequilibrium resulting from situational, developmental, or societal sources of stress. A person in this state is temporarily unable to cope with or adapt to the stressor using previous methods of problem-solving. Successful negotiation of a crisis leads either to a return to the pre-crisis level of functioning or to psychological growth and increased competence. Unsuccessful negotiation of a crisis leaves a person feeling anxious, threatened, and ineffective. Occasionally, individuals can respond to a crisis with disturbed personal coping or even with psychotic behavior.

To understand this concept fully, crisis is differentiated from various types of distress. Stress is not crisis, but pressure and tension. Everyone experiences stressful conditions that demand attention and can even be exhausting, but these are not crises. An emergency is a life-threatening situation that requires an immediate response to ensure a person's survival, but it is not a crisis, although it has the potential to precipitate one. Finally, a crisis is not a mental disorder—it can happen to people who have never had a mental disorder as well as to those who have a mental illness.

Types of Crises

Aguilera (1994) identifies three types of crisis situations. The first is developmental/maturational involving usual life changes that a person encounters with appropriate help and support from significant others. Normal transitions such as the birth of a second sibling or start of preschool are predictable, and potential problems associated with these can be anticipated and prepared for. The second category (situational) is usually unexpected, such as a baby who dies of sudden infant death syndrome. The third is social/adventitious, which may or may not be anticipated, but involves communities that experience natural or human-created disasters.

Developmental/Maturational—These crises are characterized by transitions that are universal and can therefore be anticipated and prepared for by everyone. Erickson (1963) and other developmental psychologists outlined stages that all persons experience. Behavioral manifestations and rituals associated with transitions between developmental stages vary among cultures.

Situational—This type is typically unexpected and unprepared for by all involved. A situational crisis might be precipitated by an event that threatens one's personal or physical being (such as diagnosis of a fatal illness, disability due to an accident or disease) or one's interpersonal or social integrity (such as divorce, death of a loved one). Situational crises are often encountered in clinical contexts such as hospitals and in informal contexts where clergy meet with members.

Social/Adventitious—The September 11, 2001, attack on the U.S. is a recent example of a precipitating event that triggered a crisis among large groups and communities of people. Catastrophic events such as environmental disasters (hurricanes, floods) and human-created disasters (terrorist attacks, group killings in the workplace, airplane crashes) are uncommon and unanticipated. Multiple losses with major changes in the community are the result of a social/adventitious crisis. Unlike maturational and situational crises, social/adventitious crises do not occur in everyone's lives. They are accidental, uncommon, and unanticipated events that involve larger groups rather than maturational and situational crises, which usually involve individuals and families.

Stages of Crisis Development

Caplan (1964) describes four stages that characterize an individual's or family's response to a precipitating event:

1. An external cause leads to a rise in tension and discomfort, which in turn initiates habitual problem-solving responses.
2. There is increased discomfort as coping skills are unsuccessful and the stress remains unresolved.
3. Other problem-solving strategies are mobilized in an attempt to reduce the tension and discomfort. The crisis may be averted by one of the following: reduction of the external threat, success of new coping strategies, redefinition of the problem, or giving up goals that are unattainable.
4. Without resolution, the tension increases to a breaking point, and the individual experiences severe emotional disorganization.

Background

In 1942, a fire broke out in the Cocoanut Grove Melody Lounge, a nightclub outside of Boston. Military personnel and civilians who came to dance and drink were trapped in an inferno because the nightclub's managers locked all of the exit doors, fearing that customers might leave without paying for their drinks. Almost five hundred people perished in the conflagration. Lindemann (1944) and his colleagues at Massachusetts General Hospital provided an immediate response to the families and friends of those who died. They found that the survivors who developed pathological symptoms in the aftermath had not progressed through the normal process of grieving—mourning, experiencing the pain of loss, accepting the reality of death, and eventually adjusting to life without the loved one.

Caplan (1964) developed a conceptual framework of crisis intervention that is used by most practitioners in the field today. Although Caplan's model has been criticized (Hoff, 2001) for its use of disease-oriented concepts based on general systems theory, its public health focus has been widely accepted. Caplan's community-wide approach of intervention involving nurses, teachers, police officers, and others emphasizes primary prevention and ways of preventing pathological responses to crisis events.

In the 1960s, the community mental health movement emerged, coinciding with Caplan's publication of *Principles of Preventive Psychiatry* (1964). The Community Mental Health Centers Act in 1963 mandated that the care and treatment of the mentally ill be shifted from hospitals to communities in the U.S. Legislation made federal funds available to provide comprehensive services in community mental health centers, including twenty-four-hour emergency care, telephone hotlines, and outreach activities by mental health workers.

Crisis Intervention: Important Tools

The most important tools for clergy who encounter persons in crisis are:

1. An ability to pinpoint the most salient features of a problem, since information is often presented in a piecemeal fashion.
2. Knowledge of community resources in order to make the best referrals for people in distress.
3. A basic familiarity with treatment options for specific problems.
4. A willingness to follow up.

Assessment Phase

Often information about a crisis is presented in an informal context, such as a congregational activity, and might even be provided by someone other than the person(s) in distress. Problematic symptoms do not necessarily point to a crisis, but when they do, the presenting signs are frequently the "tip of the iceberg." At this point, clergy can gather pertinent facts to determine whether there is an actual crisis. Due to time and other constraints, the initial assessment is usually a brief one. Nevertheless, sufficient knowledge of a situation can be gleaned by focusing on specific areas of crisis assessment.

Behaviors

People in crisis exhibit signs of distress. Changes in day-to-day functioning and pathological symptoms (for example, anxiety, nightmares, depression, excessive alcohol intake) can be assessed by clergy regardless of their familiarity with a person. For instance, upon meeting someone in crisis for the first time, information can be gathered from the person and, with permission, from his or her family and significant other.

Precipitating Event

To help identify what triggered a crisis, clergy should explore a person's needs, events that threaten him or her, and the point when symptoms first appeared. Four human needs are: role mastery, self-esteem, dependency, and biological function. Clergy can help those in crisis identify unmet needs by asking about aspects of life that they consider a success (role mastery and self-esteem), their relationships with others (satisfying and interdependent), and their degree of safety and security in life (biological). In a nonthreatening manner, clergy can ask about what has changed and recent events that have been upsetting. Helping an individual connect events with distressing thoughts, feelings, and ineffective coping behaviors can lead to a better understanding of the precipitating cause.

Balancing Factors

Every attempt must be made to help a person stabilize and regain equilibrium. Aguilera (1994) outlines balancing factors that contribute to this, noting that the strength or weakness in any of these could precipitate a crisis or contribute to its resolution.

1. Perception of the event: After identifying the precipitating cause, it is important to find out what it means to a person in crisis. According to Slaikeu (1990), it is a serious error to assume an understanding of what an incident means to someone. Example: An abused woman can view divorce as relief from battering, although another wife can perceive divorce as a threat to her financial needs, loss of her husband, and challenges for which she is unprepared. An event that seems trivial to one individual may be "the straw that broke the camel's back" to another. Differing perceptions of similar incidents may be due to the connection between issues from the past and the current event. Example: The wife who saw divorce as a threat, loss, and challenge might have a poor self-image as a result of experiences during childhood that trigger painful memories, and her emotions take on a greater intensity than in another woman. Since cognitive processes mediate between an incident and a person's response, knowing how it is perceived is crucial to crisis assessment and intervention.

2. Support systems and resources: An individual experiencing a crisis alone is more vulnerable to unsuccessful negotiation than a person with help. Working with someone else increases the chances that a crisis will be resolved in a positive way. Living situations and social supports can be assessed for their usefulness in crisis intervention and in determining who will and will not strengthen someone in crisis.

3. Coping mechanisms: An assessment of a person's strengths and coping ability will guide clergy in planning an intervention.

Planning Phase

Crisis assessment and intervention may be viewed as an hourglass in which thousands of sand particles in the wide portion at the top must pass through the narrow middle before they reach the wide bottom of the glass. During the initial assessment, a clergyperson is presented with multiple problems that may seem overwhelming. The task is to assist an individual in narrowing the scope of the problem. After it has been limited to the most pressing aspects, he or she can be helped to widen the scope by considering multiple options.

According to Ripple, Alexander, and Polemis (1964), an experience of extreme discomfort, accompanied by the hope of goal attainment, motivates a person in crisis to seek help. Thoughts, feelings, and beliefs often flow freely from those who seek help as conflicts between expectations and belief systems are challenged, while at the same time the hope of goal attainment is also present.

Intervention Phase

The free flow of thoughts, feelings, and beliefs by those in crisis is typically associated with high levels of anxiety, anger, or frustration. In his model of crisis intervention, Roberts (2000) prescribes a cognitive approach to crisis resolution. It involves three phases: understanding the event with all of its details, defining its personal meaning; and replacing irrational beliefs with rational ones.

Evaluation and Follow-up Phase

Roberts (2000) suggests that crisis workers should clearly communicate to a person in crisis that they are always available if further help is needed. However, it perhaps would be better to schedule a follow-up appointment within weeks to assess whether the referrals or other interventions were helpful. If that is impossible, a clergyperson can make telephone contact with an individual. Anniversaries (one month, one year) of traumatic events are difficult times for those who have experienced violence or losses. Clergy can tell persons of their desire to meet with them during this time.

Modalities of Crisis Intervention

Crisis intervention modalities are based on the understanding that health care workers must aggressively go to those in need, rather than wait for people to come to them. Similar to clergy, health care workers intervene in a variety of settings ranging from hospitals to residences.

Mobile crisis teams provide interventions to individuals, families, and communities. They may deal with someone who is threatening to jump from a building or to kill family members or coworkers. When mobile teams respond in a timely manner to defuse a tense situation, lives can be saved, incarcerations avoided, and persons stabilized. Mobile teams are usually able to provide on-site assessment, crisis management, treatment, referrals, and educational services. They typically work closely with police and community agencies.

Telephone services, such as suicide and crisis hotlines, are especially useful when those in need of help wish to remain anonymous. Telephone specialists are usually volunteers (professional and paraprofessional) who have received extensive training in oral communication skills, since visual cues are unavailable during their assessment and intervention. In addition to listening skills, they are trained to conduct a crisis assessment, use rating scales to evaluate suicide lethality, and select appropriate referrals for specific problems.

Two types of group work that have received attention in the recent literature (Everly, Lating, and Mitchell, 2000) are Critical Incident Stress Debriefing (CISD) and Critical Incident Stress Management (CISM). CISD is designed for situations in which an incident that has the potential to precipitate a crisis has affected persons in stressful occupations, such as police and fire and ambulance personnel (Mitchell and Bray, 1990). Recently, CISD has been applied to whole communities, including survivors of environmental disasters and traumatic events. The objective of CISD is to provide a rapid response after the occurrence of a critical incident. Its goal is to reduce the likelihood that survivors will react to the event in a negative way. Typically, a CISD team of four to six volunteer professionals is activated upon the request of first responders or community survivors within twenty-four to forty-eight hours of a critical incident, and a meeting is scheduled at a designated place. The debriefing session is a structured one that might last three to four hours. Each participant is invited to share thoughts, feelings, and perceptions of the event. In a group setting, misconceptions related to the incident are clarified. The CISD team provides relevant information about physical and emotional effects of experiencing a traumatic event as well as about long-term effects of prolonged stress. From the beginning to the end of the debriefing session, the CISD team validates the feelings of those involved in the critical incident.

CISM is a broader and more comprehensive form of group crisis intervention that includes CISD as one of its components. Disaster responses, such as mobilizations of teams to traumatized communities, formation of support services, provision of informational meetings, and consultations are examples of the multifaceted approach of CISM. Mitchell and Everly (1996) provide specific guidelines for CISM interventions.

Other types of crisis services include child abuse hotlines, rape crisis programs, battered women's hotlines and shelters, substance abuse crisis lines, and anxiety and depression lines (both national and local resources). The types of services offered vary by location, so it is important to research the availability of help for specific problems in advance of needing it.

References

Aguilera, D. (1994). *Crisis Intervention: Theory and Methodology* (7th ed.). St. Louis: Mosby.

Caplan, G. (1964). *Principles of Preventive Psychiatry.* New York: Basic Books.

Erickson, E. (1963). *Childhood and Society* (2nd ed.). New York: Norton.

Everly, G. S., Lating, J. M., and Mitchell, J. T. (2000). Innovations in group crisis intervention. In A. R. Roberts (Ed.), *Crisis Intervention Handbook: Assessment Treatment and Research* (2nd ed.) (pp. 77-97). New York: Oxford University Press.

Hoff, L. A. (2001). *People in Crisis: Clinical and Public Health Perspectives* (5th ed.). San Francisco: Jossey-Bass.

Lindemann, E. (1944). Symptomatology and management of acute grief. *American Journal of Psychiatry, 101,* 101-148 (reprinted in H. J. Parad, ed., [1965] *Crisis Intervention: Selected Readings.* New York: Family Association of America).

Mitchell, J., and Bray, G. (1990). *Emergency Service Stress.* Englewood Cliffs, NJ: Prentice Hall.

Mitchell, J. T., and Everly, G. S. (1996). *Critical Incident Stress Debriefing: An Operations Manual.* Ellicott City, MD: Chevron.

Ripple, L., Alexander, E., and Polemis, B. (1964). *Motivation, Capacity, and Opportunity.* Chicago: University of Chicago Press.

Roberts, A. R. (2000). *Crisis Intervention Handbook: Assessment, Treatment, and Research.* Oxford: Oxford University Press.

Slaikeu, K. A. (1990). *Crisis Intervention: A Handbook for Practice and Research* (2nd ed.). Needham Heights, MA: Allyn and Bacon.

Making a Referral to a Mental Health Specialist

"An effective referral is an act of pastoral care."

Ronald R. Lee, The Journal of Pastoral Care

Aclergyperson is more likely than a psychologist or psychiatrist to have an individual who is seriously emotionally distressed seek her or him for assistance. Most of those who consult clergy do not subsequently contact a mental health professional (Hohmann and Larson, 1993). Numerous studies indicate that fewer than 10 percent of those who seek pastoral help are referred to mental health specialists (Weaver, 1995). Experts estimate that the rate of referral should be much higher than 10 percent, given the severity of the problems brought to pastors (Hohmann and Larson, 1993). At the same time, clergy indicate that they believe seminary training does not adequately prepare them to respond to the serious emotional and family problems encountered in ministry (Orthner, 1986). Seventy to ninety percent of pastors surveyed recognize a need and indicate a desire to have additional training in mental health issues (Weaver et al., 1997).

It is essential for the responsible practice of ministry that clergy and other religious professionals be prepared to recognize the emotional needs of persons in distress and to make effective referrals. The central task of a pastor within a mental health network is to identify the needs of individuals who seek assistance and to connect them to a larger circle of specialized helpers. This section makes several suggestions as to how clergy can become a part of a mental health network.

(1) Develop a working relationship with at least one—but preferably several—mental health professional who has a comprehensive knowledge of the services available in your community and is willing to work with you as a colleague. Some psychologists and psychiatrists have specialized training in treating survivors of psychological trauma.

A psychologist is a doctor with a research degree (Ph.D. or Psy.D.) who is trained in evaluating and doing therapy with individuals and families. A psychiatrist (M.D.) is a physician with special training in mental health issues and can prescribe medications. A social worker (M.S.W.) is a professional trained in coordinating access to available community services, and some with special training have clinical practices. A marriage and family therapist has usually earned at least a master's degree training to work with marital and family problems. And some nurse practitioners have received specialized training in counseling. There are also more than seven thousand parish-based nurses in the United States, and the movement is growing rapidly (personal communication, Dr. Harold Koenig, November 2002). However, the mental health specialists that clergy most commonly work with are pastoral counselors who have at least seminary training (M.Div.) and frequently are licensed to practice in one of the other mental health disciplines (Orthner, 1986).

Seek out professionals who are open to persons of faith and have some appreciation of the scientific data that demonstrates religious commitment can be a positive coping resource in times of crisis. Don't be timid; be assertive. Interview a mental health professional on the telephone before you refer someone who trusts you to make an educated referral. Keep a record of available providers to whom you can refer in an emergency. Ask the specialists direct questions to assess their skill level, expertise, and fee schedule. Inquire in detail about their experience, training, and education. For example:

- What sorts of cases have they worked with in the past? What are their specialties?
- Have they worked with individuals and families suffering from psychological trauma?
- How do they develop treatment plans for various crisis situations and post-traumatic stress disorder?
- How easily can they be located in an emergency?
- Are they willing to do some low-fee work?

(2) It is important to create a list of professional and community resources before you are faced with a mental health emergency. Equip yourself with such knowledge as: the location of the nearest hospital emergency room, in case a person becomes suicidal or psychologically traumatized; the location of the closest outpatient mental health center; which social services are available and how they can be accessed in an emergency; and the local relief or safety plan in the event of a community disaster. Most regions publish lists of resources available in case of a catastrophic event. These should be used to develop appropriate plans of action with your mental health colleagues in the event of a disaster.

(3) Continuing education is a necessity. Unlike growth in other areas of pastoral ministry (such as administration, preaching, teaching), clergy report that no matter how long they serve, they believe that their counseling skills do not improve without continuing education (Orthner, 1986). Referral skills are closely related to evaluative skills, since clinical

evaluation usually guides the course of action, particularly the treatment goals and objectives. Research has demonstrated that training clergy in diagnostic skills enhances their ability as pastoral counselors as well as their effectiveness in making referrals (Clemens, Corradi, and Wasman, 1978). Clergy with the highest rates of referral have attended a mental health workshop or seminar during the past year (Wright, 1984). Pastors must understand that a timely referral is an act of responsible pastoral care (Lee, 1976). Clergy can serve most effectively in the mental health network as skilled facilitators who identify the needs of persons and then connect them to a larger circle of specialized helpers.

(4) Pastor, thou shall refer thyself. Clergy in emotional turmoil are limited in their ability to help those in need of assistance. A significant number of pastors report having a poor psychological profile. They feel isolated, suffer emotional distress and poor self-esteem, lack hopefulness, and find it difficult to reach out for help (Orthner, 1986). This data indicates that numbers of clergy and their spouses need counseling, whether they recognize it or not. By contrast, pastors who have greater competence as counselors are more willing to seek outside assistance for their personal and family problems and are much less subject to alienation and burnout. Apparently, those who trust in their ability to help others are most likely to seek help for them-selves as well as enjoy greater satisfaction in ministry (Orthner, 1986).

Resources

—American Association for Marriage and Family Therapy; 112 South Alfred Street, Alexandria, VA 22314; (703) 838-9808; www.aamft.org; offers continuing education programs for those who work with families.

—American Association of Pastoral Counselors; 9504A Lee Highway, Fairfax, VA 22031; (703) 385-6967; www.aapc.org; provides information on qualified pastoral counselors and church-related counseling centers.

—American Psychiatric Association; 1000 Wilson Boulevard, Arlington, VA 22209; (703) 907-7300; www.psych.org.

—American Psychological Association; 750 First Street, NE, Washington, DC 20002; (800) 374-2721; www.apa.org.

—Association of Professional Chaplains; 1701 Woodfield Road, Suite 311, Schaumburg, IL 60173; (847) 240-1014; www.professionalchaplains.org.

—Canadian Association for Pastoral Practice and Education; 660 Franklin Street, Halifax, Nova Scotia B3H 3B5, Canada; (866) 44-CAPPE; www.cappe.org.

—Interfaith Health Program, Rollins School of Public Health; 1256 Briarcliff Road, NE, Building A, Suite 107, Atlanta, GA 30306; (404) 420-3846; www.ihpnet.org.

—International Parish Nurse Resource Center; Deaconess Parish Nurse Ministries, 475 East Lockwood Avenue, St. Louis, MO 63119; (314) 918-2559; www.ipnrc.parishnurses.org.

—International Society for Traumatic Stress Studies; 60 Revere Drive, Suite 500, Northbrook, IL 60062; (800) 742-4089; www.istss.org.

—National Alliance for the Mentally Ill; Colonial Place Three, 2107 Wilson Boulevard, Suite 300, Arlington, VA 22201; (800) 950-NAMI; www.nami.org; provides educational materials to clergy and religious groups, enabling them to dispel myths about mental illness and to guide churches and synagogues to serve the mentally ill.

—National Association of Social Workers; 750 First Street, NW, Suite 700, Washington, DC 20002; (202) 408-8600; www.socialworkers .org.

—National Center for Post-Traumatic Stress Disorder; VA Medical Center, 215 North Main Street, White River Junction, VT 05009; (802) 295-9363; www.ncptsd.org.

—National Organization for Continuing Education of Roman Catholic Clergy; 1337 West Ohio Street, Chicago, IL 60622; (312) 226-1890; www.nocercc.org.

—Samaritan Institute; 2901 South Colorado Boulevard, Denver, CO 80222; (303) 639-5240; www.samaritan-institute.org; helps communities develop interfaith counseling centers.

—Sidran Institute; 200 East Joppa Road, Suite 207, Towson, MD 21286; (410) 825-8888; www.sidran.org; focuses on education, advocacy, and research related to the early recognition and treatment of traumatic stress disorders.

—Stephen Ministries; 2045 Innerbelt Business Center Drive, St. Louis, MO 63114; (314) 428-2600; www.stephenministries.org; offers training in counseling skills for local church members for peer ministry.

References

Clemens, N. A., Corradi, R. B., and Wasman, M. (1978). The parish clergy as a mental health resource. *Journal of Religion and Health, 17(4)*, 227-232.

Hohmann, A. A., and Larson, D. B. (1993). Psychiatric factors predicting use of clergy. In E. L. Worthington, Jr. (Ed.), *Psychotherapy and Religious Values* (pp. 71-84). Grand Rapids, MI: Baker Book House.

Lee, R. R. (1976). Referral as an act of pastoral care. *Journal of Pastoral Care, 30(10)*, 186-97.

Orthner, D. K. (1986). *Pastoral Counseling: Caring and Caregivers in The United Methodist Church*. Nashville: General Board of Higher Education and Ministry of The United Methodist Church.

Weaver, A. J. (1995). Has there been a failure to prepare and support parish-based clergy in their role as front-line community mental health workers? A review. *Journal of Pastoral Care, 49(2)*, 129-149.

Weaver, A. J., Samford, J., Kline, A. E., Lucas, L. A., Larson, D. B., and Koenig, H. G. (1997). What do psychologists know about working with the clergy? An analysis of eight American Psychological Association journals: 1991–1994. *Professional Psychology: Research and Practice, 28(5)*, 471-474.

Wright, P. G. (1984). The counseling activities and referral practices of Canadian clergy in British Columbia. *Journal of Psychology and Theology, 12*, 294-304.

Self-Care

Clergy have many responsibilities and require good self-care practices to keep them emotionally healthy and effective. In a national survey of almost two thousand United Methodist pastors, Professor Dennis Orthner (1986) at the University of North Carolina found that pastoral work can be rewarding but is highly demanding. Clergy are required to fulfill many responsibilities to parishioners and the community, which places extensive requirements on their time and energy. There are few occasions when pastors are not "on call," and they often must deal with persons who are severely troubled (Weaver, 1995; Weaver, Koenig, and Ochberg, 1996).

On average, United Methodist clergy spend 56.2 hours per week in ministry and twelve evenings a month away from home on church duties (Orthner, 1986). About 1 in 4 of the surveyed pastors worked more than sixty hours a week. In addition, although clergy rank in the top 10 percent of the population in terms of education, they are 325 of 432 occupations in terms of salaries received (Morris and Blanton, 1995). In part because of time pressures and financial distress, the burnout syndrome has become increasingly associated with pastoral work (Jones, 2001).

In addition to their regular responsibilities, clergy are major care providers to "at risk" groups of traumatized persons; including victims of violence and natural disasters, substance abusers, new immigrants, persons with chronic mental illness, the homeless, those with life-threatening illnesses, and survivors of unexpected deaths (Weaver, Koenig, and Ochberg, 1996). Understanding the consequences of listening to trauma stories as well as witnessing their effects become essential to clergy survival as healthy individuals. Trauma work can be dangerous to the listener and to the witness, and these hazards are such that a pastor needs to be both informed of the risks and provided ways to minimize the harmful effects (Figley, 1995).

Researchers have found that clergy are frequently the first persons to help a family or an individual with a severe personal crisis (Weaver, 1995). Pastors are most often called upon in crisis situations associated with grief, depression, or trauma reactions, such as personal illness or injury, death of a spouse or close family member, divorce or marital separation, serious change in the health of a family member, and death of a close friend (Weaver, Revilla, and Koenig, 2002). People in "crisis" involving the "death of someone close" reported nearly five times more likelihood of seeking the aid of a clergyperson (54 percent) than from all other mental health sources combined (11 percent) (Veroff, Kulka, and Douvan, 1981). According to the National Funeral Directors Association, clergy officiate at an estimated 1.5 million memorial or funeral services annually in the U.S. This means that clergy have contact each year with millions of Americans who have lost friends and family in a traumatic death (K. Walczak, personal communication, March 1, 2002).

In spite of the pressures and the extraordinary demands, most clergy continue to find their work satisfying. Three of four United Methodist pastors indicated in a confidential survey that they were either "extremely" or "quite" satisfied in their ministry and the congregation they served (Orthner, 1986). Nearly 60 percent of the United Methodist pastors reported high levels of self-assurance, which is associated with positive self-esteem, hopefulness, and well-being, while 24 percent experienced a moderate level of self-assurance. Of great concern, however, are the nearly 1 in 6 clergy who showed signs of serious distress with high levels of isolation, loneliness, fear, feelings of abandonment, anger, and boredom. These pastors without a strong sense of well-being and lacking personal adjustment will have a hard time finding satisfaction in their work or personal life.

Of particular concern are newer clergy who are often more vulnerable to emotional distress and burnout than more experienced clergy. For example, researchers found high levels of pervasive anxiety among counselors early in their professional life, with significant reductions in anxiety among those who were more experienced (Skovholt and Ronnestad, 1995). Experts in the helping professions have been found to have more efficient reasoning processes and are better at solving problems than novices (Etringer, Hillerbrand, and Claiborn, 1995). Also, experienced professionals are better at understanding more of the complexity of a situation, even if it is ambiguous, than the beginner who must rely on the expertise of others. Experience helps reduce anxiety because professionals can increasingly rely on their own mastery of appropriate responses. The most common profile for burnout among psychologists includes being young, having low income, engaging in little personal psychotherapy, and feeling overly committed to clients (Ackerley, Burnell, Holder, and Kurdek, 1988). This is the likely profile for clergy experiencing burnout as well.

It is important, given the high emotional demands on clergy offering pastoral care and counseling to the traumatized, that they develop sound self-care skills. Here are some suggestions:

- Spend time with others. Coping with stressful events is easier when people help one another. Ask for support and assistance from your family, friends, colleagues, or community resources. Join or create support groups.

- Talk about how you are feeling. Helping professionals know that human feelings are powerful. Venting is cathartic—it is a helpful process by which people use words and nonverbal communication to let go of distressing emotions.
- Take time to grieve and cry, if needed. To feel better in the long run, you must let these feelings out instead of pushing them away or hiding them.
- Receive spiritual direction from a trusted confessor or mentor. Or, treatment by a mental health professional who is open to a person of faith can be an important act of self-care (Muse, 1992).
- Set small goals to tackle big problems. Approach one thing at a time instead of trying to do everything at once. If you are attempting to do too much, eliminate or delay the things that are not absolutely necessary.
- Eat healthfully and take time to walk, stretch, exercise, and relax, even if just for a few minutes at a time. Make sure you get enough rest. You may need more sleep than usual when you are under high stress.
- Do something that just feels good, like taking a warm bath, sitting in the sun, or spending time with a pet. Celebrate your sense of humor. Laughing, being playful, telling jokes, and being humorous are particularly positive activities for those whose work environment is filled with difficult human problems (Kramen-Kahn and Hansen, 1998).
- Clergy can benefit from clinical pastoral education (CPE). In a national study of pastors serving in churches, the 1 in 4 who had taken CPE was much less isolated and more willing to seek assistance from mental health specialists when he or she had a problem than were those without CPE training (Orthner, 1986). In addition, CPE experience is predictive of greater confidence as a counselor in the parish, while other seminary course work has not been shown to have the same effect.
- A clergyperson doing pastoral counseling should be provided with professional consultations or supervision. It is vital that pastors know the limits of their expertise and are willing to refer to other professionals. They should also be trained in the areas of professional ethics and in the psychological concepts of transference and countertransference, without which clergy may be blind to some of the inherent hazards in the counseling process (Seat, Trent, and Kim, 1993).

Helpful Books

Clergy Killers: Guidance for Pastors and Congregations Under Attack (G. Lloyd Rediger, Louisville: Westminster John Knox Press, 1997).

Clergy Self-Care: Finding a Balance for Effective Ministry (Roy M. Oswald, Bethesda: The Alban Institute, 1991).

The Contemplative Pastor: Returning to the Art of Spiritual Direction (Eugene H. Peterson, Grand Rapids: William B. Eerdmans, 1994).

Pastor: The Theology and Practice of Ordained Ministry (William H. Willimon, Nashville: Abingdon Press, 2002).

Pastoral Stress (Anthony G. Pappas, Bethesda: The Alban Institute, 1995).

Recalling Our Own Stories: Spiritual Renewal for Religious Caregivers (Edward P. Wimberly, San Francisco: Jossey-Bass, 1997).

Rest in the Storm: Self-Care Strategies for Clergy and Other Caregivers (Kirk Byron Jones, Valley Forge: Judson Press, 2001).

Season in the Desert: Making Time Holy (W. Paul Jones, Orleans, MA: Paraclete Press, 2000).

Walking Through the Valley: Understanding and Emerging from Clergy Depression (Robert L. Randall and James B. Nelson, Nashville: Abingdon Press, 1998).

The Way of the Heart (Henri J. M. Nouwen, New York: Ballantine Books, 1982).

Wounded Healer (Henri J. M. Nouwen, New York: Doubleday, 1979).

References

Ackerley, G. D, Burnell, J., Holder, D. C., and Kurdek, L. A. (1988). Burnout among licensed psychologists. *Professional Psychology: Research and Practice, 19(6)*, 624-631.

Etringer, B. D., Hillerbrand, E., and Claiborn, C. D. (1995). The transition from novice to expert counselor. *Counselor Education and Supervision, 35*, 4-17.

Figley, C. R. (Ed.) (1995). *Compassion Fatigue: Coping with Secondary Traumatic Stress Disorder in Those Who Treat the Traumatized*. New York: Brunner/Mazel.

Jones, K. B. (2001). *Rest in the Storm: Self-Care Strategies for Clergy and Other Caregivers*. Valley Forge: Judson Press.

Kramen-Kahn, B., and Hansen, N. D. (1998). Rafting the rapids: Occupational hazards, rewards, and coping strategies of psychotherapists. *Professional Psychology: Research & Practice, 29(2)*, 130-134.

Morris, M. L., and Blanton, P. W. (1995). The availability and importance of denominational support services as perceived by clergy husbands and wives. *Pastoral Psychology, 44(1)*, 29-44.

Muse, J. S. (1992). Faith, hope, and the "urge to merge" in pastoral ministry. *Journal of Pastoral Care, 46(3)*, 299-308.

Orthner, D. K. (1986). *Pastoral Counseling: Caring and Caregivers in The United Methodist Church*. Nashville: The General Board of Higher Education and Ministry of The United Methodist Church.

Seat, J. T., Trent, J. T., and Kim, J. K. (1993). The prevalence and contributing factors of sexual misconduct among Southern Baptist pastors in six southern states. *Journal of Pastoral Care, 47(4)*, 363-370.

Skovholt, T. M., and Ronnestad, M. H. (1995). *The Evolving Professional Self: Stages and Themes in Therapist and Counselor Development*. New York: Wiley.

Veroff, J., Kulka, R. A., and Douvan, E. (1981). *Mental Health in America: Patterns of Help-Seeking from 1957 to 1976*. New York: Basic Books.

Weaver, A. J. (1995). Has there been a failure to prepare and support parish-based clergy in their role as front-line community mental health workers? A review. *Journal of Pastoral Care, 49(2)*, 129-149.

Weaver, A. J., Koenig, H. G., and Ochberg, F. M. (1996). Posttraumatic stress, mental health professionals and the clergy: A need for collaboration, training and research. *Journal of Traumatic Stress, 9(4)*, 861-870.

Weaver, A. J., Revilla, L. A., and Koenig, H. G. (2002). *Counseling Families Across the Stages of Life: A Handbook for Pastors and Other Helping Professionals*. Nashville: Abingdon Press.

Summary and Conclusions

Religion plays a vital role in the lives of individuals and their families, especially in times of extreme stress and crisis. Given that clergy are often the first professionals sought for help in the aftermath of a traumatic event, those in ministry need to understand the key issues to be addressed. Information is needed about diagnosing and assessing problems, types of treatment that can be initiated in the faith community, when referral is required, and to whom to refer. This text identifies sixteen traumatic events that can cause psychological trauma, provides illustrative cases, lists resources available, and suggests when and from whom to seek additional professional assistance. There is an emphasis on self-help resources available on the Internet, an increasing source of information today.

Because of the valued role that religion plays in the lives of many, it is essential that pastors, chaplains, parish nurses, and others in ministry be knowledgeable about the healing aspects of faith for families and individuals as they cope with horrific events. Religious faith is a primary, positive coping strategy for many persons with PTSD. In emotional trauma, an individual's sense of order and continuity of life is shattered. Questions of meaning and purpose arise as a person experiences a loss of control over his or her destiny. Faith communities are powerful preventive and healing resources that are relied upon to help meet the emotional needs of many suffering these difficulties. In addition to offering the social support of community, religion can provide to the trauma-stricken an effective means to understand death, which enhances well-being, lowers distress, and may facilitate faster recovery. Several studies have found a strong link between the ability to make sense of the loss of a loved one through religious beliefs and positive psychological adjustment.

Pastoral care is a responsibility of the whole religious community. Clergy can offer guidance and direction, but the task of caring for those suffering from psychological trauma requires a larger group of helpers. Much emphasis is given to prevention through education within the community of faith. The book offers concrete suggestions about how the issues addressed can be understood as forms of ministry for the entire congregation.

Glossary of Terms

Active listening: Attentive listening with an attitude of wanting to understand what a person is saying.

Acute stress disorder (ASD): A mental disorder that is formed by the same types of stressors that cause PTSD. However, in this case, the symptoms occur during or immediately following the trauma. The primary criteria are the same as those for PTSD, except that the disturbance lasts for at least two days and no more than four weeks.

Adjunctive therapies: Therapies that may be used in addition to individual psychotherapy with a primary therapist, such as art therapy, psychodrama, dance therapy, or assertiveness training.

Affective disorder: A mental disorder involving mood.

Anniversary reaction: The experience of reacting with feelings or behavior on the "anniversary" of a previous event. A common anniversary reaction is temporary depression.

Anxiety: The state of feeling apprehension, agitation, uncertainty, and fear at the thought of some future or uncertain event or situation.

Anxiety disorders: A usually treatable group of anxiety-related mental health problems affecting 1 in 10 Americans. They are caused by a combination of biological and environmental factors.

Bereavement: A normal emotional reaction to the loss of anyone who is very important to a person; this usually refers to the grief that follows the loss of a family member or other loved one.

Child abuse: Maltreatment of a minor involving physical, sexual, and/or emotional injury.

Child neglect: The withholding of adequate care from a minor. It usually refers to physical needs such as food, clothing, medicine, and supervision.

Cognitive: Having to do with the ability to think or reason; sometimes used to describe memory process; the operation of the mind as distinct from emotions.

Cognitive Behavior Therapy (CBT): A form of psychological therapy that focuses on directly modifying both thought process and behavior.

Collaboration: The shared planning, decision-making, problem-solving, and goal-setting by persons working together.

Compulsion: An intrusive, repetitive, and unwanted urge to perform an act that is counter to a person's usual conduct.

Coping: The process of using personal, spiritual, and social resources to manage stress.

Countertransference: Feelings that a counselor or therapist develops toward a client, such as overconcern, sexual attraction, or anger. Such feelings can interfere with the process of counseling if not recognized and addressed.

Crisis: A disturbance caused by a stressful event or a perceived threat to the self.

Crisis intervention: Emergency assistance that focuses on providing guidance and support to help mobilize the resources needed to resolve a crisis.

Culture: An ordered system of shared and socially transmitted symbols, values, and meanings that give a worldview and guide behavior.

Delusions: Fixed, false beliefs from which an individual cannot be dissuaded.

Depression: Emotional disturbance in which a person feels unhappy and often has trouble sleeping, eating, or concentrating.

Derealization: A feeling of estrangement or detachment from one's environment; a sense that the external world is strange or unreal.

Diagnosis: The process of collecting data to identify and evaluate a problem, and the conclusion reached as a result of that process.

Diagnostic and Statistical Manual of Mental Disorders, Fourth Edition, Text Revised (DSM-IV-TR): The official manual of mental health problems developed by the American Psychiatric Association. This reference book is used by mental health professionals to understand and diagnose psychological problems.

Disorder: A mental health problem that impairs an individual's social, educational, or mental functioning or significantly interferes with her or his quality of life.

Dissociation: The separation of ideas, feelings, information, identity, or memories that would normally go together. Dissociation exists on a continuum: at one end are mild dissociative experiences common to most people (such as daydreaming or highway hypnosis) and at the other extreme is severe chronic dissociation. Dissociation appears to be a normal process used to handle trauma that over time can develop into maladaptive coping.

Dysfunctional: Abnormal or impaired functioning.

Ectopic pregnancy: When the site of implantation is outside of the womb.

Emotional shock: A description of a reaction to trauma.

Empathic listening: Listening that conveys genuine concern for the feelings of another.

Empathy: The ability to put oneself in another's place and feel what another person feels.

Exposure therapy: A type of treatment that includes gradually bringing individuals into contact with a feared object or situation. The persons learn that the object or situation can be faced and that avoidance is unnecessary.

Family therapy: A therapeutic method that involves assessment and treatment with immediate family members present. This model of therapy emphasizes the family as a whole rather than focusing on one person.

Flashback: A symptom of PTSD in which a person experiences dissociative states that last from a few seconds to several hours or even days, during which time components of the event are relived and the person behaves as though experiencing the event at the moment.

Generalized anxiety disorder (GAD): An excessive or unrealistic worry that is unrelated to another illness and can last six months or more

Hallucinations: Abnormal perceptions that occur as symptoms of schizophrenia, mostly in the form of hearing voices or seeing objects.

Hypervigilance: Increased watchfulness.

Magical thinking: The erroneous belief that one's thoughts, words, or actions will cause or prevent events outside the laws of cause and effect.

Neurotransmitter: A chemical substance released by nerve cell endings to transmit impulses across the space between nerve cells, tissues, or organs.

Normalizing: A therapeutic strategy that depathologizes problems in a way that changes perceptions of a situation and defuses the difficulty.

Numbing: A symptom common to individuals with PTSD. It represents an individual's attempt to compensate for intrusive thoughts, memories, or feelings of the trauma by shutting down and becoming numb to internal or external stimuli.

Obsession: The mental state, occurring in obsessive-compulsive disorder, of having persistent and virtually uncontrollable recurrent thoughts about something or someone.

Palpitations: An abnormally rapid beating of the heart.

Panic disorder: A condition characterized by episodes of immediate and intense anxiety at inappropriate times. A person may experience palpitations, feelings of faintness, chest pains, and a sensation that death is imminent, even when there is no apparent threat or danger. Individuals who experience four or more unexplained attacks in a month, as well as those who have fewer attacks but live in constant fear of such an episode, may be suffering from the disorder.

Paranoid thinking: Exaggerated belief or suspicion that one is being persecuted, harassed, or unfairly treated.

Parish nurse: A nurse working in a congregation promoting all aspects of wellness. Parish nurses train and coordinate volunteers, develop support groups, liaison within the health care system, refer to community resources, and provide health education.

Phobia: An intense, irrational fear of a harmless object or situation that the individual seeks to avoid.

Post-traumatic stress disorder (PTSD): An anxiety disorder in which symptoms develop following a psychological trauma. The essential features of PTSD include increased physical arousal, intrusive reexperiencing of the traumatic event, and avoidance.

Prognosis: A forecast about the outcome of a condition, including an indication of its probable duration and course.

Projection: The act of attributing one's own thoughts or impulses to another.

Psychiatrist: A medical doctor who has special training (medical residency in psychiatry) to handle psychological problems. A psychiatrist can hospitalize patients and may treat with medications, psychotherapy, or both.

Psychoanalysis: An approach to psychotherapy that emphasizes unconscious motives and conflicts. In this therapy, the effort is on bringing unconscious material to awareness in order to increase conscious choice.

Psychological trauma: An event that is outside the range of usual human experience and that is so distressing as to cause emotional difficulties by overwhelming a person's ability to cope.

Psychologist: A doctor with an advanced degree (Ph.D. or Psy.D.) who is trained to use a variety of treatment modalities, including individual and group psychotherapy, cognitive therapy, behavior modification, psychodynamic psychotherapy, and family systems. She or he also does psychological testing.

Psychopharmacology: The management of mental illness using medication.

Psychosis: A mental condition that involves hallucinations, delusions, or paranoia.

Psychosomatic: A physical disorder of the body caused or aggravated by chronic emotional stress.

Psychotherapy: A process in which an individual seeks to resolve problems or achieve psychological growth through verbal communication with a mental health professional.

Rape: Sexual intercourse or other sexual acts without a person's consent. Rape is an act of violence, not sex.

Reframing: Putting behavior into a new, more positive perspective, thus changing the context in which it is understood.

Regression: A process in which a person exhibits behavior that is more appropriate to an earlier stage of development.

Schizophrenia: A chronic mental disorder associated with a loss of contact with reality in the form of hallucinations and delusions.

Self-esteem: A person's self-evaluation or self-image.

Self-help groups: Therapeutic groups without the leadership of health professionals.

Separation anxiety: Inappropriate and excessive anxiety concerning separation from home or from those to whom an individual is attached.

Social phobia: An intense anxiety of being judged by others and publicly behaving in a way that could lead to embarrassment or ridicule.

Social worker (M.S.W.): A mental health professional who is trained to understand and emphasize the effects of environmental factors on mental problems. They often assist individuals and their families in locating and accessing available community services.

Specific phobia: An illogical yet intense fear of an object or set of objects (such as dogs or insects) or a situation (such as flying or closed spaces); also known as single phobia or simple phobia.

Stress: Tension resulting from a person's response to his or her environment.

Substance abuse: Excess, abnormal, or illegal use of drugs or alcohol.

Thought-stopping techniques: A self-taught method that can be used each time a person wishes to stop unwanted thoughts.

Trauma: A serious physical or emotional occurrence that causes substantial damage to a person's psychological or physical state, often causing lasting aftereffects (for example, war, disaster, car accident, rape, assault, molestation, loss of a significant other [child, spouse, parent]).

Traumatic event: An event characterized as being a trauma.

Index

abuse. *See* alcohol abuse; child abuse; elder abuse; substance abuse; verbal abuse

acute stress disorder (ASD). *See* post-traumatic stress disorder (PTSD)

adolescents
  and violence, 21

aging population
  rates of, in USA, 165-66

alcohol abuse
  as effect of PTSD, 35, 138
  in law enforcement officers, 141
  and motor vehicle accidents, 52
  after rape, 122
  use of, in coping with violence, 74
  in veterans, 148

Alzheimer's Disease, 166

anger, 44
  as response to tragedy, 66, 75

anniversaries
  of traumatic event, 50

antidepressants
  effects of, for PTSD, 42-43
  types of, 53
  use of, after pregnancy loss, 109

anti-gang programs, 76

anxiety
  in burn survivors, 157-58
  and cancer, 91
  after rape, 121
  about terrorism, 65
  symptoms of, and bereavement, 101

anxiety disorders
  treatment for, 52, 65

battered wives
  and clergy help, 25

bereavement
  complicated, 100
  cross-cultural responses to, 102
  definition of, 99
  symptoms of, 99-100
  traumatic, 99-100
  uncomplicated, 100

bereavement process
  after violent loss, 81-82
  in parents of suicide victims, 85
  See also grief reactions

brain
  abnormal functioning of, and neglect, 32

bruises, 163-67

Buffalo Creek dam break
  and PTSD, 34

burn out. *See* compassion fatigue

burn survivor, 155-61
  patient support groups of, 157
  psychological complications in, 155
  See also fire injury

cancer
  in children, 89-97
  in ethnic groups, 94
  and faith as coping strategy, 24, 93
  patient, congregational support of, 92-93
  and PTSD, 92
  rates of, in children, 91
  survivors of, and therapy, 93
  treatment effects of, 90

caregiver stress
  and abuse of elders, 165
  and respite care, 166

ceremony for the dead, 151

child abuse
  and lack of attachment, 32-33
  and psychological problems, 32-33
  survivors of, and religious faith as coping strategy, 24

children
  coping mechanisms in, 59

Church Arson Prevention Act of 1996, 130
  See also church fire

church fire, 129-30

clergy
  coping skills of, 176

209